REBOOT RANCH

A story of rescue, inspired by true events

Eileen Watkins

Published by Who Chains You Publishing
P.O. Box 581
Amissville, VA 20106

www.WhoChainsYou.com

Written by Eileen Watkins
www.efwatkins.com

Book cover and interior design by Tamira Thayne
www.tamirathayne.com

ISBN: 978-1-946044-75-4

Printed in the United States of America

First Edition

THIS BOOK IS DEDICATED TO ALL
individuals and organizations who rescue and rehabilitate
horses and other equines, whether to adopt them out or
simply to provide them with safe homes for the rest of
their natural lives. At present, even the best efforts of
these dedicated individuals cannot keep pace with the
desperate need for their services. Let us hope and strive
for changes in our society that will help reduce the number
of abused and "unwanted" animals.

"The Star Thrower" (or "starfish story"),
retold here by Walt Patterson, is part of a
16-page essay of the same name by
Loren Eiseley (1907-1977), published in 1969
in *The Unexpected Universe*.

TABLE OF

CONTENTS

PROLOGUE

THE ACCIDENT

"Next up, Anna Loehmeyer on Ebony Duke."

Anna reached forward to pat her horse's sleek, black neck and trotted him into the ring. After they passed the judge's box, she nudged Duke into an easy canter.

The fall day carried a damp chill and the morning's rain had left the footing mushy in spots. A couple other riders had lost speed on the course when their horses slipped on the turns, so Anna reminded herself to be careful.

On the other hand, this was the class jump-off, so every second would count.

Circling just inside the gate, she heard a high-pitched shout of "Go, Aunt Anna!" She threw a quick smile to her teenaged niece, MJ, who stood along the rail with her parents, the Kleins. Anna's blonde younger sister Erika resembled her closely, while MJ took after her dark-haired father, David Klein.

Anna scanned the crowd in vain for another face. Her husband, Richard, knew where and when she was competing today, but after their argument the night before, he'd slammed out of the house and never came back. She had stayed up until two, calling his cell phone repeatedly with no answer, and finally cried herself to sleep.

Even so, she'd gotten to the stable by six to help her trainer, Brittany, groom Duke and trailer him to the show grounds. This was only his and Anna's second B-rated show, and they had worked hard to prepare. Cancelling would not have been an option.

Anna looked as polished as any of the other riders here today—tack and boots gleaming, cream breeches spotless, long hair netted beneath her helmet. No one watching would suspect that her eyes still ached from tears and fatigue.

And so far, she'd done pretty well—she'd made it to the jump-off!

The jangle of a handbell signaled her to start the course. *Focus, Anna. You could win this class.*

She aimed Duke at the first jump, a simple fence, and he powered toward it. Anna counted his strides in her head, rose in her stirrups at the takeoff, gave with the reins as he stretched his neck and vaulted into the air. He landed lightly and she headed him for the second hurdle, a solid wall.

Duke flicked his ears at the multicolored, artificial flowers along the foot of the wall, but kept his momentum. He almost never shied at, or refused, a jump. In her younger days, Anna had taken lessons on many different mounts, suffering bruises, sprains and even a broken collarbone. Duke, her "gift horse," was the best she'd ever ridden. He had talent, intelligence, heart. Also plenty of "go," though he always waited for Anna's signals. Was it just his fine breeding and training, or also the bond that had grown between them over the past three years?

Richard often commented that Duke was worth every penny he'd paid for him, "If only because he makes you so happy, sweetheart."

Richard...where on earth is he?

Anna sent her horse toward a spread fence and felt him lose some traction on the wet footing. They might pick up some time faults. Well, nice as it would be to take home a blue, it was more important to get around clean.

And to get around safely. Anna thought again of the news she'd meant to tell Richard the night before. His unexpected nastiness during their argument, though, had made that impossible.

When Duke jumped the spread his rear hoof tapped a rail, but she didn't hear it fall. Their time must be okay, too, because the spectators applauded once more. She galloped him toward the in-and-out, passing Brittany, who coached her from the rail: "Easy does it, Anna."

She took a firmer hold on the reins, though maybe too late. Duke cleared the first fence of the in-and-out, but over the second she heard a pole fall.

Rats, four faults.

I'm tired, that's all...

But how could Richard storm out like that, just because I asked a few questions? Like I didn't have the right! He keeps taking those mysterious phone calls at home, and rushing off to "meetings" at all hours...

What is he up to? Is it an affair, or...

She turned Duke almost too late for the triple bar. Anna felt him hesitate and thought he might actually refuse. She squeezed hard with her calves and he bunched his great muscles to spring.

They cleared the first two rails. But, in mid-air, Anna knew they would hit the third.

The crash seemed to happen in slow motion. Duke's shoulder dropped away and Anna flew over it. On the way down, something hard rammed her in the stomach. She plowed into the thick, damp footing of the ring, and everything went black.

When she came around a few seconds later, a slim, short-haired woman was taking her pulse; the stranger wore a hooded rain jacket with a medical caduceus on the front. She saw Anna's eyes open and asked if anything hurt. Shaking her head, Anna tried to sit up...and a blaze of pain made her see stars.

"Stomach." She sank back down, taking shallow breaths.

The medic called over her shoulder, "We need a gurney!"

Anna glanced to one side, looking for Duke. He stood several yards away, head drooping, Brittany holding his reins. A man in jeans and a white sweatshirt—maybe a vet?—ran his hands down the black gelding's legs.

While EMTs lifted Anna onto a gurney, the Kleins hurried to her side. MJ, especially, looked wide-eyed and pale. Anna felt terrible for her niece, and even for the other spectators. Nothing worse than seeing a rider crash so badly that she had to be rushed off to Emergency. Anna almost wanted to apologize to everyone for having ruined their pleasant afternoon.

Trim and stylish Erika stood by in stunned silence. It was paunchy David, always so upbeat, who reassured Anna as she went into the ambulance. "We'll see you at the hospital." His cheeks rounded in a forced smile. "Don't worry—you're gonna be fine."

The doors shut and the siren started up, with just an occasional *whoop* of warning. Smart, Anna thought. Scare the other horses, and they'd end up with more fallen riders.

Poor Duke, I hope he's okay! If I hurt him...

So stupid of me. I should have cancelled today! I was in no shape to ride—my heart wasn't in it. Too many other things on my mind.

A fresh stab of pain sliced through her midsection. Less like the impact of the wooden pole, though; more like a really bad cramp. The kind of cramp she hadn't felt for a couple of months now.

"Oh, God..." she said aloud, tears springing to her eyes.

The nearest EMT heard and reached for an IV stand. "Are you hurting, ma'am? I can give you something for that."

Anna didn't resist, but she knew no drug would help this pain.

Damn it, Richard, where are you?

CHAPTER ONE:

TWO YEARS LATER

The big, cream-colored SUV rolled to a stop in front of the old ranch house. Through her window on the passenger side, MJ took in the faded yellow siding, scraggly foundation bushes and patched screen door. A horse blanket sagged over the railing of the open porch, which ran the width of the house.

MJ hadn't remembered the place as being quite so run down. Her mother Erika, behind the wheel, gave her head a shake that made the blonde waves bounce.

"Still time to change your mind, kid. Anna will understand."

MJ had the same thought, but only for a second. That would mean breaking a promise to her aunt. Besides, she'd have to go home and do things her mother's way, her teachers' way, her therapist's way. Be practical, conform, "get with the program." Go to a good college, get a job where she could make lots of money working in an office.

The kind of life that killed my father.

MJ blinked away a rebellious tear and set her jaw. "I'm not backing out now. Anna's counting on me."

"Suit yourself. But it's going to be a long summer for you out here in the middle of nowhere. We didn't pass any shopping malls or pizza parlors in that pathetic excuse for a town we drove through."

They had visited the farm just once before, when Anna bought it a year ago. For some reason, though, the drive out seemed to take more time today—probably just because MJ was more conscious of the distance.

She reminded her mother, "Some kids spend their 'gap year' backpacking through the Himalayas. Would you rather I did something like that?"

"This *is* safer, I guess," Erika admitted. "Though out here, you might die of boredom."

MJ hopped from the passenger seat and slammed the door behind her. With a resigned air, Erika also got out and followed her daughter up the weedy flagstone walk and the front porch steps.

The thick sisal welcome mat at the door, with a silhouette of a trotting horse, had been swiped often by muddy boots. MJ's mother stepped onto it gingerly as she pressed the doorbell. The chime echoed inside the house, but even after a second try, no one answered.

"She's not home." Erika sounded almost hopeful.

"Nice try, Mom. We *are* later than we said we'd be. She's probably out by the barn."

A flicker of distaste crossed Erika's lightly made-up features as she gazed past MJ. The large gray barn, also old but refreshed with white trim, sat about a hundred yards off, on the other side of the dirt road. Alongside her daughter, she walked down the gentle slope.

Meanwhile, MJ's spirits lifted. The June air, muggy back where she lived, felt cleaner out here. The fresh breeze also carried a distinctive, earthy-sweet scent from the trio of large, rectangular paddocks just beyond the barn. In the first, two animals were turned out together. One was a buckskin Quarter Horse named Dash that she had seen on the farm's website; he shared his space with a brown-and-white pinto pony. A second enclosure held a thin but alert chestnut who let out a whinny as the girl and her mother approached.

When they reached the first paddock, the buckskin and the pony ambled over, hoping for treats. MJ wished she had thought to bring some carrots. "Hi, guys, what's up?"

The animals poked their heads between the boards of the fence; it had an electric wire, but that seemed to be turned off. She rubbed the buckskin's dark, velvety nose and he wriggled it in pleasure. But when she played with the pony's heavy white forelock, she caught her breath in shock. One eye was missing, the socket stitched shut long ago in a permanent wink.

That's right, Anna mentioned the pony on her website, too. What's her name? Patches?

Erika muttered about getting mud and manure on her designer boots. She paced over to the barn door and called out impatiently, "Annie! Are you—?"

"I'm here, I'm here." The answering voice had a similar pitch but a more cheerful lilt. "Sorry. I was rinsing Valentine's hay."

When Anna Loehmeyer emerged from the barn, MJ noticed again the similarities and differences between her aunt and her mother. They weren't twins, Erika having passed the "dreaded" milestone of forty just recently and her sister three years ago. Still, they shared the same tall, slim build, elegant features, wide green eyes and long blonde hair. Anna's style always had been more down-to-earth, but MJ thought she'd taken it to a new low since moving out here. Today, she wore stained jeans tucked into short, thick-soled paddock boots. Her loose T-shirt was a faded rose color and spotted with water. Her face was bare of makeup and wisps of pale hair strayed from her practical ponytail.

Still, her wide grin looked beautiful to MJ.

"Great to see you guys!" Anna started to hug her sister, then drew back with a laugh. "I'm a mess, I know."

Erika looked grateful for this consideration. MJ rolled her eyes and hugged Anna anyway. A little water, or even manure, wouldn't hurt her black jeans and old Evanescence rock concert T-shirt.

"Guess you found the place okay?" Anna asked.

"Yes, thank goodness for the GPS. I didn't remember it being so far. I was starting to wonder if we were still in New Jer—"

Erika broke off with a mousy squeak. The buckskin had reached through the fence to nibble her beige linen jacket. She jumped away and checked the hem for slobber.

"Bad boy, Dash," Anna scolded him mildly. "He's just hungry. It's almost time for their dinner."

Recovering, Erika ruffled her daughter's dark, ragged hair at the top, where it was dyed emerald green. "Better watch out, sweetie. He might think this is grass."

Hilarious, Mom, thought MJ. *Like that nice, even blonde shade is* your *natural color.*

Anna glanced at her sporty watch. "MJ, let's take your stuff up to the house. Your mom probably wants to start home before rush hour."

While the three of them headed back to the SUV, Erika chuckled. "Gee, Sis, almost sounds like you want to get rid of me."

Anna paused for a beat. "Not at all. You're welcome to stay for coffee, but first I do have to feed the horses. Unless you want to help?"

MJ piped up, "I do!"

"Oh, *you* will. You're going to help plenty. I just hope you're still that enthusiastic after a week or two."

"Anna's going to wear you out," Erika warned. MJ recognized another veiled hint that she wouldn't be able to hack it on the farm.

"Not me." MJ knew because she was on the short side, and could stand to lose a few pounds, people thought she wasn't very athletic. And it was true that she hated most team sports. But she'd taken riding lessons for a couple years now and had done well. She didn't mind having a teammate if it was a horse.

To prove she could pull her weight, MJ carried her luggage— her own fat purple duffle bag and one of her mother's big, hard-sided, rolling suitcases—up to the front porch. Meanwhile, Anna's cell phone rang. She fished it from her pocket and glanced at the number. Then she excused herself and stepped away to talk. Even so, her niece picked up a few scraps of the conversation.

"Everything okay?" Anna paused to listen, then blew out a breath. "Oh, man... Where are you now?" Another beat. "Yeah, it's not the best time, but...okay, see you then. Be careful." She tucked the phone away and returned to the SUV.

"Problem?" her sister asked.

"No, no. I'm just...expecting a delivery, and I hoped it would be unloaded before you came. The van's got to pull in here." She gestured toward Erika's own glossy vehicle.

"You are trying to get rid of me! Well, I should be hitting

the road, anyhow. It's a long drive back, and I left Carl alone at home."

"Yeah," MJ added drily, "no telling what craziness he'll be up to." Her younger brother seemed to be everything she wasn't—a straight-A student, athletic, and popular. She almost wished some day he *would* screw up, just to make her look better.

Still, the warmth with which her mother hugged her goodbye startled her. "Call me anytime, okay?" Erika also pecked her on the cheek before getting back in her car and heading off down the long, gravel driveway.

MJ watched her leave with a sudden, empty feeling. In spite of all their arguments over the last year or so, she was still Mom, a known quantity.

Now there was only Anna, still pretty unknown.

Her aunt, the Erika from an alternate universe, threw an arm around her shoulders. "Want to help feed the horses?"

"Yet bet!" MJ tried to keep pace with Anna's long strides on the way back to the barn. "You said you were washing hay? Why?"

"For Valentine. She's got a breathing problem. They call it COPD in humans—chronic obstructive pulmonary disease. In horses, they call it heaves."

"And washing the hay helps?"

"Even good hay usually has some dust and mold particles, and those make heaves worse. Rinsing gets rid of them."

Just inside the barn door, Anna stopped by a big, galvanized-metal tub filled with water. She lifted out a couple of flakes of dripping hay, contained in a net. MJ had tried picking up that much *dry* hay once, at the stable where she rode, and it weighed plenty. She couldn't imagine how heavy this armful must be! But Anna carried it easily toward the pen that held the thin chestnut.

"Open that gate for me?" she asked.

While MJ did, the mare trotted in their direction. Her eyes were big and bright, but her nostrils flared with her efforts to breathe. Closer up, MJ could even hear a slight wheezing sound.

Anna dropped the hay into a rack attached to a lower fence rail. "A horse with heaves should always eat with its head down. Helps keep the airway open. But not straight from the ground, because you don't want her breathing in dust."

While the mare started on her dinner, MJ stroked the golden-red coat. It looked dull rather than healthy and shiny, and she could see the rippling ribs and bumpy spine.

Anna brought over a wheelbarrow of dry hay for the other two horses. "So, MJ, you're taking a year off before college? I gather this was not your mom's idea."

Getting right to the point, huh? "She probably told you that I screwed up. I had early acceptance from a college, based on last year's grades. But this year I got a lot of Cs and Ds, so they—whatcha call it?—rescinded the acceptance."

"Well, you had a rough year, losing your dad. Didn't Erika explain that to them?"

"She did." MJ grabbed a flake and tossed it to Patches, to avoid Anna's eyes. "They said I could still get in if I spent this summer pulling up my grades and agreed to do my first year of college on 'academic probation.'"

"Uh-huh. And?"

"I figured I wouldn't do any better studying during the summer than I did all year in school. My head's just not into that stuff these days, y'know?"

"I guess." Anna still studied her.

"Mom sent me to a therapist, Dr. Mayer. He said I was depressed and maybe had a little ADD. He also thinks I have something called 'oppositional disorder,' because I argue with Mom so much." When Anna raised an eyebrow, MJ responded, "I know, right? But he did come up with one good idea. He told Mom it might help me to take a year off and relax. Get out more into nature."

Her aunt smiled. "Might have known Erika wouldn't agree to this arrangement without a doctor's prescription."

Got to change the subject, the girl thought. "Want me to fill the water buckets?"

"Sure. The hose is on the left side of the barn."

MJ filled Valentine's bucket first, and tried not to struggle too obviously as she carried it back out to the paddock. "You had this horse when we came out here the first time. Why'd you name her Valentine?"

"Because the star on her forehead looks like a heart. Also, because everybody loves her and she loves everybody." Anna scratched the chestnut along the top of her mane. "Don't you, pretty girl?"

MJ watched the mare tuck into her hay. "Good appetite."

"She still can't keep weight on, though. Uses up most of her energy just trying to breathe."

"How'd she get so sick?"

Anna shrugged. "She could be allergic to mold, dust or pollen. Or she might have been kept in a dirty stable. When horses stand around in their own waste all day, it wrecks their lungs."

"Was Valentine your first rescue? How did you get her?"

Anna's faced clouded, and it was her turn to glance away. "Mmm...long story. Another time, okay?"

"No problem." MJ knew how it was to have things in your past you didn't like to talk about. "You had another horse, too, last time. A dark brown one."

"Starbuck, the Standardbred. I adopted him out three months ago to a couple in Monmouth County. He's had a rough life, so I'm really hoping that works out."

Anna glanced at her watch again. MJ guessed she was still waiting for that delivery.

They finished with the three horses, and Anna spanked hay dust off onto her jeans. "I appreciate your coming out to help me, MJ. Even if you are just doing it under doctor's orders."

"Oh, no!" The girl stared at her. "It's not like that. I asked to come here."

"Erika said so, but I wasn't sure whether to believe her."

"She was mad that I wouldn't go to some kind of summer school. She said if I was going to take a gap year, I should at least do something 'meaningful.' I thought about that, and...the only adult I know who's doing anything *meaningful* is you."

Anna's mouth fell open; that expression morphed into a crooked smile. "Erika probably doesn't see it that way. Neither do most of my old friends—they think I've gone off my rocker. But thanks for the vote of confidence. Now, let's go up to the house and get you unpacked, before—"

A dusty blue pickup rattled down the drive, pulling an older-model, single-horse trailer. Anna straightened her spine, on guard. The truck drove all the way into the barnyard and eased to a stop.

From inside the trailer rang a barrage of loud bangs, like gunshots.

Bam! Bam! The power and fury behind those kicks startled MJ.

She glanced at her aunt. Some of the healthy, sunkissed color faded from Anna's cheeks.

Still, she spoke quietly. "MJ, I need you to go back up to the house, okay? And just keep out of the way."

loose, he trotted around briskly and tossed his head, still trying to impress the chestnut mare. But when they threw him some hay, hunger got the better of him and he gave it his full attention.

Anna feared that her niece would spend the rest of the evening staring at him, and squeezed the girl's shoulder. "You must be hungry, too. Let's go up to the house and I'll make dinner. Clint, you want to stay for a bite?'

"Thanks, but I should get started back east. I'll grab something at a diner halfway." He climbed back in his truck, but before leaving he asked, "Mind if I stop back in a few days to check on this big guy?"

"Please do." Anna laughed. "Meanwhile, I'll do my best to keep him on the property."

"I don't think he's goin' anywhere, now that he's in love with Miss Valentine."

Anna and MJ waved goodbye, then returned to the porch of the ranch house. The girl had parked her luggage there and Anna picked up the larger suitcase.

MJ grabbed the duffle. "You look kind of beat, Aunt Anna. If you're too tired to cook, we could always just get takeout."

Uh-oh, the kid was in for another trauma. "Please, just call me 'Anna.' And thanks, but cooking's easier. It's a trek to the nearest fast-food restaurant, and there isn't a takeout place nearby, either."

The girl gaped. "No pizza? Chinese?"

Anna shrugged. "None within ten miles, and they won't deliver beyond that."

"Je-e-ez."

While Anna held open the screen door, the girl carried her duffle inside, slung over her shoulder. Like a new recruit checking in for her first day at boot camp.

MJ tossed her bags onto the bed in her aunt's guest room and remembered seeing this honey-oak furniture somewhere before. Maybe in a spare bedroom of the Basking Ridge house, back when her aunt was still married to Richard.

MJ and her mother lived in a pretty big place, too, but it was new. Anna's other house had been a real colonial from the eighteen-hundreds, with white columns on the porch and oak floors. She'd filled it with a lots of great country-style furniture. *New Jersey Good Life*, the magazine Anna used to edit, had done a spread on it.

She had a terrific horse back then, too. A big, black warmblood named Duke. MJ had seen them win ribbons in a couple of jumper shows, and had been at the last one when they crashed. People didn't usually have bad accidents at those shows, because the jumps were designed to fall easily. But the pole that came down hit Anna in the stomach and she'd spent a few days in the hospital. Duke landed badly, too, and blew out a ligament. From what MJ had heard, he was never the same again.

That must have been so hard for Anna. Maybe not as hard, though, as Uncle Richard being arrested right after. What was it, a Ponzi scheme? Some kind of fraud, anyway.

MJ sat on the bed and bounced. Firm, comfy. The white sheets felt crisp and the quilt had an authentic country look. The bedside table held a ginger-jar lamp tall enough to read by. On the dresser, a vase held a bouquet of little blue wildflowers.

Anna tried to make this room nice for me. Is she grateful that I came out to help her with the farm work? Is she getting lonely out here, all by herself?

MJ had met Richard Cooper only a couple of times and never really liked him. He was good-looking she supposed, for an older guy, but she felt like he talked down to her. On the other hand, he seemed to do that even to the other adults.

MJ had never been clear on what a "financial analyst" did, anyway. She figured he advised people on investments. Uncle Richard must have done something crooked, because he went to trial. In the end, he was acquitted, but just because they couldn't prove anything. Richard was that slick.

So slick that Anna had never had a clue what he was up to. No wonder she kicked his butt to the curb, even before the trial was over.

Supposedly, a lot of people who'd taken Uncle Richard's advice

"A week or two, anyway. I can't wait—I've really missed New York. I'll get to hang with my cousins, hit some clubs. If you were around, maybe your Mom would've let you come with me."

No way, MJ thought. Erika never would have trusted her to run around lower Manhattan with Stacey, even for a couple of weeks. She probably sensed what MJ knew for a fact—that Stacey was a bit wild, smoked weed now and then, had been drunk a few times, and went pretty far with her ever-changing lineup of boyfriends.

"You'll have a better time without me," MJ said. "And I'll learn a lot here."

Stacey made a rude noise. "At the horsie retirement home?"

"They're not all plugs." MJ remembered her promise to Anna, not to mention Murphy. But this was Stacey, not Erika. "You should've seen the gorgeous guy they brought in today!"

The voice on the line perked up. "Guy? You said there were no—"

"Horse, I mean." She described Murphy's dramatic arrival and her role in preventing his escape. "Just retraining him is going to keep us pretty busy, I think."

Stacey sounded bored. "I never did get that whole horse-crazy thing. It's so preppy. If I want to ride something fast, I'll save up for a motorcycle. Think you can stick it out all summer with your aunt?"

"Sure, she's pretty cool. I think she'll make me work my butt off, but at least she kind of respects me. She's fine with giving me vegetarian food, and she gets everything local and organic."

"Gr-r-reat." Stacey drew out the word as a burn. "Maybe if one of those nags keels over from old age, you can at least have a burger."

MJ usually could handle her friend's dark humor, but this joke struck a nerve. "Okay, not funny."

"Sorry, I forgot. The pony from the camp, I know."

The phone began to crackle and MJ apologized. "I guess the reception's not great out here. I'd better hang up before this thing dies. Anyhow, give my best to everybody."

"I will. And I'll give Blond Bobby all your love!"

Stacey's sing-song promise and throaty laugh were the last things MJ heard before the phone cut out. She stared at the small, dark screen.

Stacey wouldn't do that to me, her best friend. Would she?

When Anna pushed the wheelbarrow filled with hay out to the paddocks that evening, all seemed peaceful. Murphy raised his handsome, chiseled head to watch her, ears pricked. She wondered if he was surprised that, instead of unloading at yet another racetrack, for more battles with handlers and jockeys, he had ended up in this congenial place, turned out under the stars with just a few mellow equine companions. Anna knew that, when in training, racehorses stayed in their stalls unless they were being exercised. This not only prevented them from hurting themselves, but kept all that energy pent up, so when the starting gates burst open they would be eager for a good run.

While she fed the others, she noticed Murphy kept a respectful distance from the electric fence. Either he'd already bumped it once or he'd encountered them in the past. Anna mostly turned it on at night, and kept the voltage low—she could have grabbed the wire herself without a serious jolt—but just the strangeness of the "biting fence" usually made a horse wary. Whether they could hear, smell or otherwise sense when it was live, they usually did not test it more than once.

Good. I don't want him jumping into the other paddocks to stir up the rest of the horses, or showing up outside my bedroom window in the middle of the night!

Anna brought Murphy his hay; while he nibbled it, she scratched the crest of his neck beneath the dark gray mane. Hard to believe this was the same creature who had thrown such a violent tantrum just hours earlier. Right now, he seemed happy because things were pretty much going his way. It might be different when someone asked him for something he didn't care to give, or tried to climb on his back.

Which raises another question. If he needs to be retrained, who's going to ride him?

For the first time in a while, Anna mentally revisited the moment when she'd headed Duke toward that last jump, and that

MJ fixated on the empty mug in front of her. "They beat him down, at that big company. Made him work harder and harder until he hated it. He never said so, but when he came home he was always so tired…" She felt her eyes well up and swiped at them with the back of her hand.

Anna noticed the gesture. She turned down the heat under the skillet, bent next to MJ, and draped an arm over her niece's shoulders. "Oh, honey."

The lump in MJ's throat made her voice hoarse. "I mean, who the hell dies of a heart attack at forty-eight?"

"I know. That did seem way too young."

"Mom keeps saying he worked hard to provide a good life for all of us. Like that's supposed to make me feel better. Like I wouldn't have been happy to give up the big house and some of our *stuff* just to have Dad still with us."

"Of course you would."

MJ leaned into her aunt for comfort and let the tears run for a minute more. Then she blotted them with her paper napkin and sat up straight. She'd felt freer to vent anger over her father's death with her aunt than with her mother.

Anna brought their plates of scrambled eggs to the table with two slices of toast each. Ravenous, MJ finished most of hers before she spoke again. "Mom's already back to dating. Some real-estate hotshot she met at a party for the magazine."

"That must be hard for you. But I'm sure it's no disrespect to your dad. Some women just can't stand to be alone."

"Like Valentine?" MJ smiled, with a twist.

"Sort of. Even when we were growing up, Erika always had to have a boyfriend and hated to sit home on a Saturday night. I figured she would get married young."

"You waited, though."

"Yeah." Anna's tone turned sarcastic. "Even though I had a couple serious relationships before Richard, I waited until I found what I thought was the perfect guy—my very own Prince Charming. You see how *that* turned out."

Now MJ felt guilty for bringing up a sore subject. "I'm sorry."

Tires crunched on the gravel outside. Anna scooped up the

last of her eggs with a scrap of toast, popped it in her mouth, and sprang to her feet. "That'll be the vet."

Though no taller than MJ, Dr. Julie Adams looked much fitter, despite her wire-rimmed glasses and the gray threaded through her short, dark hair. She first checked the barn's three older residents. MJ cross-tied each of them in the aisle, by turns, so the vet could examine them from all sides.

Julie ran a hand over Dash's spine and ribcage, and noted with approval that he'd gained about a hundred pounds since her last visit. "You should have seen this guy when your aunt took him in," she told MJ. "Skinny, backbone sticking up, sunken in at the flanks. And see these scars?" She touched spots just behind the girth area where dark skin showed through the buckskin's tan coat. "That's from big rowel spurs."

Anna filled in the rest. "He was a Western reining horse, but his last owner ran him into the ground. Y'know how they do those spins and rollbacks? The guy rode him so rough, Dash ended up with arthritis in both hocks. Then, when the he went lame and couldn't compete anymore, the slimeball just left him in a weedy field to starve."

"That's awful." MJ stroked Dash's big, round cheek in sympathy. She'd read about different breeds and knew a Quarter Horse usually had a strong, beefy build. "How could anybody abuse him like that? He's so sweet."

The vet checked his hind legs and commented that the puffiness in his joints seemed almost gone. "He's okay now for some light riding."

"Great," said Anna. "MJ, maybe you can help with that."

The girl rubbed her hands together in anticipation. The riding clothes her mom had packed would come in handy, after all.

Next, Julie examined the pinto pony. Meanwhile, Anna told MJ that she had rescued Patches from a livestock auction.

"I went there looking for Thoroughbreds," she recalled, "and then this guy half- dragged a pony into the ring. I thought she was just scared, until I saw her eye was gone. Poor thing could hardly see where she was going. I heard one of the 'killer' bidders tell his pal she wasn't even worth buying for slaughter, because there wasn't enough meat on her. That did it—my hand just shot up."

The vet commented that Patches' remaining eye also was clouding over, and said since the pony was at least in her twenties that could be due to old age. "Seems like she still gets around well enough, though." Julie ruffled the bushy white mane with affection.

When MJ brought out Valentine, she noticed again the mare's distended nostrils and heaving sides. Those also drew a frown from the vet.

"You've still got her on the prednisolone, right?" Julie asked Anna.

"Morning and night. I crush the pills and mix them into her grain."

Julie checked the mare's heart and lungs with a stethoscope. "You may want to take her off hay completely and try a pelleted feed instead. If that doesn't work, we'll up her meds, at least to get her through the summer."

Anna nodded. "She always suffers from the pollen and humidity. I remember when I first got her—"

A series of sharp bangs from the end stall interrupted them.

"Your new problem child?" Julie asked.

"That's him. Probably not happy about being stuck inside this morning, after being turned out all last night."

MJ put Val away, clearing the aisle, but when Anna started to lead Murphy out, the vet stopped her.

"We don't want this guy going over backward on cross-ties," she said. "I'll check him out in the stall, at least for starters."

MJ hung back across the aisle and watched the two other women step into Murphy's box. Anna held the gray's head while Julie ran her hands down all four of his legs.

"At least these feel okay," the vet said. "Maybe it's a good thing this guy never raced much. No sign that he's ever been pin-fired."

"That's something they do to cure lameness, right?" Anna asked.

Julie nodded. "Mostly for bucked shins or splints. You see it a lot in racehorses, because people train 'em and run 'em so damn young. The plates in a horse's legs are still open at two years old, and only starting to close at three. But of course, Thoroughbreds start training and even racing at two years old. No wonder young horses have so many accidents on the track."

"Why don't they wait, instead of risking the lives of the horses and the jockeys?"

"Money, of course. You know yourself how expensive it is to keep a horse, if he's not earning you some kind of income. Imagine feeding a whole stable of blue-blooded colts and fillies, for two or three years, with nothing to show for it! Besides, all your competitors start their horses at two years old, so you'd have to change the whole industry." The vet shook her head. "Lucky for me, in this part of the state, I don't get called to treat many racehorses."

Anna smiled. "Lucky for their owners! I'm sure you'd be giving them a piece of your mind."

Julie went on to examine Murphy's shoulders and back. She applied gentle pressure at various spots, as if she was not only feeling for anything out of line but also testing the gelding's reactions. He flicked his ears back with curiosity but never flattened them, thrashed his tail, or showed any other sign of real discomfort.

"Can't be sure without x-rays," the vet said, "but nothing feels tight and he doesn't act like he's in pain. Could be a problem with his teeth. In racing, they teach a horse to take a strong hold of the bit. If that hurt him, could've been enough to make him go sour."

"Yeah," said Anna, "I thought of that, too."

Julie moved around the gray's head, stroking his neck along

the way. She slipped on a latex glove, then pressed the sides of his mouth, asking him to open it.

Murphy flew backward, head almost hitting the ceiling.

Both women jumped away as he crashed into the rear corner of the stall. Even MJ sprang back across the barn aisle in shock.

The horse sat down for a second, wedged in the corner and trembling. Even after he lurched onto all fours again, he held his head out of reach and rolled his eyes—a half-ton bomb ready to explode.

CHAPTER FIVE:

VALENTINE

MJ crept nearer to the window of the stall door. "You guys okay?"

Both Anna and Julie, still on their feet, muttered that they were fine.

Through the bars, MJ saw that the trembling horse had backed into the far corner. "What happened?"

The vet's calm, dry tone reached her. "Guess he's a bit head-shy."

A graveyard chuckle from Anna. "Y'think?"

"Give me a minute with him," Julie said.

After her aunt joined MJ in the barn aisle, they watched the vet approach the big gray again. Julie stroked his neck and shoulder and talked to him until the white disappeared from his eyes. Then she reached up to grasp his closest ear—a stretch, because of her small stature—and massaged it until he lowered his head. This took about ten minutes, but MJ watched in fascination. She would never have thought the Thoroughbred could be brought under control so easily. Anna seemed to hold her breath in suspense, too, and rested a hand on her niece's shoulder.

Murphy almost went into a doze from the vet's approach. Still wearing the glove on her other hand, Julie again slipped that thumb and forefinger into the sides of his mouth.

MJ shuddered. She'd never have had the nerve to do that! She knew Julie must be feeling around for sharp edges or anything else wrong with Murphy's teeth. This time, he submitted to the exam like a placid old nag.

She released his head and wiped her gloved hand on her jeans. "He's got a couple of points that should be floated. Could be they neglected his teeth up to now because he reacted so badly."

"I've never seen a horse freak out like that," Anna said, still with a tremor in her voice. "Do you think he was abused?"

"Could be. Y'know, Thoroughbreds are tattooed inside the upper lip, and people around the track check that number a lot. Maybe somebody grabbed him too rough, and when he resisted they whacked him—which just scared him more. These guys have long memories." The vet stepped out of the stall and reached into her medical kit. "I usually don't like to sedate a horse just to work on his teeth, but in this case..."

"Do what you have to," Anna said. "I don't want you getting hurt."

MJ noticed Murphy did not mind the injection to his neck nearly as much as having his mouth touched. As his head started to droop, Julie dipped into her bag again, pulled on a pair of black Kelvar wrist guards and picked up a long, thin, metal rasp.

The gray remained on his feet, but more passive than before. Over the next twenty minutes, the vet used her careful, patient technique to slide the rasp into his mouth and "float," or file down, his back teeth. As he came out of the sedation he started to resist again, but by that time Julie had dealt with the sharp edges.

Outside the stall, packing up her gear, she said, "He shouldn't object now to being bridled—not for any physical reasons. So if he was flipping because of a sore mouth, this could solve the problem. But if he's already formed the habit...that's serious stuff."

"I know," Anna said.

Julie looked her in the eye. "I mean it. You shouldn't try to deal with that yourself. You need a real trainer, somebody who's handled those kinds of issues."

This warning made MJ worry that the horse might be too much for her and her aunt. As they all walked out to the vet's truck, Anna grumbled, "You know I'm running this place on a shoestring. How can I afford to hire an outside trainer?"

"You must've worked with one when you had your own horse,"

said Julie.

Cold anger hardened Anna's voice. "She's not around anymore."

The vet seemed to understand. "Well, here's another idea. Ever hear of Josh Buchanan?"

When her aunt just shook her head, MJ had to pipe up. "I have! Dad and I saw him give a demo a couple of years ago, at a horse expo down in Freehold. He cured an Arabian that wouldn't go in a trailer."

Julie nodded. "He's one of those 'natural horsemanship' types. Nothing magic about what he does, any more than what I did with Murphy awhile ago. It's just knowing how their minds and bodies work. Anyway, Josh sometimes retrains rescues for a reduced fee. I don't have his number on me, but he's got a website. You can tell him it was my idea."

Anna pursed her lips. "You don't think if we just give the horse a little more time—?"

"You ever retrained an OTT before?"

"What's that?" MJ asked.

"Off-the-track Thoroughbred," Anna told her, then turned back to Julie. "No, I haven't, but—"

"There's a lot to it, and Murphy's got more issues than most. You want to risk your neck, or your niece's, trying to fix him? Or adopt him out, and then have him fall over backward and crush his new owner?" Climbing back into the cab of her truck, Julie shot them a final, sharp look. "Call Josh."

After the vet left, Anna and MJ released all the animals back into their paddocks. Murphy had shaken off the sedation, and even cantered around the fenceline of his enclosure a couple of times. Anna thought he seemed delighted to be able to stretch his legs at liberty, without a rider on his back.

MJ joined her near the fence. "Julie seems nice, and really smart. She knows who you are?"

"Yeah, she figured it out a while ago. Not that she cares. Somebody like Julie never could have afforded to invest any money with Richard."

"She knew about your horse, Duke. What ever happened to him?" MJ took a grim guess. "Did he get hurt bad that day? Did you have to—"

"No, but he never really recovered." Anna gazed across the paddocks, as if to avoid MJ's eyes. "Let's go have lunch. Then I'll tell you the whole, rotten story."

They had microwaved frozen veggie burgers on whole wheat, accompanied by iced tea, and ate on the porch. The sky was clouding up, with a smell of rain in the air. Still, they could watch the horses and enjoy the cooling breeze.

A ragged-looking orange cat paused at the foot of the steps to peer up at them, but when MJ called it with a whispering sound, it fled.

"The barn cats are wild, unfortunately," Anna told her. "But they help keep mice out of the grain bins."

"We had a kitten, when I was younger," the girl recalled wistfully. "It only lived a few years, though, and after it died Mom said no more pets."

"Erika never was big on animals." Munching her burger, Anna wondered if she was soon going to run out of vegetarian meals. "MJ, do you you eat fish? Tuna sandwiches okay?"

"Yeah. Guess that's kind of hypocritical...but no chicken, beef, pork, lamb or anything like that." MJ paused. "I saw a video online, once, of what goes on in a slaughterhouse. That did it for me."

Anna's mouthful of burger stuck in her throat, and she swallowed painfully. "It's pretty bad, all right."

"D'you know, they shoot cows between the eyes with this thing called a bolt gun? It's supposed to kill them, but sometimes it just stuns them. They get hauled off anyway, like on an assembly line..." The girl's voice quavered and she glanced down at her food. "Sorry. Not a great thing to talk about while we're eating, even if it isn't meat."

"I know how slaughterhouses operate," Anna said, flatly. "That's why I started a rescue farm."

"You were going to tell me about Duke. I guess he got hurt when you guys crashed into that jump?"

Suddenly Anna wished she had never raised the topic. "He tore a ligament in his right front leg. The vet at the stable where I boarded him wanted to put him down, but I just couldn't make that decision—not with everything else going on in my life. So we cast the leg, gave him stall rest, and it sort of healed, but not completely."

MJ waited with big, unblinking eyes for the rest of the story.

"Meanwhile, Richard got arrested and our lives started to unravel. During the trial, his assets were frozen and we needed money to pay for a lawyer. We sold one of the cars, some furniture...and I sold Duke. I told myself it was the right thing to do. He was never going to jump again. And after all, Richard had given Duke to me, and now he needed the money." Anna heard the bitterness in her own voice. "I should've let Richard get a public defender, and kept my horse!"

"So, what happened?"

"Brittany, my trainer, handled the sale. She had an older woman student with no interest in jumping who just wanted a nice, safe pleasure horse. Supposedly, she'd go on boarding him at the same stable, where Brittany could keep an eye on him. I let her mail me the check. I couldn't even bear to go to the stable and say goodbye to him."

"Wow," said MJ, but as if she understood.

"Meanwhile, I got embroiled in the whole mess with Richard, trying to stand by him like a good wife. But pretty soon I realized he'd conned me just like he'd conned all those investors. Even though he got acquitted, I knew he was guilty. So I filed for divorce...which opened up another whole can of worms. Our house got sold and I moved into an apartment."

"You even quit your job, didn't you?"

"How could I go on editing a magazine like *New Jersey Good Life*? At that point, a lot of the society people we wrote about hated Richard. He'd bilked them out of hundreds of thousands of dollars, made them look like fools, and hadn't even gone to jail. I swore I had no idea what he was up to, but many people didn't believe it, and wouldn't speak to me anymore."

"That totally sucks." With a sober air, MJ took another bite of her sandwich and chewed. "So, how did Duke make out with the new owner? Does she still have him?"

If only, Anna thought. "With the trial and the divorce, it took almost a year for me to even check on him. Meanwhile, I started to get my life back together. I'd gotten some money from the divorce, and my mother also left me some in a trust fund before she died. I got the idea to buy a small farm and maybe get Duke back. I felt bad about selling him and wanted to make up for it by giving him a safe home, regardless of whether I could even ride him anymore."

When Anna stalled, by refilling her glass from the pitcher of iced tea, her niece prodded again. "What happened?"

"I tried to call Brittany and was told that she'd moved to another barn, somewhere in New England. No one at my old stable could—or would—tell me where she'd gone, and I couldn't find her online. So, I tracked down the woman who'd bought Duke and got her husband. He accused me of selling his wife a lame, dangerous horse. She'd been riding Duke, a couple of weeks earlier, when he'd stumbled. She'd come off and injured her back. Her husband was so angry, he'd sent Duke off to an auction."

"Oh, no." When MJ turned pale, Anna figured her niece knew the implications.

She'd gotten the man to at least tell her the name of the auction house. Its website didn't list any horse of Duke's description, but she still had to take a chance. She'd rented a single-horse trailer and driven two hours to the auction grounds.

Anna never had imagined such a depressing place. She didn't know what was worse—the scrawny, lame, and otherwise damaged animals, obviously bound for slaughter, or the fit, alert younger ones who might easily suffer the same fate. Someone pointed her toward a big pen where that morning perhaps a hundred horses had been crowded together prior to the sales. Only a few sad stragglers remained, each with a big, black number pasted to both hips.

Desperate, Anna also searched the individual pipe-rail stalls that housed a few healthier specimens. Could Duke have gone downhill so badly in just a year that she wouldn't even recognize him? But he still would stand out for his jet-black coat and the jagged, lightning-bolt stripe down his face. She saw no horse like that anywhere.

Finally, she found a clerk and described Duke to her. The woman flipped back through some pages on a clipboard.

"Black warmblood gelding, eight years old, stripe on face, lame right foreleg...yeah, he went on the block day before yesterday. Sold Out of State."

Anna remembered her flutter of hope. "Out of State? Where? Can you tell me—"

The clerk just frowned and shrugged. A passing worker who overheard told Anna, "That means Mexico or Canada, one of the houses. Sorry, lady, he's long gone."

For a few minutes, Anna still couldn't grasp what they were saying. Back then, she didn't even understand the terminology, but their dead voices and expressions told her all she needed to know. Duke had been loaded onto a truck—crowded in with dozens of other suffering and terrified animals—and sent to a slaughterhouse.

She sagged against the fence of the big corral. In the heat and dust, she couldn't catch her breath and felt as if she might pass out. She shut her eyes against a tidal wave of grief and guilt.

The shock of Richard's arrest, the loss of their house, their friends, and their whole lifestyle, had all been bad enough. But in the process, overwhelmed, she'd turned her horse over to people who didn't care about him the way she did.

She'd killed Duke. First, by crashing him into that damned jump a year ago. Then by leaving it up to Brittany to sell him, and not even following up afterward.

Even if I'd had Duke put down when he first tore the ligament, it would have been kinder than this. The idea of her beautiful, brave friend dying in such a horrible way turned Anna's stomach. She fought the urge to vomit in the sawdust, right in front of the barn workers. Not that it was likely to affect them much, after what they saw every day. Eyes still shut, she gripped the pipe fence as it were the rail of a heaving ship, and she might be swept overboard.

Heavy breathing, a warm breeze against her cheek. A velvet nose nuzzling her. Anna gazed up into a big, dark eye that shone with serenity and compassion.

Startled, she stepped back to assess the scrawny chestnut mare with the heart-shaped spot on her forehead. The horse wheezed a little with every breath. Probably had heaves, which would be aggravated by the hot, dusty conditions of the auction pen.

Yet that beautiful, liquid eye was full of soul. Miserable as the mare must be herself, she seemed to sense Anna's pain and to want to console her.

Was that moment some kind of spiritual awakening? At any rate, it moved Anna to take the most impulsive action of her life.

She waited an hour for the next auction. Outbid a couple of "killers" for the skinny chestnut mare. Then put her in the rented trailer and drove her home.

CHAPTER SIX:

DASH

"**S**he looked so thin and sick, I didn't know if she'd even survive the trip," Anna told her niece.

"But she did." Leaning back in her kitchen chair, MJ marveled at the full story—she'd never heard all the details before. It gave her a greater appreciation for Valentine's importance in her aunt's life.

Anna rose and stacked their empty plates. "I took her back to the stable where I'd boarded Duke. Brought in a vet and got advice on how to deal with her health issues. But to fully recover, she needed fresh air, open space. And at that point, so did I."

"You bought this farm just for Valentine?"

"Sounds crazy, doesn't it? She was a horse I might never be able to ride at all, and I certainly could never jump her or show her. I didn't even know how much longer I could keep her alive. But that day at the auction house, I needed a friend and so did she." Anna waved a hand toward the property beyond her front porch. "This farm had gotten run down, so it was going very cheap. And I wanted a place to hide away for a while."

MJ knew what that felt like. "Then you decided to rescue more horses?"

"I started using Julie as my vet, and one day she told me about a Standardbred harness racer bought at auction by a friend of hers, who turned out to be Clint. He was looking for a place to stable the horse while he tried to find it a new home. I had five empty stalls, so I thought, why not?" Anna pulled out her cell phone. "That reminds me—I need to give him a call."

While MJ finished her iced tea, her aunt tapped out a number. From the length of time she waited, she must have gotten a recording.

"Hey, Clint, just wondering if you had a chance yet to swing by the Deckers' place and check on Starbuck. If you did, let me know what's going on, okay?"

After she hung up, MJ asked if something was wrong.

"Probably not, but...I adopted Starbuck out to some folks in Monmouth County about three months back. They signed a contract promising to email a few photos every month showing his condition. They did it the first month, but since then they've sent nothing. I've emailed and left phone messages with no answer."

"Think something's happened to him?"

"I hope not. Some people take a horse with good intentions, but when their circumstances change...Anyway, Clint will follow up. He was pretty attached to Starbuck." Anna stuck the phone back into her jeans pocket. "Well, after the morning's drudgery, are you up for some fun? Julie said that Dash can handle a little riding. If he's ever going to find a new home, we need to keep up his training. Wanna help with that?"

"You bet!" MJ decided things were looking up.

"Get your helmet, while I go tack him."

"Don't I need the other fancy riding clothes Mom packed for me?"

"Nope. You'll be going Western, so your jeans and barn boots will do just fine."

By the time her niece met her at the barn, helmet in hand, Anna had fitted the buckskin with a cowboy saddle of dark, tooled leather, and a kind of bridle with no bit that MJ could see.

Anna explained, "It's a hackamore. When you pull the reins it puts pressure on his nose, and that's enough to stop him. Dash is a very mellow guy. Ever ridden Western before?"

"Just once, on a trail ride on vacation."

"Takes a little getting used to, if you've always done English. It did for me, but a local kid gave me some pointers. Dash has always gone Western, so I stick with what's familiar to him."

Her aunt led the buckskin into an empty, round pen at the rear of the barnyard, maybe forty feet in diameter. MJ had seen enclosures like this before in videos—they were used for training horses. Anna stopped Dash by a square mounting block just inside the gate. "C'mon, I'll help you up."

MJ could mount just fine with English gear, but felt clumsy holding onto the front horn and swinging her leg high to clear the taller back of the Western saddle. Anna reminded her to keep the reins in just one hand and showed her how to lay them against the side of the horse's neck as a signal to turn. "Leave them slack most of the time, and don't pull back too hard to stop, or he might back up," she said. "And sit up *straight*."

"Yes, ma'am." MJ smiled. That was one command she'd heard from every riding teacher she'd ever known.

Her aunt led them for a minute to make sure MJ was feeling secure, then let her ride on her own. "Just take him around the ring. You can do a few figure-eights, too, if you want to mix it up."

Just then Anna's cell phone chimed and she left the ring to take the call. "Clint, thanks for getting back to me. So did you—" She listened for a minute, and her voice dropped. "Un-huh...Oh, man, I was afraid of that." She faced away, as if to prevent her niece from overhearing any more.

Though wondering what was up, MJ settled in to enjoy her easy ride. Too much time had passed since she'd been on a horse. Her Dad always had supported her interest in riding more than her Mom did. Erika liked the social atmosphere of horse shows, but thought the sport itself was too messy, smelly, and dangerous.

Anna, still holding her phone, called out, "MJ, I've got to run back to my office for a minute. You okay out here?"

"Sure." The girl reached down to pat Dash's muscular, tan neck. He seemed like a nice, easygoing guy, and she instinctively trusted him.

When her aunt jogged off toward the barn, MJ wondered what was so urgent. She hoped nothing was wrong with that Standardbred in Monmouth County.

Dash tossed his dark mane amiably and continued his easy stroll around the pen. He reminded MJ a little of Marco, her favorite pony at the riding camp she'd gone to when she was twelve. The campers rotated horses, but everyone looked forward to a turn on Marco, because he was peppy but also obedient. Unlike some of the slow, sullen animals at the camp, he seemed to enjoy his work.

When MJ went back the following summer, though, Marco was gone. In fact, the whole lineup of horses and ponies had changed. A counselor explained it was too expensive for the camp to keep the horses over the winter, so every fall the old bunch went to auction. Wondering if Marco might be for sale somewhere, MJ had checked out auctions online...

And found a rescue site explaining that most horses went from auction directly to slaughter. It said people in many European and Asian countries actually ate horsemeat, considering it a "delicacy." That site also linked to a slaughterhouse video.

MJ felt her gorge rise again at the memory. *No wonder Anna cried over Duke ending up that way. I couldn't stand the idea of it happening to Marco, either.*

But that's one reason I'm here, isn't it? Anyway, I'm not going to spoil this nice ride on Dash with morbid thoughts.

Anna still hadn't returned from the barn, so MJ decided to try figure-eights. The neck-reining worked pretty well, and she was able to make Dash walk on a diagonal across the round pen, along the rail for a few strides and back in the other direction. Midway through the next diagonal, a fresh breeze inspired Dash to break into an easy jog. MJ pulled back on the reins to slow him and pressed her inside leg against the girth to guide him back on course.

Instead, he planted his feet, sank back on his haunches...and spun. He stopped so abruptly that MJ grabbed the saddle horn to stay on.

"Yow!" she gasped. "What was *that*?"

Heart pounding, she walked the buckskin forward again, but he had more spring in his stride now. His ears flicked back and forth, as if eager for some signal from her.

"C'mon, Dash, be a good boy," she begged. When he started to jog and veered off-course once more, she tightened the reins and put her other leg on him.

He whipped around in the opposite direction. Another full turn with a sudden, hard stop.

He stood still, then, but quivered as if ready to spin again. MJ gripped the saddle horn, white-knuckled.

Should I try to jump off? But if he does it while I'm in mid-air—

While she sat petrified, an angry, male voice shouted from outside the pen.

"Hey! Whad'ya think you're doing?"

CHAPTER SEVEN:

WALT

MJ dared to glance around. A guy about her age, of medium height, in faded jeans and a rust-colored T-shirt, glared at her over the fence.

He demanded again, "What're you doing?"

She answered with a shaky laugh. "Trying to stay on!"

"You're gonna hurt that horse. Does Anna know you're making him do that stuff?"

"W-what stuff?"

By now Anna had returned from the barn, and their raised voices drew her toward them. "What's the problem, kids?"

"She was doing spins on Dash!" the young guy accused.

Startled, MJ assured her aunt, "I didn't mean to! I just did this—" Again she raised the reins in one hand and put her leg behind the girth on one side.

Sure enough, the buckskin whipped in another half-circle, then stopped dead.

Anna ducked through the fence rail and grabbed the horse's hackamore. "You're telling him to spin, MJ. Keep your hands lower and your legs farther forward."

MJ saw the stranger, still outside the fence, shake his head. He must be marveling at her stupidity.

At least Anna looked apologetic. "I should've warned you. Dash knows a lot of fancy moves from his rodeo days. Now that he's feeling better, he may be happy to try to them out. But we don't want him going lame again." She patted MJ's knee. "Feel safe enough to walk him around a couple more times?"

"Sure." The girl felt relieved to know Dash wasn't really acting up, just responding to her mixed signals.

While MJ rode forward again, Anna introduced the newcomer. "This is Walt Patterson. His family has a farm up the road. Walt, this is my niece, MJ Klein. She's helping me for the summer."

The girl grudgingly waved to Walt.

He returned the gesture and called out "Sorry!" When he grinned, flashing a crooked front tooth, he struck MJ as much different from the guys she knew at school. His jeans looked broken in from real work and his T-shirt was actually tucked in. His reddish hair was cut in a nondescript, barbershop style—not rocker-long, spiky punk, or biker butch. Most unusual, he'd made no effort at all to look cool.

With a nod toward the paddocks, Walt remarked to Anna, "You got a new horse."

"Just yesterday." She told him briefly about Murphy's dramatic arrival. He seemed as impressed as the rest of them that the gray had jumped the tractor.

"Yeah, he looks full o' beans," Walt said. "He's back there racing with your pony."

"What?" Anna headed toward the paddocks to check.

MJ pulled Dash up and tried to dismount, then realized she'd also have to do that differently than she was used to. She couldn't just kick both feet out of the stirrups and swing her right leg over—not with the high back on this saddle.

Anna was too far off to notice her difficulty, but with another grin Walt said, "Hang on, I'll help ya."

Oh, great! MJ thought. *Now I've embarrassed myself again.*

He opened the gate and caught Dash's reins. "Just keep your left foot in the stirrup while you swing the other leg. He's not so big, you can just step down."

It was still a bit of a drop to the ground, though, and as she landed MJ felt fat and clumsy. She was about to thank Walt when he added, "Haven't done much riding, huh?"

Her pride flared up. "I've done plenty. Jumping, too. I'm just not used to Western! Everything's, like, backwards."

"Well, if you're gonna ride Dash, you'll have to learn."

MJ tried to think of a rude reply, but for the moment her wit failed her. She told herself Walt wasn't even cute enough to act so cocky. He was in good shape—probably from farm work—but with a slightly round, boyish face and a scattering of freckles. Anybody at her school would have gotten those front teeth straightened years ago. And up close, she saw he wore a cross on a chain, in plain view on top of his T-shirt. Not a funky goth cross or a bling-y, hip-hop design. Just a small, simple one in gold.

"Need help to lead him?" Walt asked, a teasing glint in his hazel eyes.

"Hardly." MJ let him hold the gate while she led the gentle buckskin from the pen. She told herself she didn't need to come all the way out here to be mocked by a guy. She could get plenty of that back at school.

Walking alongside, Walt asked, "Did that hurt?"

She thought he meant her ride on Dash, until she realized he was looking at the tattoo on her upper arm.

"Not much," MJ lied. Did he have to scrutinize her like she was some kind of space alien?

By the paddocks, they found Anna leaning against the fence to watch a strange performance. Murphy, though penned by himself, was indeed racing with Patches. The elegant gray Thoroughbred and the pinto Shetland tore back and forth along the fence that separated them, raising twin clouds of dust. In spite of the difference in their sizes, and Patches' poor vision, they managed to keep pace and almost mirror one another. With occasional snorts and half-rears, they would wheel at the corners and canter back the way they'd come.

Valentine, in with Patches, watched from a safe distance, but occasionally also trotted a few steps and tossed her head in excitement.

Still holding Dash, MJ stopped next to Anna. "Think Murphy misses the track?"

"Probably just likes having a pal to play with. Racehorses don't really get turned out together, once they go into training."

Walt joined them, and Anna filled him in on Murphy's history.

When he heard about the flipping issue, he gave a low whistle. "Never heard of a horse doin' that, 'cept maybe a rodeo bronc. You sure you can deal with him?"

"I guess we'll see. Our vet said I should call Josh Buchanan."

Walt gave a thoughtful nod, so MJ figured he might have heard of Buchanan, too. "Anyhow, I'm on my way into town, if you need anything."

"Not today, thanks," Anna said. "I stocked up when I knew my niece was coming."

Walt glanced at MJ again, and she dodged his amused eyes. *He's probably thinking I look like I put away a lot of groceries.*

He started toward a beaten-up, gray flatbed truck parked at the end of the drive; it made Clint's heap look like a BMW. "Well, you ever need help, remember we're all just up the road." From the truck's cab, Walt gave another cheery wave. "'Bye, MJ!" Then, with a neat K-turn, he guided the ugly, rattling vehicle out of the barnyard.

Wow, MJ thought. *No guy back home would be caught dead driving anything like that. It's really another world out here.*

Anna noted silently that Walt and her niece had not met under the best of circumstances. She could only imagine what her young neighbor thought when he'd found this girl with the black-and-green hair doing spins on a horse that had lameness issues.

MJ still looked humiliated after being scolded by a guy around her own age.

Anna gave her a one-armed squeeze around the waist. "I'm sure Walt didn't mean to be so hard on you. I guess he's protective of Dash. The Pattersons tipped off the county Humane Society about him being abused, and recommended that he be surrendered to my care. And Walt also taught me what little I know about riding Western, so I could exercise Dash."

"Does Walt's family have horses?" MJ asked.

"A few. Mostly for pleasure riding, though they've been in some local shows. They also raise some crops and have cows and chickens. I get most of my eggs from them."

Anna led Dash into the barn, where the hay-scented shade felt good after the blaze of the afternoon sun. Trailing her, MJ asked, "What did Clint say about that other horse, Starbuck?"

A wave of guilt made Anna's stomach clench. "It's bad. The Deckers, who adopted him, have him turned out in an almost-bare field with no shelter or water, and he's lost a lot of weight. Clint said when he stopped by nobody even seemed to be home."

"What are you going to do?"

"I left a message with the Humane Society in that part of New Jersey. They might be able to check out the situation and let me know what's up."

The two of them stripped Dash of his tack and gave him a quick grooming before turning him back out with Patches and Valentine. Anna's cell phone rang and she snatched it from her back pocket. It was someone named Cynthia, from the Humane Society.

Anna explained to her about Starbuck's adoption arrangement and what she'd been told about his present condition. "I was hoping someone from your office could investigate, see if there's any explanation. Maybe the Deckers have been ill, or..."

"We can have someone drive over there," the other woman said, sounding cautious. "But if these people already have a contract with you—"

"I know, it's my responsibility to get the horse back. It's just that I have a small operation, and it's a little hard for me to get away right now."

"Okay." Cynthia sounded a bit annoyed to be doing Anna's followup. "I'll let you know what we find."

As her aunt pocketed her phone again, MJ asked, "Do you have to go to Monmouth County?"

"I ought to, so I can talk to the Deckers myself. But I'd be gone most of the day, and I don't see how I can leave the farm for that long. Our horses with health issues, especially, need somebody to keep an eye on them. And now that I've got Murphy...who knows what he might get up to while I was away."

"That's no problem!" MJ assured her. "Now that I'm here, I can watch the horses. If anything goes wrong, I can just call the vet—"

The girl's eagerness to help was sweet, Anna thought, but she had no idea how much could go wrong, and how suddenly, on a horse farm. "I appreciate that, honey. But if something bad happens and Julie can't come right away, you might not know what to do. After all, you've only been here a day! Maybe later on, after you've had more experience."

They retreated to the small office Anna maintained near the front of the barn. It had come with old-fashioned pine paneling and she'd added a beige metal desk and a filing cabinet, purchased used from an office-supply place. Her printer sat on a weatherbeaten tack trunk. A far cry, Anna reflected, from the setup she'd had as a magazine editor in Basking Ridge.

Deflated by the problem with Starbuck, she sank into her rickety desk chair. Her gaze drifted to her old desktop computer, which she'd used to look up the number of the Humane Society. The screensaver showed a professional-quality photo, taken at a horse show, of Anna crouched high on Duke's neck as the powerful black cleared a three-bar fence.

MJ noticed it, too. "Great picture."

Her aunt nodded. "I keep it up as a kind of memorial, I guess. After all, it was losing Duke that inspired me to start this place."

"Really captures the action. Who took it, a show photographer?"

"No, Richard. Photography was one of his hobbies. He was good at a lot of things." Anna couldn't resist adding, "Like pulling the wool over people's eyes."

"Where did you say he is now?"

"Hawaii, of all places. Last I heard, he was starting up another financial consulting service of some kind. And he's found a new girlfriend, of course."

"Does that bug you?"

"Only when I think he might be bilking more people out of their life savings and getting away with it." Uncomfortable with the topic, Anna changed it. "I know something you might be able to help me with. Didn't you say you set up a website for one of your friends? I attempted to create one for this place, but it's pretty lame. I used to lay out a magazine electronically, but designing a good website takes a whole different skill set."

Her niece pulled a wooden shoeing bench nearer to the desk. "Yeah, your site is totally bare-bones. And you need a better name than 'Anna's Horse Rescue.'"

"Guess I've been waiting until I was sure I could make a go of the operation. Can you think of something better?"

"Maybe 'Valentine Farm?' Since she was your first rescue."

Anna made a face. "Sounds like a tacky honeymoon resort. But when I searched online, most of the obvious names—with words like 'rescue' and 'haven' and 'sanctuary'—were already taken."

"Really?"

"Oh, yeah. There are lots of rescue operations, all around the country, but still not enough. So many people get rid of their horses after they get old or lame, or they just can't afford them anymore. Meanwhile, farms keep breeding racehorses, but few win enough to earn their keep. Unless they're put down or sent to slaughter, they all have to go somewhere."

A neigh sounded from outside. Murphy's distinctive, demanding tone.

Anna slapped her knees and stood up. "Ha, dinnertime already! We'll talk about the website later. First we'd better feed those guys and ourselves."

After dinner, while MJ voluntarily washed up the dishes—having gotten over her shock that the house had no dishwasher—Anna checked on the horses one last time. Val, Dash and Patches dozed on their feet in various spots around their enclosure, while Murphy still gazed out over the fence of his own paddock.

Anna wondered if he'd settle in faster with a companion. He seemed to have hit it off with Patches, but luckily not in the same way as with Valentine. He didn't seem to regard the half-blind pony as a potential mate, just a platonic pal. And Anna knew Patches could hold her own very well against bigger horses.

I won't risk it tonight, but maybe tomorrow....

She returned to the office to finish some homework of her own. Although "Ann Cooper" had stepped down two years ago as editor-in-chief of *New Jersey Good Life*, "Anna Loehmeyer" still appeared in fine print on the masthead as one of the magazine's copy editors. Erika sent her articles on a regular basis—usually, the ones that needed the most polishing—so Anna still drew a bit of income from that source.

She appreciated this help from her sister, but the small monthly paycheck didn't go far toward covering the expenses of running the farm. The inheritance from her mother, which Anna had invested with the help of a legitimate financial advisor, provided her with a better income stream. Even that wouldn't be sufficient, though, if her rescue kept expanding.

If Starbuck has to come back now, that will bring our total number of "residents" up to five. I need to find some donors with big hearts and deep pockets. Trouble is, most of the wealthy people I know think of me as a pariah these days.

To distract herself from such depressing thoughts, Anna buckled down to editing the magazine story. It took about an hour to whip it into shape. When she emailed it to Erika, she added a note that MJ had successfully completed her first full day as a horse-rescue volunteer, and even offered to wash the dinner dishes. As far as Anna knew, the girl had not called home since arriving at the farm.

Before turning off her computer for the night, Anna yielded to a temptation that had been tugging at her all day. She checked out the website for Josh Buchanan's horse-training business.

His home page gave a summary of Natural Horsemanship, debunking the idea that it involved anything mystical. The principles, it explained, grew out of studying equines in nature and how they interacted with each other. One photo showed Buchanan holding a rearing horse at the end of a lunge line, matched with a second shot in which he sat bareback on the same animal, now relaxed and docile. In other pictures, he rode a big warmblood at a dressage "working trot," and jumped what looked like a Thoroughbred over a sizeable hurdle. You could see Buchanan himself only at a distance, but Anna got the impression of a rather tall, lean figure with curly brown hair and the kind of face people liked to call "ruggedly handsome."

A page marked "Behavioral Problems" explained his methods for curing different equine vices. The gist seemed to be regaining the horse's trust through groundwork in a round pen. Anna read until her eyes started to burn. She realized that, although it wasn't quite ten, she badly needed sleep.

As she shut down the computer, she still doubted whether she needed to spend any of her sparse income on hiring Buchanan as a trainer. But his website had given her a few new ideas, and she resolved to try them out the next morning.

Might as well find out sooner, rather than later, just how hard it's going to be to retrain flippin' Murphy.

CHAPTER EIGHT:

ROUND PEN

The next morning, Anna led the gray Thoroughbred outside. Following with Patches, MJ asked her aunt, "Why not just turn him out with Valentine? We know he likes her."

"Yeah, but maybe too much. From what Clint says, this guy wasn't gelded until he was about three, which means he could still have a bit of a sex drive."

"Patches is a mare, too."

"But she's pretty old." Anna smiled. "And from what I've seen, Murphy doesn't like her in 'that way.' Besides..."

She gestured toward the height difference between the two animals, and MJ laughed.

They brought both horses to a pasture just beyond the paddocks, fenced but not electrified. Anna just hoped the presence of a buddy would keep Murphy occupied enough to stay put.

"I forgot how messy this field got over the winter," she mumbled, half to herself. "We've got a fallen tree, and those rocks I piled up last fall... Nothing they should hurt themselves on, though."

Anna thought of taking off the gray's halter, but he could be hard to catch—better to leave it on. She led him through the gate but faced him away from the field as she quietly unsnapped his lead line.

It took him a second to realize he was free. Then he tore off across the green expanse.

Dryly, MJ asked, "Think we'll ever get him back?"

"That may be up to Patches. C'mon, bring her in."

At first, the half-blind pony trotted with confidence into the field, though after she tripped once on the uneven ground she grew more careful. About a hundred yards in, she let out a high-pitched whinny.

Murphy halted in mid-flight, then galloped back to join her. The two touched noses and he danced in place, urging his new friend to chase him. Patches did so, though it was hardly a hot pursuit. After a minute, Murphy deliberately slowed, giving the little old lady a chance to catch up.

Watching this game, Anna's heart lifted. "Yes!"

Her niece grinned. "Patches is calming him down, huh?"

"And Murphy's not a vicious psycho-horse. He's smart and he's got a good heart. We can work with that."

Anna's cell phone rang, displaying a Monmouth County area code. Cynthia from the Humane Society again.

"A couple of our guys stopped by to check on that Standard-bred," she told Anna. "The owner, Mr. Decker, had a stroke a couple months ago. He's still pretty debilitated. They spoke to his wife, who's had her hands full. Sounds like taking care of the horse has been the last thing on her mind."

Anna remembered that Bob Decker always was the more enthusiastic one about adopting Starbuck. Maybe his wife never did know or care much about the animal. "So, what can we do?"

"The good news is, she surrendered the horse to us without any protest, and we have him in our barn. The bad news is, he's about two hundred pounds underweight, he's got cracked hooves and he's real dehydrated. I don't think he can travel very far until we get him in better shape."

Anna felt a stab of anguish, imagining poor Starbuck reduced to such a condition. *I feel sorry for the Deckers, too...but damn, couldn't the wife at least have given me a call and asked me to take the horse back?*

"I appreciate anything you folks can do for him," she told Cynthia. "Whenever he's ready to travel, I'll come with my van to pick him up."

"That would be good. We're always short on stable space

here."

After ending the call, Anna explained the situation to MJ. "This is so depressing. The first horse I adopted out, and he ends up as bad as before! This rescue business is turning out to be even tougher than I thought."

"Hey, you'll get him back in shape again and find him another home." MJ nodded toward the field. "Meanwhile, check this out!"

Patches galloped alongside the big gray, still pretending to chase him and keeping him close to the fenceline. That was where most of the winter debris had piled up, but none of it seemed to deter Murphy. The toppled tree, the piles of rocks... whatever showed up in his path, he jumped. He cleared it all with room to spare, as if he was having great fun.

Anna heard the excitement in her niece's voice. "We *really* need to train him."

"Easy, kid. *I* need to train him. You can help, but only from a safe distance."

"Really? When can we start?"

"After lunch." Anna watched the Thoroughbred fly around the pasture yet again. "Of course, that's assuming we can catch him."

When they brought the two horses back to the barnyard, Anna told her niece to put Patches in with Val. She turned Murphy loose in the round pen, where he could still see the two mares.

She also passed her cell phone to MJ. "Anything goes wrong, I've got the doctor on speed dial."

The girl looked startled. "Julie?"

"No, *my* doctor."

Anna picked up a lunge whip she had left outside the pen and stepped inside with Murphy. She moved slowly and quietly, so he wouldn't overreact to the five-foot-long stick with the even longer lash coiled around it.

She had tried to memorize the instructions she'd read on Josh Buchanan's website, and others, the previous evening. It felt like a whole new ball game, though, now that this big, high-strung animal stood in front of her. The enclosure suddenly seemed smaller than before.

At first, Murphy's attention remained so focused on his equine neighbors that he hardly noticed Anna's presence. She walked toward him, raised the end of the whip slightly and pointed it at his hindquarters. That made him pivot toward her, snort and bolt to her left. Anna let him circle, not concerned for the moment about his pace. She rotated to follow his motion, keeping the whip about waist-high and pointed at his hip. Murphy flicked his ears toward her and rolled his eyes, wary.

I'm sure he's never done round-pen work before. I wonder if he's even worked on a lunge line! These were familiar parts of a show horse's training and exercise routine, but perhaps not used so much with racehorses.

MJ leaned on the fence rail, watching in fascination. When Murphy cantered roughly past her and threw in a buck, though, she sprang back. *Time to change direction,* Anna decided. *Now we'll really see if I'm any good at this.*

She switched the whip to her other hand, took a couple of steps toward Murphy and reached the long stick slightly in front of him. He slid to a stop, raising dust. She used both the whip and her body language to send him in the opposite direction. He trotted just a few steps to the right before he ducked his shoulder, dodged past her and charged left again.

"Wow," MJ called from the rail. "Why's he being so stubborn?"

"He's mostly been trained to go counterclockwise. That's the direction they run in horse races." The Internet articles had said one of the first challenges in retraining an OTTB was to get him to circle to the right.

He's got to learn this if he's ever going to be used for anything else. Reminding herself to be patient, Anna once again stepped a bit in front of the trotting horse and tried to send him the opposite way.

This time he planted his feet, laid back his ears...

And reared.

Anna froze. Even at a few yards away, the horse's front hooves seemed to paw the sky. She imagined them right over her head, and it took all her self-control to stand her ground.

In her mind, she heard the voices of her past riding teachers: *Don't let him get away with that.* She raised the whip and shouted. "No!"

The gray dropped back to all fours, but once more tried to go left. She blocked him and snapped the whip on the ground.

Murphy backed up, ears flattening. But he finally he turned and trotted clockwise.

Hot, dusty and still vibrating with fear, Anna kept working the horse for about ten more minutes. At least Murphy paid full attention to her now, ignoring anything outside the pen, and never reared again. When he trotted all the way around to the right without balking, Anna ended his lesson.

She parked the whip against the fence and walked up to the Thoroughbred, her body language quiet and voice soothing. Murphy's dappled coat was dark with sweat from the afternoon's warmth, his exertion and his nerves. But he stood still as she approached, watching with curiosity rather than fear, and seemed to enjoy her pats and praise. She led him from the round pen and put him back in his usual paddock, near his girlfriends.

"That's it?" MJ sounded relieved, as her aunt latched the paddock gate.

"He did what I asked him to, so he gets his reward."

"I had my finger on the speed-dial," MJ joked, "but you called his bluff."

"He was just copping an attitude." Anna did not want the girl to pick up on her own misgivings.

On their walk back to the house, she wondered if Murphy had just been bluffing, and if she really had "cured" him. *Or is it like Julie said? Has rearing to get his way become a habit for him by now—a very dangerous one?*

That would be bad news for both of us.

CHAPTER NINE:

Intruder

When MJ finally phoned her mother that evening, she put a positive spin on her adventures at the farm so far. "Right after you dropped me off Sunday, a friend of Anna's came by with a new horse. He's an ex-racer and we're gonna retrain him to be a jumper."

"Oh?" Erika sounded only mildly curious. "You can do that?"

MJ realized her mother had no idea just how hard the task might be. *Well, neither do I, really.* "Anna's doing most of the training, but I'm helping. And yesterday I rode a Western horse who does spins—that was pretty wild!" Laughing, the girl almost convinced herself that the experience had been more fun than frightening.

Erika still didn't express much interest. "Be nice if you were learning some actual career skills."

"Who says I'm not? This morning Anna taught me how to muck out a stall. Maybe I can get a job working backside at a racetrack."

A moan on the line. "Oh, fine. I'm sure you'll meet all the best people there!"

MJ felt the old tightness creep back into her throat—a pressure that, she realized, she hadn't felt since arriving at the farm. "Dr. Mayer said I'm supposed to relax and get in touch with nature. Anyway, I came here to figure out a lot of things, and I'm still doing that. I need more time, okay?"

Erika sighed. "I just don't want to see you fall too far behind... all your friends."

She meant, MJ knew, behind all the kids of *her* friends. That would look bad—her daughter the slacker. The loser.

"Your brother wants to say hello," Erika said. "He scored three goals in his soccer game today!"

Carl got on the phone, still breathless from victory. MJ congratulated him, though winning was par for the course with Carl. At fifteen, he also starred in basketball and track. This time, at least, MJ could share some stories of her own. She told him about Murphy and Dash, embellishing a little more than she had for her mother.

"And a neighbor came by yesterday, a guy from the next farm," she went on. "About seventeen, I guess, 'cause he was driving. A big ol' pickup truck, vintage really. Like something out of...what was that old TV show? The Waltons!"

That made Carl snicker. "Yeah, from what Mom says, you're out in the sticks. I still don't know why you want to stay there the whole summer."

"It's been fun, so far," MJ told him "'Course, I've only been here a couple of days. Maybe I will get bored after awhile. It is pretty quiet, especially at night—"

As if to make a liar out of her, a horsey scream rang out from one of the paddocks. It sounded like Murphy, she thought. But he hadn't made a peep the night before, even though he'd been new to the place.

He bellowed again, loud enough to hear even over the window fan. Sounding not exactly afraid or hurt, MJ thought, but...angry? She also heard Anna stride across the living room to the front door.

"Carl, I think there's a problem with the horses. Gotta go!" MJ ended her call and ran to help her aunt.

From the front porch, which had a dim light over the door, they both could see the dappled gray pacing back and forth in his paddock. His focus didn't seem to be on any of his four-legged companions, though. He stared up the gravel drive to where it disappeared into blackness, leading out to the road.

Peering over the porch railing, Anna warned MJ back. "The way he's carrying on, it might be a bear. They come around every once in awhile."

"What if it is?"

"The horses will be safe because I've got the electric fence on. You go in the kitchen and get a couple of those old aluminum pots, with their lids. If it is a bear, we can bang them to scare it away."

MJ did as she was told. By the time she got back, her aunt had ventured halfway down the front steps. The security light over the barn door showed nothing and no one in that area. Anna swept the nearest part of the drive with her flashlight beam, but MJ didn't see any intruders, animal or human.

Anna went out to the Thoroughbred's paddock to reassure him. "Hey, buddy, what's the matter? Did something scare you? Don't worry, you're okay in here."

Armed with a couple of pots, MJ followed her aunt. Though none of the other three horses acted as nervous as Murphy, they had bunched together toward the back of their enclosure—as far from the driveway as they could get. Dash stood on guard as if protecting the two mares, and even in the dim light MJ noticed white edging his eyes.

Somewhere down the drive, tires crunched on gravel in short spurts, as if someone was backing and turning. Then an engine roared into the distance.

MJ looked at Anna. "Do bears around here drive trucks?"

"Not here, or anywhere else." Her aunt's blonde brows drew together above her slender nose. "And if someone came in this far on foot, they had to pass through the main gate. It's not locked, but still—"

"Maybe it was Clint? Or Walt?"

"I'm sure they'd just park in the barnyard and come up to the house."

Murphy pawed the ground and gave another snort.

"Well, at least whoever it was drove away." MJ left unsaid, *If they'd wanted to do anything bad to us, they probably wouldn't have beat it so fast.*

"Yeah, maybe they were just lost. Came this far in and realized they had the wrong farm."

"Sure, that makes sense." *But even if somebody was lost, when he saw our lights on, why not come to the door and ask directions?*

Anna switched off her flashlight and started back inside. Before joining her, MJ threw a last look over her shoulder.

Murphy wandered back to his water trough and took a peaceful drink.

"If we can't train him to be a show horse," the girl suggested, "maybe you can adopt him out as a watchdog."

Her aunt's full-throated laugh made her feel a little better.

Though Anna had put on a brave front for her niece, she slept fitfully that night. The slightest scrape of a branch against the roof, or stamp of a horse outside in the paddocks, set her nerves jangling.

She had left her bedroom window open, as usual, to take advantage of the breeze, but now wondered if she should close and lock it. And maybe MJ's, too?

I'm being ridiculous. I'm sure it happened just like I said— somebody came down our driveway by accident. It's not easy to find a particular house out on these country roads, after dark. Maybe after he realized he was in the wrong place, he was too embarrassed to ask for help. Maybe he, or she, was drunk.

Like MJ said, at least when the driver heard us come out, they did leave.

Still, Anna got up to lock her window. She crept down the hall to MJ's room, cracked open the door and made sure her niece was still asleep. A big electric fan whirred in the girl's window, so at least no one was going to sneak in that way.

If anything happened to MJ, because she came out here to help me, I'd never forgive myself.

Anna reflected this must be how it felt to be a mother. Not an experience she'd had so far, and at this rate it didn't seem she ever would. Her jumping accident had terminated the only child she ever would conceive with Richard. Maybe he'd been right, that day at the hospital, when he'd told her it was just as well.

When she'd first moved to the farm, she'd often felt like this. Worried about the isolation, about strangers dropping by when she was alone, about wild animals. Over time she'd learned that she had friends just a phone call away, and that bears and coyotes found all the food they wanted in the woods, rarely approaching either her house or her animals. She'd gotten used to leaving her windows open and her doors unlocked, confident that she could take care of herself.

That had been fine, back when she'd had only herself and the horses to worry about. But now she had a taken on bigger responsibility.

She had MJ.

The next morning, while they were bringing the animals in for breakfast, MJ noticed that Dash's old green halter, usually hung over the paddock fencepost, lay on the ground. When she stooped to pick it up, she spotted some fresh footprints.

Large, with smooth soles and pointed toes. MJ hadn't seen anyone around the farm, so far, who wore boots like that. She and Anna mostly wore athletic shoes or round-toed paddock boots, and as far as she remembered, Clint had worn heavy, treaded work boots.

Did Walt have on Western boots, the day he came here? Maybe...but I don't think his feet are that big.

She showed her aunt what she had found.

Anna looked worried all over again. "The way the tracks are pointing, the guy must have stood close to the fence, looking at the horses. I wonder why that upset them? None of them seem to have been hurt in any way."

"The electric fence was on last night," MJ pointed out.

"That's right." Anna stared at the wire, as if reconstructing some scenario. "It makes a high-pitched buzz that animals can hear, but not humans. A stranger could have put his hand right on it and got zapped. Maybe he cursed, jumped away—"

"—Knocked the halter off the fencepost, and that spooked the horses?"

Her aunt nodded. "Then, when we came out, he thought we'd be angry, so he ran off."

MJ exhaled. That did sound like the most probable explanation. "Still kind of weird, but I guess people do funny things sometimes."

"Just the same," said Anna. "I'm going to start locking the main gate at night."

CHAPTER TEN:

BLINDSIDED

A few minutes later, while MJ poured grain into the corner bins of the horses' stalls, she overheard her aunt talking on the phone in the barn office.

"Today?" Anna asked. "Okay, I guess I can get there. I'll just have to arrange some things..." She punched another number, then stepped away from the open door, so her niece couldn't eavesdrop.

By the time MJ had finished feeding, her aunt joined her in the barn aisle. "The Humane Society folks say Starbuck is strong enough to travel, so I'm going to go pick him up. Mrs. Decker will be there to release him back to me."

"You're going to Monmouth County?" MJ brightened at the prospect of a trip—she hadn't been off the farm since she'd arrived.

"Yes, but I'm afraid you'll have to stay here. It'll be about two hours each way, plus whatever time I have to spend at the Humane Society settling things up, so I won't be back until late afternoon. Somebody has to keep an eye on our horses."

Of course, MJ thought, a little deflated. "Oh, well, I can do that. I know the routine by now."

"I'm sure you do, but just in case, Walt's going to drop over. I'm going to need some extra feed and medications for Starbuck, anyway, and he's offered to pick them up for me."

MJ couldn't suppress a groan. Five hours on her own with the horses, she probably could handle. But five hours of Walt's superior attitude? "Honestly, I'll be fine. I don't need a babysitter!

Especially not—"

Her aunt took her by the shoulders. "MJ, even if I thought you had enough experience by now to handle the usual things, I wouldn't want to leave you by yourself after what happened last night. The person who drove in here probably did it by accident, but if there's any chance it was some guy who figured out there are two women living here alone...you might not be safe. Understand?"

A little shaken, MJ nodded. It occurred to her, though, that her mother might not like the idea of her spending a whole day alone with a guy her own age, either. "What makes you so sure I'll be safe with Walt?"

Anna let go of her with a mysterious smile. "Oh, I'm not worried about him."

MJ blinked, not knowing how to take that reply.

"If you get bored, though, maybe he can give you a lesson on Dash," her aunt added. "Now c'mon, you can help me hitch up the trailer."

Fifteen minutes later, Anna headed off down the drive in her burgundy-colored Dodge pickup, towing an empty, two-horse trailer behind. Watching her go, MJ felt more conscious of how little she knew about running the farm by herself.

At least before she left Anna had put both Val and Murphy outside in their pens. All MJ had to do was bring out Dash and Patches when they finished eating. Murphy seemed pretty laid-back that morning, and Val, having had her morning meds, was breathing okay.

If I've got any questions, I guess I can ask Mr. Charm—whenever he gets here.

The girl wondered why her aunt had smiled in that funny way when she said she trusted Walt with MJ. *Probably 'cause I'm such a fat weirdo that no guy my age would be interested in me.* She knew Anna wouldn't think anything so cruel, but maybe Walt had said something about MJ not being his type. *Like he's so hot.*

She remembered the mocking glint in his eyes when she'd struggled to dismount from that high-backed Western saddle. Why leave herself open to more humiliation?

Dreading the prospect, she checked to make sure Dash and

Patches had finished breakfast. Then she led the buckskin out to the paddock, thinking she *would* like to ride him again, but not if it meant taking orders from that know-it-all.

For the first time since she'd come to the farm, she questioned her decision. If she were home, maybe she could have found a way to see more of Bobby. She'd almost texted him the night before, but chickened out. Well, not exactly...they'd had the commotion outside with the horses, and after that it was kind of late.

MJ went back into the barn to get Patches. *Maybe I'll call Bobby tonight. I did design his website, and it needs updating. I could call to remind him, and tell him about the stuff happening here. He might be more interested than Stacey was.*

As she slid the pony's stall door open, she remembered how Stacey had teased her on the phone about leaving Bobby up for grabs. *What if he is doing shows this summer, and Stacey's going to them, without me? Telling him what a brilliant guitarist he is, batting those fake eyelashes at him...*

MJ tried to force such thoughts from her mind. Stepping briskly into the stall, she slapped the pony on her rump to make her move over. "C'mon, Patches, let's—"

A quick, sledgehammer punch sent MJ crashing into the wall.

She crumpled to the floor and sat in the wood shavings, stunned. Soon, the dead feeling in her left shin flared into agony. It took her a second longer, though, to realize that Patches had kicked her.

The pony swung to face MJ and stood with her head cocked. Her nostrils flared as if to catch the girl's scent.

Crap, I forgot. She's blind on that side!

Patches dodged out then through the stall's open door and trotted off across the barnyard. MJ tried to get up and catch her, but the pain in her leg made her see stars. With a gasp, she sank back down in the shavings.

Just great! I'm here all by myself, Patches is running loose, and now I can't even get up. What the heck more could go wrong?

She soon got an answer to that unspoken question, when she heard a familiar voice call her name. In spite of her predicament, MJ didn't even want to answer.

But Walt put his auburn head through the open door of the stall. "There you are! Goofing off on the job, already?"

There was no reply but an honest one. "Patches kicked me. I surprised her—came up on her blind side."

"Oh, wow. Where'd she get you?" When MJ pointed to her shin, he insisted she roll up the leg of her jeans so he could look. "Nasty. You're gonna have a lump there, for sure."

"You don't think it's broken?"

"Looks like just a bad bruise to me. 'Course, I'm not a vet."

MJ supposed he was trying to be funny. "Good thing. You'd have me put down."

"Nah. Might just retire you to someplace like this, since you probably got a few more good years left. Think you can stand on the other leg?"

Leaning on both Walt and the stall's grain feeder, MJ levered herself out of the dirty shavings and hopped into the aisle. There, she sat on a hay bale with her injured leg stretched in front of her. She asked Walt, "Patches is loose out there, so could you put her in with Val and Dash?"

"No problem." At the barn door, he hesitated. "Which is her blind side?"

"The right."

After that errand, Walt offered to get MJ some ice from the house. She fished the front-door key from her jeans pocket. With a curious expression, he took it and disappeared.

A few minutes later he was back with a tray of cubes from the freezer and a dish towel. MJ hissed as he laid the ice-filled towel over the knot swelling on her shin.

"You musta been close to her," Walt said. "Otherwise it'd be worse."

"Yeah, at least I remembered that much from my camp lessons. I was right next to her, so she didn't have much room to swing."

"My brother Paulie got kicked once, almost the same way," he said. "One of our horses was dozin' in the field. Buckshot, sweet old guy, we rode him all the time when we were kids. Paulie walked up behind with no warning and got sent flying. Broke his thigh bone. It healed fast, though. He was only twelve."

MJ heard that last part as a put-down—only a kid would make such a stupid mistake. "Anna warned me about Patches, but I just didn't think."

Walt shrugged. "Even horses with two good eyes can't see straight behind them. And they're prey animals. You sneak up on 'em, they kick first and ask questions later."

The phone in the barn office rang, and he and MJ looked at each other. The machine picked up and they heard a woman's voice.

"Can you check that?" MJ asked. "Might be Anna."

A few minutes later, Walt came back wearing his trademark sly smile. "You're in luck. Vet's on the way."

"What?"

"That was Doc Adams. She asked if Anna still wants her to drop by and check over the horse she's bringing back today. I told her if she comes a little early, there's another lame one here could use some fixing."

MJ's future humiliation stretched out in front of her. "Swell. Soon the whole town will know what an idiot I am."

"Nah. Everybody who works around horses gets kicked, bitten, or stepped on now and then. Besides, if you're worried your leg might be broken, Doc Adams travels with an X-ray machine."

His words made MJ feel a little better—mentally, at least. And the ice pack did seem to be keeping the swelling down, though it still hurt like the devil. She shifted on the hay bale in vain to get more comfortable. "Wish I could make it to the front porch, where I could put my leg up."

"We can probably do that." Walt offered her a hand to stand, and let her lean on him to hop slowly out of the barn and up the path to the house. The front steps were trickier, but finally she was able to sink onto one end of Anna's rattan loveseat and stretch her injured leg across the rest of it.

Walt stood with his thumbs hooked in the pockets of his jeans and smirked, as if he'd never seen anything so pathetic. "Anna said you'd make lunch for both of us, but I guess that's not gonna happen."

Sexist. MJ taunted him back, "It's so easy, even you can do it.

Lunch is in a bowl in the refrigerator, top shelf. Plates are in the upper cabinet near the sink, silverware in the drawer below."

He accepted his orders with a brisk nod. A few minutes later, he returned carrying two plates heaped with food, along with paper napkins and two forks.

Balancing the plate on her lap, MJ had to laugh. "I don't think I can eat all of this."

"If you can't, I'll finish it." Walt sat opposite her, in one of the two rustic, twig rockers, and tucked into his food. "How come you guys lock up the house when you're only out in the barn?"

"Anna just did that today." MJ told him about the driver who'd come all the way up their road but sped off when they came out on the porch.

"Probably got lost," Walt guessed. "We sometimes get city people stopping by our place to ask directions. 'Course, there's five of us—my folks, me and my brother and sister. I can see why Anna might be more worried, with just the two of you here."

"Whoever it was, he came as far in as the paddocks." She told Walt about the horses acting up the night before, and the boot prints she'd found in the dirt that morning. Meanwhile, she stole a glance at *his* footwear. The toes were a little pointier than regular work boots, but as she'd remembered, he didn't have especially big feet.

"Pretty good detective work," he said. "Western boots, huh?"

"Yeah. Can't be that many people who ride Western in New Jersey."

Walt barked a laugh. "Are you kidding? There's tons of 'em, and Western shows, too. My dad and my brother and I do team penning, and my sister's getting real good at barrel racing. You ought to check that out."

MJ made no commitment. "I've always done English. Back home, I was starting to take jumping lessons."

Walt stood up. "I saw lemonade in the fridge. Want some?"

"Yeah, please." MJ realized she'd gobbled most of her lunch, so if he expected more he was out of luck. While Walt was gone, she tried to rearrange herself on the loveseat but gave up. With her throbbing shin, there *was* no comfortable position.

Walt came back with two tall, frosty glasses of the fresh-squeezed lemonade and handed one to MJ. "So, you here on summer vacation?"

"Not exactly," she admitted. "I messed up my grades this year at school, and blew my chance at getting into a college. Mom and I made a deal that I could take a year off—maybe make up my courses in the fall—and spend the summer working with Anna."

She expected Walt to frown and maybe even call her a slacker, but instead he lit up. "No kidding? I do the same thing. I take classes online, and Mom home-schools my brother and sister."

It surprised MJ to think someone could do that much of his course work outside of a classroom. "You don't go to school at all? Why, so you can help out on the farm?" "Yeah, and because our folks want us to have a Christian education. They don't like the stuff going on in the public high schools, with drugs, drinking, girls getting pregnant and all that. But it's cool this way. I went to a regular grade school and I couldn't stand being cooped up in a classroom that long. I like being outside most of the day and doing my school work in the evenings."

MJ held back a smile. Now she understood her aunt's comment about trusting her alone with Walt. Not that a guy who said he was a conservative Christian might never mess around, but Walt sounded pretty serious about it. "But when do you see other kids? I mean, besides your family?"

"That's no problem. Our church has a big youth center with basketball and baseball games, dances, and other stuff. And when we take our horses to shows, we sometimes meet friends there."

They heard the distant hum of a truck engine, and he leaned over the porch rail to peer up the road. "Doc Adams to the rescue! Maybe she can get you back in shape before your aunt comes home."

MJ shifted her leg again and moaned. "Hope she can at least give me some horse-sized aspirin."

CHAPTER ELEVEN:

STARBUCK

D r. Julie Adams turned the display of her portable X-ray machine so MJ and Walt could see the image. "At least there's no sign of a break."

Relief washed over MJ, but she still wondered, "Then why does it hurt so much?"

"Shin bruises are like that. Not much fat or muscle there, just blood vessels and nerve endings. You'll get a lump, and it'll turn all kinds of colors, but don't let that scare you too much." The vet unplugged her machine from the porch outlet; it looked like a big, old-fashioned box camera, but she'd explained that it was the latest digital technology. "You're doing the right thing, MJ. Keep the leg elevated for a day or so, and keep icing it for a few more hours until the swelling goes down."

"Can you give her some Bute?" Walt teased. MJ knew that was a common, strong painkiller for horses.

Julie fished in her medical bag and instead pulled out a bottle of Advil. "My own stash. I'm sure your aunt has something around the house, but meanwhile..."

"I'll get some water." Walt disappeared through the screened front door.

Julie glanced after him, then back at MJ. "Good thing Anna arranged for him to come by today. You might've been sitting in that stall until she got home."

MJ grimaced, and not just from pain. "She's going to freak out over this. She's bringing another horse for us to take care of, and now I can't even help."

The vet sat in the rocker, with a sympathetic frown. "Don't worry. You ought to be back on your feet in a day or two. You might still limp for a while..."

"I feel so stupid! At my lesson stable, we learned all about handling horses. I should have known—"

"Honey, even the most experienced person gets careless now and then. You think I've never been kicked? I could show you the hoof-shaped scars."

"Yeah, but you work with horses that are sick or hurt—"

"Like Patches, right?" Julie rested a comforting hand on MJ's sneakered foot. "It's one thing to deal with lesson horses, like at your stable at home, that are healthy and well-trained. Here, you've got animals with issues and they're gonna be less predictable." She removed her hand and sat back in her chair. "Speaking of which, how's your aunt doing with that new Thoroughbred?"

MJ wondered how much to say. Would it be disloyal to let on that Anna already had some problems with Murphy? "He seems pretty happy here. We turned him out in the big field yesterday with Patches, and they chased each other around—it was cute. And Anna did some round-pen work with him."

Julie kept her thoughtful brown eyes trained on MJ's face, absorbing this information. "Anna's got a lot of guts, I'll say that for her. Just to start up this place all by herself, and now to take on that animal."

The screen door whined, and Walt bowed like a servant as he presented MJ with a tumbler of water. She gulped two Advil tablets and washed them down. She hoped they'd work fast, because by now her whole leg felt somehow achy and numb at the same time.

The vet told Walt, "She's worried about not being able to hold her own around here for the next few days. If Anna needs a hand, would you be able to pitch in?"

"Oh, sure. Mom and Dad can spare me for a couple of hours a day. And I'm always glad for the chance to visit—" hesitating, he threw MJ a crooked smile "—my ol' buddy Dash. I used to exercise him for Anna, and I miss that."

MJ figured he was needling her, but at the moment couldn't muster a snappy comeback. After about fifteen more minutes she felt the Advil start to kick in, though, and once her pain ebbed her mood also improved.

Anna's SUV and horse trailer came rumbling down the drive. When it stopped near the first paddock, Walt jogged out to meet it.

Julie stood and stretched, hands pressed to the small of her back, as if warming up for her next patient. She picked up her medical bag and quietly told MJ, "You just stay here. I'll explain about your accident."

Anna at first did not seem to notice that her niece remained seated on the porch. She stood by the trailer and talked soberly with Walt and Julie, too far off for MJ to overhear.

Then they all went to the rear of the trailer, where Anna opened the doors. Walt dropped the ramp, and when he straightened and faced the open trailer, he stiffened. MJ wondered what had upset him, and dreaded a replay of the scene where Murphy came roaring out and almost injured Clint.

But no...Anna's trailer was wide enough for her to turn Starbuck around, so she could lead him out facing forward. She did this slowly, and MJ soon understood why. The dark brown horse stepped with care, as if his feet hurt. Once his whole body came into view, though, MJ wondered if his legs were just too weak to support him. Even from where she sat, she could make out every one of his ribs and the ridge of his spine. His neck was so wasted near the top, it almost looked upside-down. She imagined how hard it must have been for him just to keep his balance for two hours in the moving trailer.

Anna and Julie guided Starbuck down the ramp with pats and reassuring words. Even after he reached the solid ground of the barnyard, he stood quivering.

Julie had just stooped to open her medical bag when the horse's knees buckled.

"Julie ,Walt, help!" Anna cried out. "He's going down!"

As her vet and her neighbor hurried to assist her, Anna tried to coax the horse to stay on his feet. "No, baby, no...stand up. Come on, you can do it."

She wrapped her arms around the scrawny neck. The animal's big body staggered against hers and she felt his labored breathing. Even in his emaciated condition, Starbuck still weighed far too much for her to hold him up, if he was determined to lie down.

Julie and Walt pitched in, encouraging him physically and verbally.

"C'mon, pal!"

"That's a good boy...stand up!"

Meanwhile, another voice joined theirs—Valentine, neighing loudly. Anna glanced over to see the chestnut mare standing by the fence of her paddock, as close as the electric wire would allow, with her ears pricked and her nostrils flared. Eyes on the struggling Starbuck, she paced a few agitated steps, then whinnied again.

Anna finally realized that her niece still lounged on the porch. "MJ, help us!"

Over the horse's back, Julie caught Anna's eye. "She *can't* help. Forget her for now. Let's just—"

Maybe it was another rousing neigh from Val that did it. But with a burst of courage, Starbuck bunched his wasted muscles and pulled his legs back under him. He stood with his head down, breathing hard, but at least it seemed like he'd made up his mind to fight. All of them showered him with pats and coos of "Good boy!"

Julie told Walt, "Get a bucket of water and we'll sponge him. Maybe he just got too hot in that trailer." While the teenager ran off, the vet used her stethoscope to check Starbuck over. Judging from where she applied it, Anna knew she was listening to his heart, respiration and gut sounds.

"He had water to drink in the trailer." Anna hoped she wasn't guilty of some kind of neglect.

"I think he's just stressed. And his feet could be part of the problem."

"I know." Anna had noticed the cracked hooves as soon as Starbuck was led out of the Humane Society's barn. "They said he was turned out in a muddy pasture, maybe for months."

"Probably hurts him to stand. Once we cool him off, get him into a stall. If you've got one with a good, strong ceiling beam, I have a sling in my truck."

Walt hurried back from the barn with a pail of water and a sponge, and they washed foamy sweat from the horse's dark coat. Meanwhile, Anna glanced again toward the porch where MJ sat; the girl gave her a big shrug with hands upturned, in apology.

"She had a little accident." Julie glanced up from checking the Standardbred's feet. "Surprised Patches and got kicked in the leg. Nothing serious, but she's got to stay off it for awhile."

"Oh, no." Anna realized her tone sounded more irritated than sympathetic, but her first two concerns were selfish: *Who's going to help me with all these horses? And Erika will kill me—she'll insist that MJ come home!*

"Now, don't yell at her. That's what she's afraid of. I spent a lot of time convincing her that these things happen to the best of us. Don't undo all my efforts." With a wink at Anna, the vet drew a syringe from her bag and gave Starbuck a shot in his neck. "B-12. That might perk him up enough to get him moving."

For a few minutes, Anna left the Standardbred in the capable hands of Julie and Walt, while she checked on MJ. Her earlier irritation vanished when she saw the concern on the girl's face.

"How are you, honey?" she asked. "Julie told me what happened."

"I'm not too bad now. She gave me some extra-strength Advil." MJ lifted the ice pack to show the multicolored bump on her shin and Anna cringed. "It looked worse before, it's gone down a little. How's Starbuck?"

"Not so great. We're going to put him in the barn and try to make him comfortable. Are you sure you're okay for now?"

"I'm fine like this. Walt even made us lunch." As her aunt turned to go, MJ added. "I'm really sorry. About getting kicked, but about Starbuck, too."

Anna nodded her thanks. "I'll be back as soon as we get him squared away."

In the yard, Walt held a handful of hay as a lure so Anna and

Julie could lead the weakened horse into the barn. Valentine watched him go but no longer cried out; she seemed to understand that he was past his momentary crisis and in good hands. As Julie had suggested, they put Starbuck in an empty stall with a sturdy beam across the top and a hoist designed to lift hay bails into the loft. Julie brought in her sling, a web harness. Walt and the vet passed the straps around the horse's whole body and buckled them securely. Then Anna climbed a ladder to secure the sling to the beam, and tightened the hoist under the vet's directions.

"It doesn't need to support his whole weight," Julie explained. "Just to take some of the pressure off his legs and feet and keep him from lying down. In his condition, he might not have the strength to get up again."

Anna knew if a sick horse laid down too long, because of his weight his organs could start to fail. And if he was too weak or lame to stand up, he might have a heart attack trying. Once they'd put hay and water within his reach, the brown gelding looked fairly relaxed and comfortable, though the dullness of his eyes still worried Anna.

She saw Julie toting her portable X-ray machine and asked, "You used that on MJ's leg? Nothing's broken?"

The vet shook her head. "But you should bring her to your doctor, anyway."

"Oh, I will."

Once Julie had finished X-raying Starbuck's hooves and legs, she gave Anna a rundown on him. "Keep him on just alfalfa the first day or so, then add some senior feed to help build him up. Once he can stand without the sling, your farrier can start trimming back those hooves. Gonna take a long while before they're healthy again."

Anna's chest ached as she looked at the animal's feet, the horn around the outer edges shredded like cardboard. She wondered if he could ever rebound from this setback. Tears blurred her eyes, but she wouldn't shed them in front of Julie and Walt.

Both of them took off then, the vet to her next appointment and Walt to dinner with his family. Anna rejoined her niece on the porch and updated her on Starbuck's status.

"Wow," MJ said. "I feel so guilty that I can't do anything to help."

"It's not your fault. If anyone should feel guilty—" Though Anna tried to control her emotions, the floodgates opened and she buried her face in her hands.

"Anna..." The girl reached out awkwardly to touch her shoulder.

"When I sent him off to that couple down south, he was healthy. I spent almost a year getting him that way. He had good muscle, his coat was shiny, he'd gotten a spring back in his step... and look what they did to him. He's as bad now as when Clint first brought him to me. Maybe worse."

"That's horrible. How can people be so cruel?"

"I made a bad call. I trusted them, and I shouldn't have. They were supposed to send me photos, and the first time they missed, it should've been a red flag. I should've driven out there *then*—"

"But that would've been hard, right? Like you said, it's a long drive and it's tough for you to leave the ranch."

"Then I should have had Clint check on him, or the Humane Society, before it got to this point. Starbuck was the first horse I adopted out, my first 'success,' and look what happened!" Wiping her eyes, Anna reminded herself that MJ had problems of her own. "I should stop this, though. Here I am, feeling sorry for myself when you're hurt."

"Well, you're feeling sorry for Starbuck, and I can't blame you for that."

"Hell of a day, eh? Hard to imagine what else could go wrong."

A jaunty, minor-key tune, maybe the old Addams Family theme, sounded from the pocket of MJ's jeans. The girl shifted gingerly on the loveseat to pull out her cell and check the number. "Uh-oh, spoke too soon."

Anna's stomach twisted as she guessed the caller. "Let me—"

"That's okay, I'll handle it." MJ answered the phone in an upbeat voice. "Hi, Mom!"

CHAPTER TWELVE:

SISTER ACT

By the time Anna took the phone, Erika was perhaps less hysterical than when MJ first told her about the accident. But still... "You left her *alone* on that farm, out in the middle of nowhere?"

"Erika, I understand that you're upset and I'm very sorry MJ got hurt. But she wasn't alone for long. I arranged for one of my volunteers to come by in case she needed any help."

"Yeah, a teenaged boy! Honestly—"

"Walt is extremely responsible. He proved that by taking care of her when she was injured. He even arranged for a doctor to come and look at her."

"A veterinarian!" Erika shrilled. Then even she must have realized how ridiculous it sounded, because she started to laugh.

That eased Anna's worries a bit, but she knew she was walking a fine line. She wanted to tell her sister that accidents did happen around horses, and as long as you weren't seriously hurt you just soldiered on. But Erika had never done this kind of work and didn't understand why MJ wanted to. It might not take much for her to decide it was all too dangerous and insist her daughter come home.

"I'm taking MJ to my own doctor tomorrow morning," Anna assured her. "We'll go by whatever he says, and I promise I won't put her back to work until she's completely recovered."

An audible sigh. "Well, *she* didn't sound very upset, so I guess it's her call. But really, Sis—"

"I'll take more precautions in the future, and I'm sure MJ will, too." That resolved, Anna hoped to wrap up the call before her sister changed her mind. But Erika hung on silently until she had to ask, "Was there something else?"

"I almost hesitate to bring it up after this, but...You remember Lillian Gale? We met her a couple years ago at one of your horse shows."

Anna did recall the slim, meticulous little woman with the silver hair and twinkling blue eyes. The last of a very wealthy New Jersey family, widowed with no children, Lillian had helped sponsor a rider in the Olympics a few years back. Fortunately, being a very astute investor, she'd never been tempted by any of Richard's shady schemes.

"Anyway, we're doing a story on her for *Good Life*, so I met with her recently. Because she's a horse lover, I just happened to mention your farm, and Lillian seemed interested. She said she admired your efforts to 'rebuild your reputation' and 'put Richard's money to good use' by doing something charitable, and that she might consider a donation. Coming from Lillian, it could be a substantial amount."

Anna's pulse quickened. Maybe this could be the answer to her immediate funding crisis. "Thanks, Erika, that would be great! What would I have to do?"

"I suppose just meet with her, show her around the farm. Explain your business model, that sort of thing."

Of course, Anna thought. A savvy woman like Lillian Gale would want to see a business plan and financial statements. And she'd expect the farm to be incorporated as a nonprofit, for tax-deduction purposes. But over the past year Anna had been so busy just keeping fences and stalls repaired and horses fed and medicated, she hadn't had time to do most of that paperwork.

She explained this to Erika, who sounded disappointed.

"How long do you think it would take to pull things together? Lillian is interested now, but I can't promise she will be in a month or two. She might find someplace else, meanwhile, to donate her money."

"I know." Anna clenched her jaw in frustration. "Even if I got the paperwork together this week, I'm sure getting IRS approval takes time. But I really appreciate your making the connection for me. I'll do what I can."

"I've got her number in my office. I'll text it to you. You can give her a call, at least."

"I will. Thanks again, Sis."

After Anna hung up and passed the phone back to MJ, she had to satisfy her niece's obvious curiosity.

Despite her physical discomfort, the girl brightened at the news. "That would be great, wouldn't it? Is the paperwork hard to deal with? Darn, if I was in shape to do more around here, you'd probably have the time..." Her dark eyes rounded. "I bet I *can* help you. Even while I'm stuck in a chair, I can work on the farm's website! I told you, I did one for my friend's band. Everybody at school said it came out real well."

Anna had visions of lurid, flashy effects and pounding background music. "Thanks, but I don't know if—"

MJ grinned. "Don't worry. I wouldn't do the same kind of site for this place. But you need pictures of the horses, stories about their backgrounds, and more information about how to adopt a horse. You've got some of that now, but—no offense—it needs the wow factor."

Anna had to agree. As a former magazine editor, she knew how it *should* look but hadn't taken the time to update her website-design skills. "Okay, kid. Maybe tomorrow we'll put our heads together and see what we can do, providing you feel up to it. For now, let's go inside. It's getting chilly and you've got to be starved." When MJ glanced at her propped-up leg, her aunt told her, "Hang on..."

A few minutes of rummaging in her bedroom closet unearthed a single crutch that Anna had used years ago when she'd sprained an ankle. With that tool, plus her aunt's support, MJ managed to hop into the house.

By eight thirty, the girl had taken another dose of pain medication, gone to bed, and fallen sound asleep. Anna felt very alone as she headed out to check on Starbuck one last time. It was still twilight. She'd locked the main gate and turned on the electric fence, and she saw no signs of any more prowlers near the property. The horses in the paddocks seemed fine, though Valentine still stood near the fence, gazing toward the barn.

She and Starbuck were my first two rescues, Anna remembered. *They were inseparable until I got Dash. And even then, when Starbuck shipped out to his new home, Val fretted for a couple of days. I guess she remembers him... and still cares about him.*

Anna thought of the mare's agitated neighing when her old friend had stepped out of the trailer and almost collapsed. That was so like her, to get upset because another creature was in distress.

Anyone who thinks animals don't have souls hasn't met Valentine.

Moving on to the barn, Anna found Starbuck still well supported by his sling. His once mink-brown coat was marred with raw spots at his hips and shoulders, that looked as if he'd been beaten by someone or nipped by other horses. Anna knew, though, that they came simply from lying down on hard ground. He was so thin that the pressure of his own body chafed those areas of his hide. Right now, at least, he seemed peaceful. Or was it just exhausted, defeated? His big eyes still had a sickly glaze that Anna knew did not bode well.

Not having to put up a brave front for anyone else, she let the tears run again. She stroked the gelding's wispy mane and bony face and told him how sorry she was that she had let him down.

"We got you healthy once, and we can do it again," she promised. After making sure he had enough hay and fresh water for the night, she roamed back out to the paddocks and surveyed her other four charges.

She had to accept that even if Starbuck survived, he might never be rideable or even drivable again. Val and Patches also had serious physical issues. That made three of her residents who were adoptable mainly as "pasture buddies"—not something in great demand. Even horses used for beginner lessons or therapeutic riding programs needed to walk and trot without too much distress. Dash was on his way to recovery, but while he might make someone a nice trail or lesson horse, his competitive days were over.

I guess when I started this place and chose my first rescues, I was thinking with my heart, not my head. Maybe that was no accident—Richard's obsession with money and success made me swing in the opposite direction. Also, maybe at first I wasn't a hundred-percent committed to making this a real business. That could be why I didn't go to the trouble of applying for nonprofit status or even giving the place a real name.

But like it or not, she had responsibilities now. Five animals depended on her for their futures, and a couple of young volunteers also believed passionately in her cause. To make a go of this farm, she would have to call upon rusty skills and once again think like a businesswoman. Her first and only adoption had been a failure, and that wasn't a track record to attract donors.

I'd be happy if I could place any of these guys in good, safe homes, and I wouldn't quibble about what the adopters could pay. But to impress a donor like Lillian Gale, I need a real success story.

That left one candidate. Even as the idea crossed Anna's mind, the big, gray Thoroughbred swung his chiseled head to stare straight at her. With a snort, he shook out his overgrown, salt-and-pepper mane.

Her thoughts traveled to the last stall in her barn, where the former owner had left behind a dusty pile of old jump standards and cross rails. Some day soon, those might come in handy.

Murphy, you're my best shot. Providing you don't kill me first.

CHAPTER THIRTEEN:

GUILT

"**P**oor ol' Starbuck." Clint's voice cracked, as he reached into the stall and ran his long fingers through the Standardbred's forelock. "Maybe not even so old, I guess, but he's had a rough life."

Anna felt guilty all over again. Clint was the one who'd rescued the ex-racehorse from an Amish farm, where he'd been worked almost to death; she had promised to find Starbuck a new, loving home. "At least Julie said he's getting stronger. We probably can take him out of the sling tomorrow."

"That's good. He sure got a lotta ground to make up, though." As Clint stroked the horse's neck, Starbuck leaned into the touch, eyes half-shut. Anna wondered if he remembered his rescuer, or would have appreciated the comforting gesture from anyone.

"What about our other guy?" Clint asked. "Mr. Hotshot?"

Anna smiled. "Murphy's doing real well, I think. C'mon outside and I'll show you."

They passed the open door of the barn office, where MJ hunched in front of Anna's old desktop PC. The girl had propped her bad leg on a plastic milk crate, and her single crutch leaned against the file cabinet. Anna's doctor had reached the same conclusion as Julie, that MJ's injury wasn't serious and should heal quickly with rest. Meanwhile, the girl already had started punching up the farm's website.

Clint stopped to offer her get-well wishes, and shared a few war stories about his own mishaps while working on the "backside" of racetracks. MJ winced when he explained that he'd once been thrown and trampled by a colt he was exercising. "The docs had to wire my leg back together, and it came up a little short. Even since then, I walk kinda funny."

Anna pulled him away before he could scare her niece off horses forever. She told MJ, "I'm going to show him what I've been working on with Murphy."

The morning before, with Walt's help, Anna had dragged the old jump standards and rails out to the round pen. The two of them had set up four low hurdles along the fenceline, spaced at equal distances. They'd added empty barrels or hay bales to make the jumps more solid.

Now, as Clint watched from outside the fence, Anna led Murphy into the pen and turned him loose. He strode up to each obstacle in turn, eyeing and sniffing them all in curiosity.

Anna picked up her long lunge whip, keeping the lash wound around the stick to avoid startling the horse too much. She pointed the tip toward his rump and clucked to send him out to the rail.

The gray needed no more encouragement. He trotted up to the first hurdle, jumped it, cantered to the next one and did the same.

Her heart lifted as she watched the horse measure his own strides and clear each obstacle with inches to spare. He pricked his ears forward and flagged his tail, having a ball. Picking up speed, he flew around the small course a second time with no prodding. In fact, Anna had to point the whip at his shoulder and step toward him to make him slow to a stop.

When she walked up to Murphy and snapped the lead line back onto his halter, the big gray was breathing fast, but from excitement, not fatigue.

Outside the fence, Clint jutted his lower lip. "Not bad. 'Course, the way he cleared that tractor on his first day here, we knew he could jump."

"Sure, but he did that in a panic." Anna reminded herself that Clint might know what made a good racehorse, but not necessarily a good show jumper. "What he's doing here is controlled, smart. He's great at it, and he loves it!"

"Does look that way." Her friend leaned his arms on the top rail of the fence, black eyes glinting with dry humor. " 'Less you're gonna adopt him out to a circus, though, he'll hafta jump with somebody on his back."

Anna laughed, though with a twinge of anxiety. "Well, of course."

"You been on him yet?"

"Uh...no. Not so far. I thought I'd start off with the groundwork. Then this week I had to go pick up Starbuck...and MJ got hurt—"

"Sure, sure. And you shouldn't do it by yourself, anyways. Well, right now you got me to help. Wanna give it a try?"

Anna hesitated. Clint was right, she supposed. They had to find out, sooner or later, if Murphy would accept a rider without pulling any of his old tricks.

And if I'm going to get on him, I shouldn't ask MJ or Walt to risk helping me. No one better than Clint, who's handled high-strung Thoroughbreds most of his life.

Besides, Murphy had just given himself a good workout and seemed in a positive frame of mind. Anna gazed up into his big, alert eye and patted his dappled neck. Now did seem like the perfect time to try getting on his back.

So why did she suddenly feel scared to death?

In the barn's tack room, she scanned the saddles on the wall racks. Chose the all-purpose English saddle she'd used for Valentine and Starbuck. On three pegs hung an English bridle with a mild snaffle bit that she'd also used for those two horses, next to Dash's Western hackamore and Duke's dark brown show bridle.

Anna's stomach did a flip-flop as she plucked the first one from its peg. Lastly, she grabbed the helmet she'd always used for jumping.

Meanwhile, she began to understand her nerves a little better. Since her accident on Duke, she'd ridden just her three rescue horses—Val, Starbuck and Dash. Not only were they all gentle animals, but with their various ailments none ever was up to much more than an easy trot. It had been a long time since she'd climbed aboard a horse as young, healthy, and full of fire as Murphy.

Don't make so much of it. You'll just get on, walk him around a little and get off. Start gaining his trust. That will be plenty for the first day.

But from what she'd heard, that part would be the biggest challenge. Murphy's last couple of jockeys never had gotten beyond those first few steps. They'd never made it out of the racetrack paddock, and one had gone in an ambulance, straight to the ER.

Passing the office, where MJ was still working on the website, Anna tried to be quiet. Still, the slight jingle of the bit and stirrups reached the girl's keen ears and made her swivel in her chair.

Her wide eyes took in all the gear, "What's up?"

"Nothing much," her aunt lied, with a casual smile. "We're just going to saddle Murphy and see how he handles it. Don't let me distract you—stick with your project. I'll be back later to see what you've done."

The last thing she needed, Anna thought, was her niece watching in horror if something did go wrong.

Out in the paddock, Clint still held the gray by his lead rope. Both looked a bit impatient.

"Thought you got lost," Clint teased.

Anna ignored the ribbing. Her arms full and knees shaky, she sidled through the pen's gate and shut it behind her. "These should do."

"Yeah, that's a good saddle." Clint ran a hand down one of the fairly long and wide flaps. "Give you something to grip onto, not like those little ones they use at the track."

He's thinking the same way I am.

Murphy pawed the ground and tugged on the line. Clint noted, "He was calmer with you. Could be, he don't like men."

"Is that possible?"

"Sure. Horses can tell men from women. And even though there's more girls working at tracks these days, if he got handled mostly by guys and they gave him a hard time—" Clint rubbed the gray's neck again "—he might've decided we're all bad news. So, you could be in luck, there."

"Good. I need all the luck I can get."

Anna set the English saddle just behind Murphy's withers and slid it into place. It fit him pretty well and didn't seem to pinch anywhere. Moving slowly, she pulled the girth not quite tight. She talked to the horse softly all the while, as if he were a green colt.

"You do this good," Clint told her.

"I broke Starbuck to saddle," she reminded him. The Standardbred had only gone in harness before he came to her farm. "Of course, he always had a nice temperament."

With Clint's help, she passed the bridle reins over Murphy's neck and took off his halter. When she offered the bit he stiffened, and Anna held her breath. Would he shoot backward, the way he had in the stall when Julie reached for his mouth? Or even rear?

Prepared for anything, she slipped the middle finger and thumb of her left hand into the sides of his mouth, finding the gap between the front and back teeth. She slid the bit into place, pulled the bridle over his head with her other hand, and quickly fastened the straps. Murphy chomped the bit but didn't make a fuss.

With her mount tacked up, Anna gazed up at the waiting saddle as if it were the peak of Mt Everest. She checked his girth and tightened it another notch.

"Want a leg up?" Clint asked.

"Let's use a mounting block. I want to try something."

Anna brought the heavy green block from its spot near the gate and set it in the center of the paddock. While Clint held the reins under Murphy's chin, she stood on the block and rested just her upper body across the saddle—again, as if working with an untrained horse. The gray's ears flicked backward, but in curiosity, not anger. She gradually put more weight on his back, keeping low.

"How's he seem?" she asked Clint.

"Fine. He's a good boy, right Murph?"

Finally Anna swung her right leg over his back. No problem. She straightened and felt very high up. Murphy was taller than her other rescues, maybe by a full hand. But Duke had been about the same height.

She'd leave her feet out of the stirrups. Just in case she had to bail, fast.

"There ya go!" Clint grinned in approval. "Wild Horse Anna."

Murphy shivered the skin above his withers. Anna scratched him there and took hold of the reins at the buckle.

"Wanna walk on?" Clint's voice held a hint of caution. "Might be better."

"Yeah, let's."

As Clint faced away and started forward, still holding the reins close to the bit, Anna felt like a child being led on a pony ride. Murphy switched his tail and stepped forward grudgingly. From the high-spirited, athletic creature who had sailed happily over the small jumps, he moved now like a barn-sour old nag.

In pain? Not likely—he would have reacted as soon as I leaned on the saddle.

Anna squeezed with her legs.

Murphy planted his feet. When Clint coaxed him forward, the gray threw his head high, probably jabbing himself in the mouth with the bit. His ears went flat back.

Anna's heart hammered. Over the din, she barely heard Clint's commands. "Make him walk! Can't go up if he keeps movin'. Give 'im a kick."

She felt the huge body beneath her bunching up and pulling back, and had a visceral memory.

Duke crashing into that spread jump...somersaulting over his head...that pole punching her in the stomach...

Anna dropped the reins and vaulted out of the saddle. When her boots hit the ground, her knees almost gave way and she gasped for breath.

Murphy snorted and still pulled back against Clint's hold. But he hadn't gone up. Maybe, Anna thought, because he hadn't needed to. Just the threat had made her lose her nerve.

Clint scowled and shook his head.

"I'm sorry," she told him, still trembling.

"Now Anna, whad'you teach this horse today? Huh? You taught him that if somebody gets on him, all he's got to do is act a little feisty and they'll jump right off an' leave him alone. He never has to do a day's work again."

"I know, but—"

Clint straightened his bucket-shaped sun hat and hitched up

his jeans. "Here, you hold him and I'll get on him."

That startled her. Was he bluffing? "No, Clint! With your bad leg? You can't take the chance."

"Well, somebody's got to. Otherwise, no matter how good this guy can jump, he's got no future. He might not go to slaughter, but he'll get put down, just the same."

The older man's face and tone softened. "Look, I know you ain't used to dealing with a horse like this. He's got some scary issues. An' I know if you get hurt, you got nobody else to run your farm. But Anna, honey, if you won't get on him, you better find yourself somebody who will."

From the barn doorway, MJ watched the brief argument between her aunt and Clint. Then he got back in his truck and drove away. Anna's shoulders sagged as she untacked Murphy, led him to his regular paddock and turned him loose with a hard slap on the rump.

Knowing her aunt probably would head for the barn next, MJ hurried back to the office as fast as her crutch would allow. She sat again at the computer when Anna stopped in to check on her progress.

"How's it going?"

"Great." MJ gave her a bright smile. "I've got a few ideas. I've been checking out websites of other horse-rescue places. Boy, you were right, there's a lot of them."

Pulling up the bench to sit beside her, Anna nodded sadly. "And still not enough to keep up with the need for them."

MJ tried to shake off that discouraging thought. "Anyhow, I made a list of the interactive features they've got on their sites that we should have, too." She opened the home page of a ranch in Colorado, one of the best she'd come across. "See how this one has a whole section of the horses available for adoption? It gives their rescue histories, their present conditions, and what kind of care and training they need."

Her aunt responded with a tight smile. "Dunno if that's such a good idea, with our bunch. Might discourage people too soon."

Anna really seems down this afternoon. More than before she went out to meet with Clint. MJ persisted, though, and tapped the screen. "This place also has a link to send donations—either money or supplies, like hay and medicines—and to foster a horse or to volunteer. Since we're on such a tight budget, it would be good for our site to have those things, too."

"You could be right. Though before we start accepting cash donations from strangers, I need to send off that nonprofit paperwork."

"You will." MJ felt determined to boost her aunt's spirits. "Another cool thing—they've got video of some of their horses. Maybe we could put up a video of Murphy and Patches playing. I bet people would love that! Or maybe of him going over those jumps by himself, like he did this morning."

Anna rocked back a little on her bench, hands cupping her knees. "Clint told me you were watching us, just now."

Was she angry? MJ lowered her eyes. "You sounded like maybe you didn't want me to, but I couldn't resist. You did more than just tack Murphy up, you got on him! That's good, isn't it?"

"Yes and no. Clint wanted me to ride him around a little, but I chickened out."

MJ knew that hollow feeling. A few times in her riding lessons she'd been afraid to try stuff the instructor wanted her to do. "Well, he gave you a hard time."

"Clint? Yeah, but I had it coming, I guess."

"I mean Murphy. He threw his head up, got all tense and pulled back. I was scared you might not get off in time."

She saw surprise in Anna's face. "It looked that way to you?"

"Yeah, I was holding my breath." The girl laughed. "I'm already limping around here. If anything happened to you...Jeez, we'd have Walt running the place."

Anna's shoulders relaxed and she gave her niece a hug. "Thanks, kid. Whether or not you're right, at least you made me feel less like a total coward."

"No way. You tried, didn't you?"

"I *did* leg him forward, but when he stiffened like that, I panicked."

"I don't blame you, with his reputation," MJ said. "I sure wouldn't have known what else to do."

"I guess somebody else—somebody who wasn't like me or Clint—just would've whipped him."

The girl shuddered to imagine how Murphy might react. "Could be what made him crazy in the first place."

"Exactly." Anna sighed. "Clint was right about one thing, though. I've got to fix that horse's issues or he'll never be adopted." With a determined air, she stood up and headed for the door.

That surprised MJ, who wanted to show Anna a few more things on the computer. "Where're you going?"

"Up to the house, to get a phone number. Like the old saying goes, I've gotta talk to a man about a horse."

CHAPTER FOURTEEN:

THE NATURAL

Tall and straight as a Central Casting cowboy, Josh Buchanan stood with his hands on his hips and surveyed the setup of Anna's round pen.

"Good size," he said. "Looks like you've got what you need here. Except for the jumps."

"Murphy took them, all on his own," Anna told the trainer. "He was loving it!"

"Maybe, but you're rushing him." For the moment, Buchanan did not even look at her. A peaked baseball cap and wrap-around sunglasses shielded his eyes from the afternoon sun, but Anna could tell when he shifted his gaze to Murphy's paddock. "He's just off the track, and he's only been here...what, a couple of weeks? He needs down time. And if he's never done anything but race, he shouldn't be jumping—not even that high. You need to condition him to it gradually."

Anna knew better than to mention that the horse had cleared about five feet the first day he'd arrived at the farm, and wood piles as high as these hurdles when he'd been running loose in the field.

At least the celebrity trainer hadn't come decked out like one of those Western "horse whisperers," she thought. More like the typical English riding instructor, in a dark green T-shirt, snug, faded jeans and low paddock boots. When he'd introduced himself and shaken her hand, she'd read the small, white print on the front of his shirt that said, *Because I'm the trainer, that's why.*

Now Buchanan swung toward her again. "Mind if we haul those jumps outa there?"

They got assistance from Walt and even MJ, who still favored her leg a little but no longer needed her crutch. Once they'd cleared the ring, Buchanan asked Anna to bring in the gray Thoroughbred.

Murphy seemed to know something was up, and danced as she led him across the barnyard. He pricked his ears toward the uprights and poles stacked outside the fence. After Anna turned him loose in the pen, he sniffed the ground where the hurdles had stood.

Buchanan grunted something, and she asked, "Excuse me?"

"Smart." Then he glanced back toward MJ and Walt. "Got a big coil of rope? Or a long lunge line?"

MJ took off for the barn, returned with a thick coil of blue webbing, and handed it to the trainer.

"Perfect." A white smile broke through the lean, tanned planes of his face. MJ flushed at the mild praise, probably starstruck to be helping out the semi-famous Josh Buchanan.

He took off his sunglasses and tucked them into his hip pocket. "Okay, let's get to know this guy a little."

When Josh let himself into the pen, the gray flared his nostrils and snorted. Anna recalled Clint's comment, *Could be he don't like men.* Murphy did seem more wary of Josh's presence than he ever was of hers.

She thought the trainer might walk right up and try to touch him, maybe clip the lunge line to his halter. She wondered if she could be sued for whatever might result. Instead, Josh loosened a few coils from the line, flipped them toward Murphy and clucked sharply.

The horse wheeled and tore off around the ring to the left, his preferred direction.

Anna didn't need to warn MJ and Walt to keep clear of the fence—they watched from several feet back. The powerful gray swept around the forty-foot pen like he was coming down the home stretch at the Preakness. Buchanan remained still at the center, but tracked Murphy with his eyes.

When the horse started to slow, Anna exhaled in relief. But Josh tossed out the lead line to get him moving again.

"This is so cool!" Walt half-whispered, next to her. Anna saw he was riveted, his hazel eyes keen. "I've heard about this stuff, but never saw it in person."

"What do you mean?" MJ matched his hushed tone.

"He's using eye contact and body language to keep the horse out on the rail. Showing him who's in charge."

For a while, it seemed as if Murphy intended to argue that point. He cantered swiftly around Josh, now and then threatening him with a loud snort or a buck. The trainer remained unimpressed, and whenever his pupil tried to stop, chased him with the loop of webbing once more.

This went on for about ten minutes, until MJ said, "Look, I think he's getting tired."

Though Murphy still trotted at a good clip, he dropped his head and stretched out his neck.

Walt practically chortled. "See how he's licking and chewing with his mouth? That means he's giving up, he wants to stop."

MJ stared at her friend. "How do you *know* all this?"

At last, Josh allowed the gray to slow down. Then he half-turned away from the horse and stood quietly, gathering up the lead line.

Still on the rail, Murphy halted and stared at the trainer's back.

Anna held her breath again. If the horse really did have a problem with men, might he attack Buchanan? Was the trainer taking a big chance, turning his back that way?

Murphy strolled into the center of the ring and stopped just behind Josh's shoulder, almost as if he'd been called. Only then did Buchanan acknowledge the horse again, stroking his neck and scratching him on the withers. Murphy lowered his head as if relishing the attention.

Anna could hardly believe it was the same animal. Even in his better moods, he never had behaved that meekly for either Clint or her.

So much for his not liking men. Or maybe it's the first time he's met one that he does like?

Josh dug into his pocket and fished out a few pieces of carrot. Murphy chomped them happily.

"That was my problem," Anna joked to MJ. "I forgot the bribe!" She wondered why *she hadn't* thought to have a reward for Murphy, if and when he did well.

Josh smiled and gave his student another pat. "Nice mover. Sure, he's got some attitude, but he's not crazy. And believe me, I've handled some that were."

Anna felt embarrassed, in front of MJ and Walt, that the trainer had made so much more progress than her in such a short time. She told Buchanan, "Well, he *likes* going to the left, the way he was trained. You should try working him to the right."

The tall man bobbed his head once. "I'm sure that's tougher. But I think your boy's had enough for today. Might as well end on a good note." As Josh strolled back to the gate, the lunge line coiled in his hands, the horse followed him.

Cynically Anna told herself, *He just wants more of that carrot!*

The trainer let himself out of the paddock, and Walt frowned. "Aren't you going to get on him?"

"I don't think anybody should get on this horse yet. From what I've heard, he'll need a lot more work first." Buchanan turned to Anna. "What was he like at the track, d'you know? I mean, in his races."

She thought the question odd, since she had no intention of ever forcing Murphy to race again. "Clint told me he did well, at first. Came in second in his maiden race, won the next one, but finished last in his third. After that, he never got onto the track again. He flipped in the paddock, with two different jockeys, and hurt the second one pretty seriously."

Shaded by the cap's visor, Buchanan's brows drew together. "Sounds like something happened between his second and third races to make him go sour. Maybe he spooked and got beat up for it. Or some physical problem cropped up in the third race, so he ran badly. If his owners didn't spot it, or didn't give him time to heal, maybe he was still sore when they saddled him up the next time."

"Sure," Walt chimed in. "That must be it."

"But he's been vetted a couple of times since," Anna protested. "He should be fine now, but he still acted up when I got on him."

"Whatever happened, his body may have healed, but he's still afraid." Working in the day's heat had left a sheen on Buchanan's face; he pulled off his cap and massaged his short brown curls. "Flipping is a bad vice—you don't get much worse. But keep in mind, the horse probably doesn't know he could kill the rider. He just wants that guy off his back in the worst way, so bad he's even willing to risk hurting himself! An animal like that has lost his trust in people."

MJ hung on the trainer's every word. "So, he isn't mean, after all?"

Buchanan tilted his head at the girl. "Not to get personal, but I saw you limping a little. Has he kicked or bitten you? Or anybody else here?"

Looking surprised, she laughed. "No. I did get kicked, but it was by the pony."

Walt spoke up again. "Murphy tried to nip me a couple of times, but I just poked him in the nose. I got fast reflexes."

"He might've just been playing," the trainer said. "If he really wanted to nail you, he could have."

Josh's explanation gave Anna a new slant on things. "At least it sounds as if you think he can be...rehabilitated."

"Don't see why not. It'll take time, though."

That deflated her hopes a bit. "H-how much?"

Josh handed the lunge line back to her. "I can take him to my place for two months. I've got courses set up there to do more groundwork and special desensitizing exercises. Then I can get him started under saddle."

For some reason, his confident air rankled Anna. She remembered how Richard used to hold forth on subjects about which he knew very little. She almost snapped at Josh, "He doesn't need that, does he? He's already been ridden."

"By jockeys and exercise riders. Why do you think he tensed up when you got on him? He's never had a person's full weight on his back, never really had a leg on him. He's got to re-learn everything, from the ground up."

Though Anna realized all of this made sense, it wasn't what she wanted to hear. "But...two months?"

"Like I said, you can't rush him. I'm betting that's what his first owners did, and you see how that turned out."

Anna noticed that, from a couple of yards away, MJ and Walt stared at her. They probably couldn't believe she was arguing with this expert, who'd written magazine articles and taught clinics at horse expos around the country. She got her irritation under control. "Josh, can we talk about this in my office?"

"No problem."

As they walked to the barn, she recalled that her parents sometimes would retreat to another room to avoid arguing "in front of the kids." She also realized this was the first time since she'd moved to the farm that she'd been around an attractive man her own age. Was that part of the reason she felt annoyed with Josh—leftover trauma from all she'd gone through with Richard?

In the office, Anna sat in her desk chair and Josh took the nearby bench.

She decided that, with this outspoken guy, honesty would be the best policy.

"Look," she began, "I do want what's best for Murphy. It's just...I'm operating on a very tight budget. Besides taking on this horse as a favor to my friend Clint, I've had another returned to me after his adoption didn't work out. So, in the past couple weeks, I've gone from caring for three horses to five. And at least two of them may be too ill to ever move on to new homes."

Buchanan nodded sympathetically. "Running a rescue, if you do it right, is a tough business. Too many people, even though they have good intentions, don't know what they're getting into."

Though stung by the implication that she might be in over her head, Anna pressed on. "Of all the animals I've got here, I feel Murphy has the most potential to find a good home. It sounds as if you believe in him, too, and I *would* like you to work with him. I've seen the training fees listed on your website, and I was kind of prepared for those. But for him to spend two months at your farm—! I'm sure you'd also have to charge me board, and right now there's no way I can afford that."

Josh fell quiet for a minute. Meanwhile, his gaze drifted toward the screen saver on the desktop computer—Anna and Duke sailing over a colorful spread fence, in a long-ago horse show.

"That you?"

She nodded. "The first horse I ever owned. He was sold during my divorce. I lost track of him for a while...and later found out he went to slaughter." An ache started behind her eyes, as it usually did whenever she recalled Duke's fate. "He's the reason I started this farm."

Buchanan seemed to mull this story for a moment, then sighed. "I always make faster progress with a horse at my place, because it's a controlled environment with no distractions. But I can see you're in a tough spot, Anna. How about this: I'll take Murphy for two weeks. I think that would be the minimum to get him, at least, safe to ride."

She exhaled. "That does sound more manageable."

"After I bring him back here, I'll show you what I've been doing, so you can pick up where I left off. If you're going to keep taking rescues, you should know some of those techniques, anyhow."

"Fine," Anna said, with more confidence than she felt. "I can do that."

"I'll also stop by, maybe once a week, to see how you're coming along with him. I never want to see my students backslide." He showed a glimpse of white teeth again. "You're lucky I'm just in the next county. For a client fifty miles away, I've *got* to keep the horse while it's in training. I couldn't work out an arrangement like this."

Smooth, how he managed to remind me that people bring their horses to him from all over the East Coast. "I really appreciate it. So, what would the cost..."

Josh shrugged. "Since it's not a typical contract, I'll have to write something up. I'll email it to you tonight. If it looks okay to you, I can come with my trailer and get Murphy tomorrow morning."

They left the barn more in accord than when they had gone in.

Outside, they parted with a handshake, and MJ and Walt looked relieved.

After Buchanan drove away, the girl asked, "Is he gonna take Murphy away for two whole months?"

"Nope. I bargained him down to two weeks. Then he's going to show me what to do and I'll take over."

"That'll be great," Walt beamed. "Can I hang around and watch? I mean, when Josh is here?"

Still a bit miffed by his blatant hero worship, Anna told him, "Sure. Come around tomorrow morning—" she threw MJ a sly look "—when he tries to load Murphy into a trailer!"

Reminded of the horse's explosive arrival, the girl pulled a horrified face. "Oh no..."

Oh, yes, Anna thought. *Let's see how our famous horse whisperer deals with that.*

CHAPTER FIFTEEN:

STORMY WEATHER

Thunder rolled and MJ glimpsed an occasional lightning flash outside her bedroom window. With Anna working on her laptop in the living room of the ranch house, the girl had retreated to the privacy of her bedroom to phone Stacey. Her friend asked what she'd been up to, and MJ recapped the day's high point—Murphy entering the trailer for his trip to Josh's stable.

"At the beginning," MJ said, "we were all scared that Murphy would hurt Josh, or tear the rope out of his hands and run away. But Josh kept him circling on the long line, so he never had a chance. And every time he quieted down, Josh would rub him and pat him."

"Uh-huh." Stacey sounded like maybe she was doing her nails or checking her text messages.

MJ didn't even care, wanting to share the experience with her best friend. She shifted to a more comfortable position in her bed, propped up by two pillows.

Another peal of thunder, and crackling on the line. "Stacey, you still there?"

"Yeah, but this connection stinks."

"We're having a storm out here, that's all," MJ told her. "Anyway...Josh started to lead him into the trailer, but Murphy pulled back and freaked out again, so Josh made him circle some more. He did this again and again for fifteen, twenty minutes. When Murphy finally put his front feet inside and sniffed at the hay in the net, Josh let him step off again as a reward. Then they circled and came back—"

"I got it." Stacey sighed on the line. "Again and again and again."

"But it worked! It took almost an hour, but at the end Murph got all the way on and stood quietly. Josh closed the trailer and they drove away."

"Da-h-h-hling," Stacey turned it into a yawn, "that is the most *fascinating* story I've heard all week."

MJ knew it was a burn, but couldn't help laughing. "I guess you had to be there. It *was* fascinating to us—me and Anna and Walt and Clint. We all learned how important it is to be patient with a horse." She settled back against the headboard of her rustic iron bed and stretched out her bare legs, in shorts, on top of the old quilt. She noticed with satisfaction that the lump on her shin had disappeared and even the bruise was fading. "The sad part is, he's only been gone a few hours and I miss him already."

Stacey perked up. "Who, this Josh? I thought you said he was, like, forty!"

"What?" MJ felt herself blush. "C'mon, I mean Murphy. I guess that sounds dumb, but he kept things lively around here."

"He does sounds livelier than most of the other males you mentioned. What's the story with that other guy, Walt?"

"Eh, he's just a neighbor, been helping out here since my accident. Now, *he's* the one who's going to miss Josh."

Stacey chuckled. "Oh, he's like that, huh?"

Honestly, MJ thought, did she have to make everything about sex? "No, not 'like that.' God, Walt is such a straight guy! One of those born-again types. But I think he totally wants to *be* Josh, now. It's like he's found his calling."

Stacey obviously felt a change of subject was overdue. "Speaking of guys, did you know RaserzEdge played the Mercury Lounge last weekend?"

MJ's gaze flitted to a printout on the wall that she'd made on her aunt's computer, the home page of the band's website. She'd taped it up next to her dresser as a kind of poster. Bobby Raser, glowering rocker-style from behind jagged blond bangs, posed with his guitar in front of the four-man group. "N-no, I didn't.

Where's that?"

"In the Village, kid—Manhattan. What a great gig, right? And they sounded so-o-o good!"

A lump rose in MJ's throat. "You went?"

"How could I not? It was just a couple of subway stops from my Dad's apartment. A bunch of kids from school came in for the show, too. It was such a cool club, they didn't even card us." Stacey giggled again. "I got pretty wasted. Bobby called an Uber to get me back to my Dad's place in one piece." In what sounded like an afterthought, she added, "You shoulda been there."

While MJ tried to come up with a reply, thunder crashed outside again and Stacey's voice faded in and out. At least they shouldn't lose power, though—Anna had an emergency generator.

She told Stacey, "This connection is getting pretty dicey."

"I know, I can hardly hear you. Listen, I've got another call, anyhow. Text me if there's anything new, okay? I mean, besides some guy getting a horse to walk into a trailer." With a breezy laugh, Stacey clicked off.

Sitting on her bed in silence, with another flicker of lightning outside her window, MJ mulled over her friend's words.

"You shoulda been there."

Yeah, maybe I should have been at Bobby's gig. At least I should have known about it. After all, I'm supposedly managing the band's website. If they got this big break, why didn't he even tell me?

MJ had texted Bobby a few times since she'd moved to the farm. When he'd replied briefly or not at all, she'd told herself he must be busy.

Guess he was, all right. With his band...and maybe with Stacey?

Her eyes shifted to the dresser mirror. The girl who looked back had dropped a few pounds over the past couple of weeks, despite Anna's good, healthy cooking. Even with her bum leg, MJ had kept doing a fair amount of hard work around the farm.

On the other hand, her hair was a mess, dark roots overtaking the green tips. If she wanted to re-do it, where would she find the right hair color, out here in the sticks? Jeez, where would she even find a stylist to give her the right kind of cut?

Stacey thinks I'm turning into some boring hick. Is she right? Coming out here, I cut myself off from the kind of fun she's having. Am I losing touch with all my friends?

Of course, MJ thought, she had new friends now—Anna, Clint, Julie, Walt and even Josh. Stacey probably would call them hicks, too. MJ couldn't think of them that way, though, people trying so hard to help animals nobody else wanted. But they sure were a hundred-eighty degrees different from her friends back home, and even from the rest of her family.

She'd felt charged up after watching Josh's success with Murphy that morning, but the brief conversation with Stacey had brought her down again. So low that MJ did something she'd avoided since coming to the farm.

She called her mother.

As fashion editor, Erika split her workday between time in the office and photo shoots in the field with the stylists and models. After work, she usually made dinner for Carl and drove him to his sports activities. Tonight, though, MJ actually reached her at home between obligations.

MJ reported that her leg was about good as new and she was trying to make updates to the farm's website. "Anna needs to upgrade her computer," the girl complained. "It's hardly got enough memory for what I'm trying to do. With any kind of bad weather I have to reboot, like, every fifteen minutes."

"Well, it's good that you can help her." Erika's voice sounded optimistic. "You've always had a knack for computers. That's a direction you could pursue, you know, when you go back to school."

To avoid further discussion of her college plans—or lack of them—MJ explained that Anna had brought in a trainer to work with the new horse. "The guy picked Murphy up this morning. He's going to work with him at his own farm for two weeks."

"Yes, Anna mentioned that." Erika sounded only slightly more interested than Stacey had. "Funny, that she had to get some kind of expert. I mean, if the horse was already ridden in races, wouldn't it easy to teach it to do...less dangerous things?"

Anna still didn't tell her about the flipping, of course. "It's complicated, Mom. Racers just know how to run flat-out. Anna wants to make him into a jumper, like her horse Duke. Murphy can jump on his own, but he has to learn to pace himself, change directions quickly, and really listen to his rider."

"I enjoyed watching Anna ride, but I never understood what-all went into it." Erika paused. "You really think this trainer can fix the horse so it can be adopted, or sold, or something?"

The sincere interest behind the question took MJ by surprise. "Yeah, I do. Murphy didn't even want to get in the trailer this morning, but finally he did."

"She said this Josh has a great reputation, that he's some kind of horse whisperer."

"They call it natural horsemanship, but yeah, he's written books and made videos. He even gave a demonstration at that big expo, a couple of years ago, that I went to with Dad."

"Oh?" Now Erika sounded more impressed. "Well, Anna said she needs to place at least one of her horses in a good home, soon, and feels Josh can help. I'd just like to make sure she gets her money's worth."

"Er...yeah. I hope so, too."

After getting off the phone, MJ wondered about her mother's odd comment. Why should Erika take such an interest in Josh's credentials, Murphy's future, and what Anna did with her money?

Unless it's not Anna's money. She was so worried about how to pay Josh...

Maybe she hit Mom up for a loan?

CHAPTER SIXTEEN:

TEMPTING OFFER

After she and MJ finished feeding the next morning, Anna brought the horses back out to the paddocks. With the storms the previous evening, she'd kept them all in the barn overnight. The confinement hadn't agreed with Valentine; even that brief exposure to shavings underfoot had aggravated her COPD. Her nostrils flared and her sides behind her ribcage heaved with the effort of breathing.

The hotter and more humid it gets, the sicker she gets, Anna thought. *Julie said for the summers we might have to switch her to a stronger steroid. It's more likely to cause side effects, though...*

Even under the weather, Val still looked bright-eyed compared to her even frailer pal, Starbuck. At least now he was able to stand and walk on his own.

This morning, Anna decided to try a new arrangement. She'd noticed Patches staring over at the neighboring pen, as if missing Murphy, so she moved the pony into that enclosure with Dash. Now that Starbuck seemed stronger, and Julie's checkups found no signs of contagious disease, Anna decided to turn him out with Valentine.

Summer had begun, and flies had started to annoy the horses, so she covered the scrawny brown gelding with a fly sheet. The small pressure wounds on his hips and withers had started to heal, and she didn't want biting insects to open them up again. As she fastened the straps to secure the light mesh around his body, Anna recalled buying it when she first got Valentine. In those early days, the neglected chestnut mare had suffered from the same problem.

Val seemed happy to be reunited with her old friend, and the two stood nose-to-nose for a full minute. Anna could imagine them telepathically sharing stories of their hardships. After awhile, they sidled together head-to-tail, so they could whisk the flies from each other's faces.

She should be good for him, maybe give him more of a will to live. From what Julie says, he'll need it.

Anna reminded herself that today she had to get to work on that nonprofit application. *Maybe after lunch, on my laptop.* Right now, MJ was back on the office computer. The girl had promised to reveal her website updates that afternoon, complete with a new name for the farm. Anna worried about what that might be, though she supposed almost anything would be an improvement over "Anna's Horse Rescue."

MJ's right. We need something catchier to get people to at least open the landing page, plus well-written text and some up-to-date photos of our horses that might move people to adopt them—

The distant rattle of a vehicle made her swing around. An older-model black Ford SUV jounced up the driveway, hauling a single-horse trailer.

Oh, no. Another rescue? Anna couldn't imagine taking on another troubled horse right now. *And they have nerve, to show up without even calling first. Unless it's a desperate case...*

The vehicle stopped in the barnyard and out hopped a short, chunky woman in faded jeans and a plaid shirt with the sleeves rolled up. She glanced around at the two occupied paddocks before wandering over to Anna.

Her smile revealed a slight gap between her front teeth. "You Anna? Hi, I'm Mandy."

A bit wary, Anna shook the woman's hand, as sun-weathered as the rest of her. It was hard to guess her age; she moved with a youthful energy, but fine lines crinkled around her eyes. Her hair showed an inch or two of brown at the scalp, then hung lank, in a brassy shade, down to her collarbone.

MJ emerged from the barn just then. The sight of the unfamiliar woman and trailer made her ask, "What's going on?"

"Nothing, MJ." Anna smiled to reassure her. "I'll be with you in a minute, okay?"

Her niece returned to the barn, but lingered in the doorway.

Anna turned her attention back to the newcomer and her small, somewhat dented trailer. "Got a horse in there for me?"

The woman barked a surprised laugh, a whiff of stale nicotine on her breath. "Oh, no. I come t' buy one from you!"

That tipped Anna off that Mandy didn't have much idea what kind of a place she'd come to. "Well, I appreciate your interest, but this is a rescue farm. We don't sell these horses."

"Whad'ya mean? You take in ones that are sick or hurt, an' you get 'em back in shape, right? But then, what? You don't sell 'em?"

"No, we *adopt* them out to new homes."

"Adopt 'em." The little woman smirked. "You mean, like with kids?"

"Almost like that, yeah. We try to place each horse in a home that will work out well for them, depending on their age, health and fitness to work. I have to warn you that, right now, most of the animals here do have health issues."

Mandy nodded toward Val and Starbuck. "I can see these two don't look so good." She scanned the neighboring paddock. "An' that pony's got something wrong with his eye?"

"She's missing an eye, yes. But she gets around just fine, and she's healthy otherwise. She'd make a great pasture buddy for—"

"How 'bout that buckskin?" Mandy strolled over to the pen that Patches now shared with Dash. "He looks in decent shape."

Anna followed her. "Yes, Dash has been doing well, though he's still got some lameness issues. He's okay for light riding. But anyone who adopts him will have to commit to continuing his rehabilitation. He needs corrective shoeing and a monthly injection in his hocks."

Mandy considered this. "Sure, I can do that. He moves around pretty good, though. C'n I go in and look him over?"

Though still put off by the woman's brusque manner, Anna opened the paddock gate and let her inside.

Usually, Dash walked right over when Anna came into his space, but today he kept his distance until she called to him. Even then he hesitated, so she met him halfway to slip the halter over his short, broad head. She held him while Mandy studied his body condition, which had filled out nicely over the past month. The buckskin flicked his ears, which told Anna he was tracking the visitor with his side vision.

At least Mandy appeared used to horses, from the way she ran her hands down his legs and lifted his hooves to check his feet. She noticed the small, dark patch visible through his buff-colored coat, just behind the girth, and touched a finger to it.

Ears going flat, Dash struck forward with his hind foot in a cow-kick. Mandy jumped aside and cursed.

"Sorry!" Anna stepped in between them. "He's never done that before, but he is sensitive about those scars."

"Scars?"

"He's got the same thing on the other side. His last owner used rowel spurs pretty harshly. That's one reason we ended up with him."

Most people, in Anna's experience, would have responded with a sympathetic comment. Mandy just threw her a sideways glance as if she didn't quite believe the explanation. "Sounds like he goes Western, anyway. Got a saddle, so I can try him out?"

She's not easily discouraged, Anna thought. "I'm afraid I can't let you ride him until you've gone through the application process."

"C'mon. I've handled horses a lot tougher than this one. Or d'you think I'm gonna fall off on purpose, and sue you?"

Just the fact that her visitor would conceive of such an idea troubled Anna, but she kept cool. "Those are the rules. If you just want to see Dash working under saddle, I can ride him for you."

Mandy grew impatient and waved a hand. "Never mind. Just tell me what this 'adoption' process involves."

The two of them left the paddock and Anna latched the gate behind them. Meanwhile, she spotted MJ still watching from the barn doorway.

"There's some kinda fee, I'm sure," Mandy prompted.

Anna remembered that she'd let Starbuck go to the Deckers for four hundred dollars, and they hadn't valued him much. She wasn't going to make that kind of mistake again. "Like you said, Dash is in the best condition of any of our rescues. He was trained as a reining horse and has excellent bloodlines. So, the adoption fee for him is eight hundred."

A bit to Anna's surprise, the woman nodded. "Okay. I can give you that right now, in cash."

"It's not that simple. If you're interested, though, you can leave a deposit of one hundred and take an application." She called out to MJ to get one of the forms from the office. "It's pretty detailed, so you may want to bring it home and take your time filling it out."

Mandy scuffed one booted foot against the other, as if this was not what she'd wanted to hear. While they waited, Anna asked her, "Would you be boarding the horse, or do you have a farm of your own?"

"We...I got a little place." She hesitated before adding, "Out toward Hackettstown."

"That's a drive. What brought you here? Were you looking at other horses in this area?"

"Nah, just thought I'd check out your farm. Saw your website an' thought it sounded like a nice idea, rescuing horses."

But you didn't call ahead, Anna thought. *Not even to make sure I'd be here.*

MJ came back with the application and handed it to the visitor. When Mandy saw the single-spaced document, which took up both sides of fives pages with many blanks to be filled, her frown returned. "Jeez, what *is* all this?"

"Just factual information," Anna explained. "Your previous experience with horses, who else might be riding the horse, where you'll be keeping him, what other horses you own...things like that."

"My birthday, my Social Security number, my employer...Looks like you want everything but my blood type." She flipped through the pages with a mounting air of outrage. "Have I ever been accused of animal cruelty...have I ever been arrested...!"

Anna shrugged. "It's a standard form. We have to take every precaution. Sometimes people come to a rescue saying they want to adopt a horse and end up sending it to slaughter."

"Why the hell would I do that? He's a show horse with good breeding, right?"

"Well, you wouldn't be able to show him anymore, not in his condition. That would be stated in the agreement, too. It also stipulates that if, at any time, you become unable to care for the horse properly, we'll take him back." *And if we find that you're not taking care of him, we have the right to take him back.*

Mandy shook her head in obvious frustration, and thrust the papers back into Anna's hands. "Look, I can pay twice the fee you asked for. More! I got eighteen hundred dollars with me. Would I pay that much for a horse I was gonna send to slaughter? But I drove a long way and I don't feel like goin' back with an empty trailer."

To Anna, the situation didn't smell right. "You seem to want this particular horse very much."

"I do. He's just what I been looking for." The visitor glanced around, as if making sure MJ had gone back into the barn. She tugged a tooled-leather wallet from her jeans pocket, pulled out wad of bills, and dropped her voice. "How about you just take this, I'll bring him home with me, and we call it a done deal?"

Anna stared at the cash, enough to help cover the farm's bills for the next few weeks. She thought of the extra medicine Starbuck and possibly Val were going to need. Also of the loan she'd just accepted from her sister, which she wanted to pay back as soon as possible.

In the paddock behind them, as if he'd read her mind, Dash gave a loud snort. *Don't worry, pal. I won't let this tough chick take you anywhere.*

"Sorry," Anna told Mandy. "This is how a rescue operates. If it isn't what you expected, I'm sure you can find someone else around here to sell you a horse, with no questions asked."

Mandy glared at her for another minute, as if she couldn't believe Anna had turned down the cash. Finally, she stuffed it back in her wallet and jammed the wallet into her pocket. "You're kinda nuts, you know that?"

She stalked back to her vehicle and shot Anna another venomous look through the windshield, before swinging the SUV and trailer around and bumping off down the drive.

The spray of gravel startled the horses, and Anna stepped back inside the buckskin's pen to rub his neck and soothe him. "Good riddance to her, eh, Dash?"

She took off the horse's halter and hung it back on the fencepost. She remembered that MJ had found it on the ground, the night after they'd heard the mystery visitor outside. Anna glanced down at the packed dirt of the paddock. Mandy had left behind distinctive footprints. Western boots, almost like those of their late-night visitor from a few weeks back.

Had to be a coincidence, though. Mandy's prints were much smaller.

But something else nagged at Anna. *She called Dash a "show horse." And he was, a couple years ago, under his full, registered name.*

But I never mentioned any of that to her, did I?

CHAPTER SEVENTEEN:

WEB PRESENCE

MJ leaned back in the desk chair and gaped at Anna. "She was gonna pay almost two thousand dollars for a horse she didn't even ride yet? I mean, that wouldn't be much money for a *good* horse, no offense to Dash. But after you told her he was lame, and couldn't work too hard..."

Anna pointed out, "And after he tried to kick her."

The girl shook her head. "I groom him all the time, and he *never* does stuff like that."

"I know. Can't blame him, though. By the time this Mandy left, I was ready to kick her, myself." Anna sank onto the old wooden bench. "I've come across people before who didn't understand how a rescue operates, but she was just weird."

"Too bad, though. I guess we could've used the money, huh?"

Anna did not let on that the thought had crossed her mind, too. "I wouldn't trust her to take Dash to the end of our driveway and back. She wanted me to sell him outright, meaning no contract, and no right to check on him or to take him back if she mistreated him. That would go against everything we're trying to do here."

"And she said she came all this way just because she saw the farm's website?"

"Yeah, even that sounded fishy. You and I both know, the site's not that riveting."

A spark lit up MJ's dark eyes, beneath her overgrown bangs. "Well, that was before. Check out the new version and tell me what you think."

She shifted the computer mouse, and the screen filled with a striking color photo of Murphy galloping across his green field. The breeze lifted his black-streaked mane and tail and his long legs stretched in a ground-covering stride. The banner at the top of the page spelled out REBOOT RANCH in rustic logs. Just below, more conventional type added *Horse Rescue* and gave the farm's address, phone number and email.

Though Anna reserved judgment on the new name, she had to admire the overall look of the splash page. "Where did you get that great photo?"

"Took it with my cell phone last week, just before Murph shipped out. I've been playing horse paparazzi around here for a while." She guided the cursor to a vertical row of horseshoe-shaped buttons down the left of the screen. "See, here are all your important links. 'About Us' has the history you already wrote of the farm. 'Why Horse Rescue?' tells how many unwanted horses are born in the U.S. every year, and reasons why people neglect them or give them away. I researched that stuff myself."

As MJ called up each page, Anna felt guilty for ever doubting her niece's talents. She'd done a very professional job.

"I didn't know which horses you wanted to say are up for adoption," the girl went on, "so I just made a section called 'Our Horses,' and put them all there."

She brought up a recent photo of Valentine, taken inside the paddock for a full-body view. The mare half-turned her head toward the camera and the shot captured her sweet, soulful expression. MJ also had taken Patches from her "good" side, the heavy white forelock hiding her stitched-up eye socket.

On this page, Murphy posed in the big field under a blue sky like a mottled silver statue, neck arched and eyes on the horizon, with what Thoroughbred breeders called "the look of eagles." By contrast, Starbuck stood in his stall half-supported by his sling, head drooping, although MJ's upbeat text emphasized how everyone at the farm was working to nurse him back to health.

"The only one I could do as a before-and-after was Dash," she explained. "You had a shot in your file of how skinny and beat-up he looked when you first got him, so I posted that next to one I took of him last week. Shows how much he recovered by being here at the farm. That's good, right?"

"Very good." A lump rose into Anna's throat. "MJ, this is all excellent work."

Her niece blushed, as if beneath her show of confidence she had worried that Anna might not like the results. "Thanks. I enjoyed it, and at least it kept me busy while my darn leg was healing."

Anna read the entry about Dash. "You say he was a top reining horse that went lame from hard use, but is now on the mend. Mandy called him a 'show horse' and I wondered how she knew. This explains the mystery—she must've read it on your new website."

"No-o-o-o, that's not possible. I wouldn't go live with this version until you approved it. Right now, there's still nothing up on the Web except the old one, *Anna's Horse Rescue*."

"Really?"

With a couple of clicks, MJ switched to the original version. It featured just one picture of Dash, slightly better than the pathetic "before" shot, but still with ribs and scars visible. The minimal text said nothing about his show-ring career.

Anna scrutinized the old entry in vain for some clue to explain Mandy's interest. "I don't get it. As soon as she saw Dash, she seemed determined to have him. And to take him with her, as soon as possible."

"Maybe she recognized him."

Anna stared at her niece.

"He was in shows around this area, right?" MJ reasoned. "If she's a Western rider, maybe she went to some and noticed him winning ribbons. Later, she came across your website, saw that old photo, and thought she could pick up a great horse cheap."

"And she didn't bother to ride him, because she already knew he was well-trained," Anna finished.

"Good thing you didn't sell him to her! She might've tried to show him and he might've broken down again."

With a nod, Anna straightened on her rough seat and mulled this explanation. It still seemed like a stretch, but that could be the answer.

Only...if Mandy she saw Dash years ago in a horse show—when he was fit and healthy, and performing under a different name— would she have recognized the bony, battered animal in this photo as the same horse?

Walt was coming over in a little while to exercise the buckskin, Anna remembered. He might be able to provide some answers.

Meanwhile, MJ reminded her aunt, "You didn't say anything about the name I came up with."

"You mean, 'Reboot Ranch'?" Anna stalled.

"You hate it."

"No, but...it sounds kind of Western, doesn't it? Like it should be in Arizona, not New Jersey."

"But like you said, there are so many other rescues out there— not just for horses, but for dogs and cats, too—that a lot of good names are taken. I was working out here yesterday during the storms, and this computer kept going down. After I rebooted it, like, the third time, the name just came to me." MJ turned up her palms in a pleading gesture. "I thought it had a ring to it."

"It does." Anna hated to dampen her niece's enthusiasm. "Maybe it's the log letters putting me off."

"They are kind of kitsch-y." MJ giggled. "I can get rid of those."

"It is...clever. Let me think about it." Anna ruffled the top of the girl's head, where by now the black roots had forced out much of the green. "How's your leg doing these days? You look like you're getting around pretty well."

"Oh, it's fine. I'm ready to go back to mucking stalls and pushing wheelbarrows."

"That can wait until tomorrow. I was thinking maybe you'd like to get back on a horse."

MJ's eyebrows jumped. "You bet! But—"

"I know Dash took you for a spin last time, and Starbuck and Patches aren't rideable. But Val's not doing too badly today. You can ride her for a while."

While her niece hurried back to the house to change, Anna tacked up the chestnut mare with the all-purpose English saddle and bridle. To her surprise, MJ showed up in the barn doorway wearing breeches and high boots, along with her helmet and a faded rock T-shirt.

"Mom, packed 'em for me." The girl grinned. "Might as well use them."

Out in the barnyard, Anna gave her niece a leg up. "You'll have to stick to a walk. She shouldn't work any harder in this warm weather."

"No problem." MJ stroked mare's neck, then straightened her spine and squared her shoulders. Her excellent posture in the saddle impressed Anna.

She led the two of them into the round pen and watched for a few minutes. MJ let Valentine ramble on a loose rein, guiding her along the fence with just an occasional squeeze of her legs. And Val, despite her health problems, walked on cheerfully without much prodding.

"If you get bored," Anna told her niece from the rail, "she's had some dressage training. You can collect her a little, do leg yields and figure-eights."

"Sweet," MJ called back.

Confident the pair would do just fine without supervision, Anna retreated to her office to get started on the dreaded IRS paperwork.

She sat at the desk and brought the new home page back up on the screen; shook her head again over the words "Reboot Ranch" printed in log letters. *Not sure I can live with that! On the other hand, I do have to enter some kind of business name on the nonprofit application.*

Oh, well, I'll leave that part until last. I have plenty of other, more complicated material to get through first. She opened the online IRS document and scrolled through all the questions she had to answer. Even leaving out the categories that didn't apply to her particular business, it still came to well over twenty pages of dense legalese. Anna would have to check with her tax account for some of the information.

No wonder I kept putting this off. And Mandy had the nerve to complain about our measly five-page form!

From outside, Walt's voice reached her ears. She guessed by his buoyant tone that he was teasing MJ again. *Too bad they don't get along better,* Anna thought. *On the other hand, maybe it's a good thing they don't.*

Eager to be distracted from her task, she left the office and met Walt in the barnyard.

"I was gonna use this ring to exercise Dash," he complained lightly, "but it's occupied."

Anna smiled. "Poor MJ's been frustrated ever since she hurt her leg, so I thought she needed some horse time. You can take Dash out on the trail."

"Excellent." He led the Quarter Horse into the barn while Anna brought out the Western tack. As Walt tossed a saddle blanket over the buckskin's back, she gave him a quick summary of her conversation with her would-be customer that morning.

"Your Dad was the one who found Dash half-starved in that field, wasn't he? And reported it to the county Humane Society?"

"Just about a year ago. I remember how upset he was when he came home, muttering that he couldn't believe people could sink so low."

"The farm was pretty close to here, wasn't it?"

"I think so. Dad passed it driving back from a delivery to a customer." Walt took the heavy saddle from Anna and met her eyes. "I know what you're thinking...but it wasn't anywhere near Hackettstown."

That came as a small relief. "I did wonder if there could be any connection. D'you remember the name of the owner?"

"Nope, but Dad would. I'll ask him."

A minute later, Walt led Dash out to the yard and sprang into the saddle as if he'd been riding all his life—which, Anna knew, he had. MJ halted her mare by the fence to watch.

Valentine let out a ringing neigh and Dash answered her.

"Hey, you fast filly," MJ scolded her. "I thought Starbuck was your boyfriend now!"

"She plays the field," her aunt punned.

Walt held his horse back and glanced down at Anna. "Can MJ come along?"

She thought about it. "I guess so. Honey, want to go out on the trail with Walt?"

"You bet. The trail part, I mean. The Walt part..." She made a so-so gesture with her hand.

"Better be nice to me," he parried. "I'm the one who knows the way back."

Anna let MJ and Valentine out of the pen, and the horses fell in step next to each other, more in tune than their riders.

"Just walk," Anna warned. "Dash might be able to handle more, but Valentine can't."

"Yes, ma'am," Walt said.

"And don't go too far."

She watched them set off for the shady gap between the tall maples and stopped herself from calling out any more instructions.

I haven't been on that trail myself in at least a month. What if there's a lot of fallen debris in their way? What if Valentine gets tired and stumbles?

Relax, Anna. They're on quiet horses that get along well. They're only walking, and even if something does go wrong, Walt will know how to handle it. He came to the rescue when MJ got kicked, didn't he?

Anna realized that was the germ of her worries. The last time she'd let her niece out of her sight for very long, the girl had been injured. Nobody would have expected that, either. When you worked with horses, crazy things sometimes did happen.

But my sister doesn't get that. She was pretty mad about the accident. If MJ ever got hurt again, or even had a close call, Erika might insist she move back home.

At this point, I'd really miss her. And not just as another pair of hands.

CHAPTER EIGHTEEN:

TRAIL RIDE

On Valentine, MJ followed Walt and Dash into the fringe of woods that bordered her aunt's property. The shade came as a relief after the heat of the barnyard, and from her high seat she could appreciate the breeze that ruffled through the trees overhead. She felt comfortable on Val, because she'd worked around her for weeks now and knew how kind and level-headed she was.

MJ always felt a special, nonverbal communication with a horse, from her first few minutes on its back. She could tell if it was nervous, sulky, overeager or sneaky—just waiting for a chance to bang her leg against a tree, or spin around and race back to the barn. Valentine, in spite of her labored breathing, seemed like a happy creature. She walked along with pep, as if delighted by the change of scene. She probably felt reassured, too, by Dash's presence.

"This trail goes almost all the way to my family's place," Walt called back. With a nod to the right, he added, "Out that way is Pasquales' farm. They've got a dairy."

"Oh, yeah? I think that's where Anna gets her milk and ice cream."

Walt half turned in his saddle, as if to check on her. "Done much trail raiding?"

"A little. At my stable I took lessons in a group, and mostly we stayed in the ring. But once in awhile we'd all go out on the trail together."

"Got the regulation pants and boots, eh? You look more comfortable than when you were on Dash."

"I like an English saddle better than Western. I can feel the horse's movements more—there's not as much in the way."

She saw Walt shrug. "Depends on what you're used to, I guess. How long you been taking lessons?"

"About two years. We were just learning to jump when I stopped."

"You didn't want to do that?"

MJ decided there was no harm in explaining. "My Dad used to take me to the county stable. He'd hang around and watch, and on the way home we'd talk about how I did. Even if I thought I'd screwed up, Dad would always say something to make me feel better."

Around the next bend, big tree limb lay across the narrow path. Walt slowed to let Dash step over it, and Valentine followed at the same careful pace.

"Your Dad's not around anymore?"

"He died, almost a year ago. Had a heart attack at work." MJ heard her voice thicken and pushed down the painful memories. "After that, I quit riding. It wouldn't have been the same, going to the stable without him."

"That's too bad." After a beat, Walt asked, "Couldn't your mom still take you?"

MJ sniffed. "It wouldn't be her thing. She'd rather go to my brother's hockey or baseball games. Mom and I don't have a lot in common. Without Dad around to make peace, we get on each other's nerves. That's one reason I'm out here for the summer."

"I get that," said Walt. "I don't fight with my folks much, but I've got a brother and two sisters. It's a rare day when at least two of us aren't arguing about something. We always make up, though. I bet you and your mom will, too."

"Maybe." MJ mused, "It's funny how much better I get along with Anna. I guess it's mean to say it, but I almost feel more like I could be her daughter."

"She's quite a lady, all right. Starting up the farm all by herself—"

Something rustled in the bushes up ahead. Dash sidestepped and Val halted with ears pricked. MJ remembered what her aunt had said about bears in the area, and her blood chilled.

If a bear sprang out at them, what would they do? Would the horses scare it—or vice versa?

"What's the matter?" she called to Walt, who'd gotten the buckskin under control.

"Dunno. But you stay here. I'll ride on ahead and check."

She let him go, meanwhile stroking Valentine's coppery neck to keep her calm. She could feel tension in the mare's body and knew she was waiting to be told whether it was safe. *So am I, girl.* MJ watched Dash's tan rump and black tail recede farther down the trail, and suddenly wished she'd told Walt not to leave her alone.

Another rustle, but fainter, as if something was moving away. A minute later, Walt returned. "Didn't see anything, but whatever it was, I think it's gone. Probably just a deer, though Dash is usually calm around those."

The trail widened now and they were able to ride side-by-side. "I just realized," he said, "I don't even know your last name. I guess it isn't Loehmeyer."

"MJ Klein. If you must know, it stands for Martha Joan, but nobody's called me that since I was ten."

"Klein, huh? So...you're Jewish?"

MJ felt a twist in the pit of her stomach. The way he asked... was he prejudiced? Among the well-to-do but multicultural kids she knew back home, the issue never even came up. But none of them wore little gold crosses around their necks or got home-schooled for a "Christian education."

"My dad was," she answered, coolly. "Mom is some kind of Protestant, but we didn't go to church very much. Once in a while, we'd go to a seder at my grandmother's house, and we had a Christmas tree every year. But those were just traditions. Neither of my folks was really religious."

Walt seemed to mull this over. "I guess there are a lot of people like that, but...I can understand somebody believing in *another* religion better than believing in *no* religion."

Feeling judged, MJ stiffened in her saddle. "It's no big deal. You can still be a good person. My Dad was one of the best people I ever knew."

"No offense. I'm sure he was."

They'd reached a straight, hard-packed section of the trail. Dash pranced and tossed his head, as if eager to shift into a faster gait.

"He's feeling good." Walt smiled. "Sometimes I jog or lope him down this stretch."

"If you want to, go ahead," MJ said. "I can just wait here for you to come back."

"Don't be so sure. Valentine might try to race him! She is a Thoroughbred, y'know."

"She is?" MJ found it hard to believe the mellow mare was the same breed as Murphy, who seemed more typical.

"Anna mentioned it one day. She figures that's why Val is so gutsy, even though she's sick. She said Thoroughbreds have a lot of heart. They'll hang in and tough it out, no matter what."

MJ rubbed the crest of her mare's neck, feeling even prouder to be on her back. Then a memory sobered her. "Y'know, when I was researching stuff for the farm's website, I read that more than a thirty thousand Thoroughbreds are born on racing farms in this country every year. About a third don't make any money on the track, so they're sold at auction. Some probably get retrained for other things, but lots of 'em—beautiful, healthy horses, and not even that old—get shipped off to slaughterhouses."

Walt's frown showed that this pained him as much as it did her. "Pretty awful, huh?"

"Yeah. This same survey said a hundred thousand horses of all kinds end up unwanted and neglected every year. I can't even wrap my mind around that."

He turned his gaze down the trail again. "I think a lot of people get horses with no idea of how to take care of them, or how much work and money is involved. When they get in over their heads, bad things happen. That's why it's great that people like your aunt are trying to help."

"But it sounds impossible, doesn't it? Our farm isn't that big, so we can only take in a few at a time. And even with all the other rescue groups around the country, there still must be a lot of horses that go off to slaughter, or just suffer and die from neglect."

Following her impassioned speech, MJ looked across to see Walt staring at her sadly. She lifted her chin. *Pull yourself together, girl! He thinks you're a head case, getting so worked up over something you can't do anything about.*

They reached a shallow creek where water rippled lazily over the rocks. Its satiny beauty took MJ by surprise, and she slowed her horse to appreciate it.

Walt did the same. "Let's stop and let them drink. It's such a hot day."

MJ drew up alongside him and let her reins go slack. Their mounts dipped their noses into the creek, sipping delicately for such big animals.

Walt relaxed in his saddle, one hand holding his reins on top of the roping pommel. "I guess it's like the starfish story."

"The what?"

"You never heard it? Gee, I thought everybody knew the starfish story. My mom told it to me when I was a kid, and I heard it again in a Bible class later on."

"It's got something to do with horses?"

He grinned, showing the crooked front tooth. "I'll give you the short version. An old man is walking on the beach, and because there was a big storm, all these starfish are washed up on the sand. Thousands, as far as he can see. Now, the starfish can't breathe out of water, so they're gonna die, right? But up ahead, he sees this little boy walking on the beach, picking up one starfish at a time and throwing it back in the ocean.

"The old man feels sorry for the boy. When he catches up with him, he puts a hand on the kid's shoulder and says, 'Son, it's no use. Don't you see, there's too many. The whole beach is covered with them! You can throw 'em back all day and it still won't make any difference.'

"The boy just shrugs. He bends down, picks up another starfish and throws it into the water. And he says to the man, 'It made a difference to that one.'"

MJ sat speechless, stunned at how well Walt's little parable captured the pain and frustration of their rescue work. She felt almost uncomfortable, too, that this strange guy with the freckles and bad haircut—who acted as if he'd never even met anybody Jewish before—could have shared such a kernel of wisdom.

Not that he made the story up himself! At least he admitted that.

When Valentine raised her head from the creek and gave a cough, MJ was glad for the diversion. "She probably liked that story. Anna sure made a difference to her."

"Is she okay? Her nostrils are kind of fluttering."

MJ felt relieved that he focused on the horse. "Yeah, she's breathing a little hard. We should start back."

On the return trip, they again passed the spot where they'd heard the noise in the bushes. This time, MJ could detect nothing more ominous than birds flitting through the trees, and the horses showed no fear.

As soon as she and Walt reached the barnyard, they stripped the tack from their hot mounts. MJ called dibs on the wash rack, an outdoor pipe enclosure where horses were hosed down, because she wanted to cool off Valentine as quickly as possible. Once the mare began breathing more easily, MJ turned the rack over to Walt and Dash. She put Val in the paddock with Starbuck, who welcomed back his friend with a soft nicker.

In the barn's tack room, she hung up the English saddle and bridle. Meanwhile, she heard chuckling from the direction of the office. Strange, because she figured her aunt was in there alone.

MJ put her head in the office door and found Anna grinning at the computer screen. "Did that paperwork finally drive you out of your mind?"

"Almost, but that's not why I'm laughing. Josh emailed me a video of the work he's been doing with Murphy. Check it out."

MJ sat on the bench. "I guess if he reared up and mashed the poor guy, you wouldn't be so happy."

"Oh, Josh still hasn't gotten *on* him." Anna restarted the video and rolled her chair to one side so her niece could watch.

The old desktop model was so short on memory that the footage froze every couple of minutes, but MJ could tell it also had been edited to give just the highlights of several training sessions. Except this was like no training she'd ever heard of before.

Josh worked with Murphy in a round pen set up with some of the strangest paraphernalia MJ had ever seen. PVC archways had been draped with long, colorful streamers or strips of sheeting. From tall jump standards projected horizontal rows of those foam noodles people used in swimming pools. There also was a huge, red plastic ball; a big blue tarp tacked flat to the ground, like a make-believe pond; and a long wooden plank balanced at the middle on a pole, like a very low see-saw.

"You did tell him we wanted Murphy to be a jumper?" MJ asked. "Not a circus horse?"

"Josh is desensitizing him. This is supposed to make him less nervous and get him to trust people again."

As they watched, the trainer brought his charge up to the giant ball, letting him paw at it and bounce it. He also led the horse through one of the streamer obstacles, then in between the foam noodles, which brushed Murphy's sides as he passed. In each case, the gray shied, backed up or wheeled a couple of times before he went through successfully. Once in awhile, Josh exchanged a comment with the person shooting the video, an unseen woman.

Walt joined them in the office. "Hey, lookit Murphy go! That's the way they train trail horses, y'know."

"I don't think we'll be using him for a *trail* horse," MJ scoffed, still skeptical about Josh's approach.

Anna reproved her with a glance. "You came to a few of my horse shows, MJ. You know how they dress up those jumps with flowers and stripes and other stuff, to distract the horse and make the course harder. Murphy needs to learn to ignore all that nonsense and keep his mind on his job."

The video ended with a close-up of Josh patting the horse's flat cheek and rubbing his forehead. The high-strung gray stood with his eyes half-closed, seeming mesmerized by the trainer's touch.

"As you can see, your boy is making good progress," Josh

summed up. "He's learning to deal with new stimuli without freaking out, and to look to his handler to keep him safe. Now that he trusts me, I've got no qualms about getting on him—I'll do that tomorrow. Will keep you updated on our progress."

As the video ended, Anna leaned back in her chair and smiled. "Fingers crossed!"

"It'll be fine," Walt predicted, with his snaggle-toothed smile. "My money's on Josh."

"You kids have a good ride?" Anna asked him.

"Yeah, great."

"No problems?"

MJ held her breath, until Walt gave a nonchalant shrug and said, "Nope." He avoided her eyes, though, by checking his watch. "Well, I'd better get home. Got a couple of chores to finish before dinner."

"You'll remember to ask your Dad about...that thing?" Anna reminded him.

"I'll ask him." With a wave, he headed out to his truck.

MJ didn't bother to ask what the "thing" was. Probably just some piece of equipment Ann wanted to borrow.

She was relieved Walt hadn't mentioned the mysterious stirring in the woods that had spooked their horses. *Maybe he forgot about it already. Or he wasn't as scared as I was, and just chalked it up as a fun adventure.*

Or maybe he knew Anna would make a big deal of it and would not want me to go out on the trail again.

So, is it possible that Walt...told a lie?

There might be hope for The Sunday-School Kid, after all!

CHAPTER NINETEEN:

LOSS

The shrill neighs of terror shredded Anna's heart. Murphy struggled to escape, but the streamers from one of Josh's pipe-frame contraptions had wrapped around the horse's neck. He stamped his hooves, thrashed his whole body and twisted his head, trying to get free, but the strips of fabric only wound tighter around his throat. His calls turned to wheezes as he fought to survive, and his white-rimmed eyes pleaded for Anna to save him.

She tossed in her bed as if she was the one caught in a trap. When she woke, in a sweat, she began to realize it had been just a nightmare.

Most of it, anyway. Those strangled cries were real, but they weren't coming from Murphy. He was many miles away, she remembered.

Anyhow, she knew her horses well enough to recognize the "voice" as Valentine's.

Groggy, and wearing sleep shorts and T-shirt, Anna shoved her feet into her old sneakers and dashed from her room. In the hall she ran into MJ, who was dressed about the same way.

"Something's wrong..." the girl slurred, still half asleep.

"I know." Anxious to bolt straight outside, Anna hesitated and held her niece back, too. "Wait. Go get those pans from the kitchen and meet me by the front door."

Anna doubled back to her bedroom and snatched from a dresser drawer her only available weapon, a large can of red-pepper spray. She'd heard it could stop a bear or a coyote as well a human being. She wondered which of those she might find outside, bothering the horses.

Then she remembered that she'd left the electric fence turned on. Of those three possible intruders, only one would know how to switch it off.

She grabbed her cell phone from her bedside table, too.

Back in the living room, MJ stood by the front door holding a pot and a pan, fear in her wide, dark eyes.

Another strained cry from Valentine drifted up from the paddocks.

"If it's a bear," Anna whispered, "bang the pots together and yell as loud as you can. That should scare it away. Heck, that should even scare a person away."

"A person? You don't think—"

She dropped a hand on MJ's shoulder. "I've got my phone. If it's anything worse than a stray dog, I'll call 9-1-1."

Anna eased the screen door open and slipped out onto the porch, her niece a couple of steps behind. The morning air felt cool and dank, and a gray dawn haze shrouded the barnyard. At first glance, Anna saw no human or animal threat lurking near the paddocks, but the chestnut mare kept up her commotion. The two horses in the other pen watched as she trumpeted again, then pawed and struggled with something big and dark on the ground.

Something that could only be—

"Oh, God." Anna dropped her spray can on the porch and ran down the front steps. As she got nearer, she could see through the fence rails that Starbuck lay stretched out in the dirt.

"MJ, stay back." Her hands shook as she switched off the current to the fence. Meanwhile, she thought she saw the fallen horse raise his head a little.

Her hopes lifted, too. Maybe she could still do something to help him?

Valentine stood over her companion, her sides heaving in distress. As soon as Anna stepped through the gate, she could sense that all life had left Starbuck's body. He looked flat, as if he already were sinking back into the earth. She wondered for a second if some animal *had* attacked him, because his fly sheet was ripped to shreds near the shoulder.

Then it all became clear. Valentine reached down again to grab the webbing strap of the sheet with her strong teeth, and tried to haul her friend back to his feet. She couldn't move him much, but the slight rise and fall of his limp head sickened Anna.

"No, honey, no. Don't do that." She wrapped her arms around the mare's neck and used all her strength to push Valentine away. "You can't help him. He's gone."

Face pressed against the damp neck, Anna could feel the mare's wheezing breaths and hammering pulse. Behind them, the paddock gate whined open and shut, and MJ's choked voice said, "Oh, no! Oh, damn—"

"Yeah, we lost him." Anna wiped her eyes with the back of her hand. "Get Val out of here, would you? Put her in with the other guys. But be careful. She's upset right now."

The mare already seemed more resigned to the situation, though. Except for a backward look, she offered no resistance to being led away.

Left alone with Starbuck, Anna knelt and tried to get an idea of how long he'd been dead. Less than an hour—the body was only slightly cool. If they hadn't been asleep, if they'd known he was in distress, could they have done anything to save him?

Maybe not, given his wasted condition. Even now, after weeks of good care, his ribs still showed under his dark coat, through the rip in the fly sheet, and his stretched neck almost looked caved in.

She bit back a sob. *I let you down, buddy. Leaving you with that old couple, not checking up on you until it was too late. I'm so, so sorry!*

MJ returned, a sheen of tears on her cheeks, too. "What d'you think happened?"

Anna stood up, with a shake of her head. "Maybe Julie will know. But from what she said last time about his condition, his heart might just have given out."

"You don't think we let him out of the sling too soon?"

"He seemed ready, but...with a very weak horse, sometimes they lie down and don't have the strength to get up again."

MJ glanced toward the neighboring pen. Val stood with her

head over the fence, nostrils flared, and watched their every move. "From back by the porch, it almost looked like...like she was trying to help him up."

"She was." Anna's vision blurred again, as she took out her cell phone and tapped Julie's number on speed dial.

When the vet arrived, about half an hour later, she concluded that Starbuck had died of multiple, overlapping causes. Crouched by the body, Julie muttered, "What a shame. I thought we had a chance to save this guy, but I guess he was just too damaged."

The last word struck Anna hard, as both painful and accurate. Unfeeling humans, over the years, had damaged Starbuck so badly that his poor body gave up. She heard a sniffle from MJ, beside her, and put an arm around the girl.

"Thanks, Julie, for all you did to help him," Anna said.

"Wish I could've done more." The sturdy little woman packed up her medical kit and stood erect. "I know this is a rough question, but what do you want to do with him?"

Yes, Anna realized, that had to be decided soon. Even emaciated, the horse must still weigh seven or eight hundred pounds, and in this warm weather his carcass would soon become a problem. "God, I don't know. I guess I was naïve, or in denial, but I never thought much about how to handle something like this. Can I bury him here on the property?"

"I'm not sure that would be allowed. He didn't have any contagious diseases, but we've put so much medication into him, it might be considered a pollution hazard. Also, while burying him here sounds like a nice thing to do—" she glanced with meaning toward MJ "—sometimes it isn't such a pleasant thing to see."

Anna considered that. Would she just be putting her young niece through more trauma?

"If you want," Julie went on quietly, "I can call a service to remove him. They're close by and should be here pretty quick. You can take MJ up to the house until it's over."

Anna agreed to this. "One thing—can I keep his fly sheet?"

The vet first looked quizzical, then smiled gently. "I'll see to it."

Anna and MJ brought the rest of the horses into the barn for their morning meal, though Valentine still acted restless and ignored her special, enriched senior feed. No harm in leaving them all inside, Anna thought, until Starbuck had been taken away.

Back at the house, she and MJ also felt little appetite for breakfast. Even when they heard a deep-throated engine cross the barnyard, they avoided discussing the Standardbred's sad fate. Half an hour later, when they stepped outside again, the gate to his paddock stood open. Drag marks from some kind of sled, and wide tire treads, gave evidence that he had been taken away. The fly sheet lay neatly folded over the top of the paddock gate.

Anna turned out the remaining horses together in the second pen. She hoped the company would help bring Valentine out of her funk. *I don't need her wasting away, too.*

Meanwhile, MJ lifted Starbuck's red webbing halter from the post of the empty paddock and turned it over in her hands. "We're back down to three. Same as the morning I came out here."

"We are, aren't we? At least we should get Murphy back next week."

"Wow, I guess so, huh?" That perked up MJ a little. "Think Josh will have him all trained by then?"

"Two weeks' board at Josh's farm is all I can afford. So, whether Murphy's trained by then or not, he'll be coming back to us."

When Walt stopped by later, planning to exercise Dash, Anna told him what had happened that morning.

He leaned against the paddock fence with a pained expression. "Aw, darn, that's awful. I'm really sorry."

"Thanks. I feel terrible about it. Starbuck was the first horse I adopted out, and I failed him. On top of that, I had to have him carted away like...well, like garbage. It was the sensible thing to do, but still..." She laid her hand on the fly sheet, where it rested on the rail of the gate, and explained how Valentine had ripped it trying to help her pal. "This is all we've got left of him, now."

"You need to say a real good-bye to him," Walt told her. "Where's MJ? I've got an idea."

They chose a spot in one corner of the big meadow, beneath a spreading maple tree, and Walt dug a hole about two feet square. Anna placed the folded mesh sheet inside and MJ added the red halter. After Anna shoveled dirt back into the hole, Walt tied together two branches to form a small cross, and planted it in the center of the mound. MJ picked some daylilies from a sunnier part of the field and laid them on the token grave. Hands folded, Anna recalled aloud what Clint had told her of Starbuck's history—his early success as a pacer at the Meadowlands, then his many years pulling a carriage on an Amish farm in Pennsylvania.

"Before I got him, he was never ridden." Her throat constricted around the words. "After he grew strong enough, I started getting on him. He was such a gentle soul, and he tried hard to figure out what I wanted. I think he was smart, too, because he caught on pretty quick. He could have made somebody a great pleasure horse or trail horse...he *should* have."

When she choked up too much to go on, Walt stepped in to recite "The Lord is My Shepherd" and then the Our Father. Anna joined in the latter, but noticed that MJ had to mumble her way through, as if she'd never learned the prayer by heart.

"Thanks, Walt," Anna said, as they walked back from the meadow. "You were right. That's just what we needed."

He shrugged. "At our farm, we've had so many animals over the years that a lot have died on us. But whenever it's a special one we really loved, my folks have some kind of ritual to say goodbye."

"I'll have to call Clint, and I know this will be tough on him. He tried so hard to give Starbuck a better life, and he counted on me to help."

They'd just reached the barnyard again when the phone in Anna's back pocket warbled for her attention. Erika's number. She stalled until the two teens had gone up to the front porch of the house before she answered. "Hi, what's up?"

"I might ask you the same thing, Sis." Erika's bright voice carried an edge of annoyance. "I gather that you never called Lillian Gale."

"Uh, yeah...sorry about that. I've been trying to finish that IRS paperwork, but I've been so busy..."

"Honestly, Anna." Her sister's exasperation, though, seemed tinged with humor. "Well, no matter how busy you are, you're coming with me to a big party this Saturday."

"What? Oh, no...I can't get away. Besides, I'm seriously not in the mood. We lost one of our horses this morning."

"Lost?" Erika probably pictured it running away.

"Starbuck died. He'd been very sick for awhile, but..."

"Oh, dear. That's too bad, but you'll have to pull yourself together. What is it they say—'cowgirl up'? Because Lillian Gale will be at this party, and you're going to pitch your rescue farm to her, for all you're worth."

Anna reminded herself that Erika was trying to help. "I haven't even sent in the nonprofit application yet."

"No big deal. At least you can soften her up. This might be the best chance you'll get." Erika huffed again. "Sis, do you want to make a go of this farm, or don't you?"

Yes, that was the jackpot question. "A party, huh? With other grownup human beings? That'll be a change." Anna sighed. "Okay. Where and when?"

CHAPTER TWENTY:

PARTY

When her aunt stepped out the front door onto the porch, in a feed store T-shirt and cutoff shorts, MJ saw Mrs. Patterson's eyes widen. She whispered to her son, loud enough for the girl to overhear, "Anna's going to a fancy party dressed like *that*?"

Sitting across from them in the twig rocker, MJ giggled. "No, first she's going to stop at our house and my mom's going to dress her up. Y'know, like the fairy godmother did with Cinderella."

Anna brushed a long blond strand behind her ear, and told Mrs. Patterson, "When I moved out here, I got rid of most of my nice dresses, and the only one I have left is too big now. It's the rescue-farm fitness program—just combine back-breaking labor with constant anxiety."

"It should work so well for me!" MJ sniffed.

"Oh, you've toned up, too," Anna reassured her niece.

Walt, next to his mother on the loveseat, chimed in. "Sure, you look fine."

His mild compliment took MJ by surprise. She had noticed that Walt ragged on her less these days. Well, good. If they were going to be thrown together so much, they should at least try to be friends.

Then she saw Mrs. Patterson shoot her son a narrow, even disapproving look.

MJ figured that Dottie Patterson probably cared as much about the latest styles as her son did. This afternoon she wore loose, high-waisted pants—the kind Erika would call "mom jeans"—with a short-sleeved, flowered blouse tucked in at the waist. She had the same scattering of freckles across her nose as Walt, and the same straight auburn hair, though hers was shoulder-length with a few strands of gray.

Meanwhile, Anna rolled her eyes as if the makeover was a bit silly. "Erika's lending me one of her designer dresses and a pair of heels. She said something about having her hair stylist stop by the house, too."

"You'll probably look terrific," MJ encouraged her.

"Well, I'd better get going." With a lingering trace of reluctance, Anna started down the steps. "Four already...It'll take me more than an hour to get to Erika's, and the party's at seven. She'll probably need all the time in between to whip me into shape."

As her aunt climbed into the dusty burgundy truck and drove off, MJ shook her head. *Imagine if Anna pulled up in front of the catering hall in that pickup. Another reason why she has to ride there with Mom!*

"What's the occasion, again?" Walt's mother asked, after another sip of iced tea. "Anna said it was some kind of charity dinner."

"For autistic kids," MJ told her. "*New Jersey Good Life* is one of the sponsors. That's the magazine Anna used to edit. My mom still works there."

Mrs. Patterson nodded, seeming to approve of the worthwhile cause. No doubt that held more interest for her than the idea of mixing with a roomful of rich and glamorous types.

The three of them sat on the porch in awkward silence. MJ still didn't know how it had been arranged that Dottie Patterson would spend the evening out here with her and Walt while Anna was away.

Crap, I'm almost eighteen. Mom trusts me to stay home with just Carl all the time. Okay, maybe Walt isn't my brother, but still...

When the girl had protested, Anna reminded her that the last time she'd been gone just a few hours, MJ had an accident. In case that didn't convince her, she also brought up the mystery visitor who had driven onto their property one evening.

Those were plausible reasons for caution, and MJ pretended to accept them. But she suspected that, in addition, Anna didn't want her staying alone that long with Walt. Or maybe his mother didn't.

Hah. Like they have anything to worry about!

"Anna seemed nervous," Walt commented. "I guess she doesn't go to many big parties."

"She used to," MJ said. "For the magazine and for her husband's work. But I guess she feels out of practice."

"A shame she has to worry about people judging her," said Mrs. Patterson. "Your aunt's pretty enough as she is. Is she widowed?"

"Divorced." Would that be a black mark against her, in Dottie's book? No way would MJ get into the rest of that dicey story. If Mrs. Patterson found out Richard Cooper had been indicted for fraud, she might never set foot on Anna's property again.

"That's a shame. And they never had any children?"

"No. I guess with them both working so much, they kept putting it off."

"Mm. Too many people do that, these days. Put off having kids for the sake of their careers." She made air quotes around the last word. "Then, when they finally decide they're ready, it's too late."

It irked MJ that Mrs. Patterson would question Anna's decision without knowing anything about her particular situation. Did Walt's mother disapprove of birth control, too? MJ knew some very religious people did, and Walt seemed to have a lot of brothers and sisters.

He also looked uncomfortable with the subject. Gripping his empty Coke bottle, he bounced to his feet. "Getting late, Mom. Time to feed the horses."

She checked her watch. "You're right. And after that I'll make dinner. You kids must be famished."

No doubt these two criteria had prompted Anna to choose Mrs. Patterson as their "babysitter"—she had plenty of experience at both farm work and cooking. Though MJ knew Anna had left their dinner pretty much ready to serve.

The three of them headed out, MJ grateful for some physical work to interrupt Mrs. Patterson's cross-examination. En route to the paddocks, though, she caught the woman staring at her.

"Were you painting something?" Dottie asked, in an innocent tone. "Got some green stuff on the ends of your hair..."

MJ couldn't suppress her inner rebel any longer. "Oh, it's usually a lot greener. I haven't been to the salon lately." She wore a short-sleeved T-shirt, and on an impulse rolled the sleeves higher, to make sure Dottie also saw her tattoo.

Walking ahead of Mrs. Patterson, the girl didn't even glance back to check her reaction. But Walt caught MJ's eye and stifled a laugh.

She tried to share his amusement, but feared this could turn out to be a very long night. She hoped her aunt wasn't been "judged" nearly so much at her fancy fundraiser.

At the catering hall, Anna glimpsed herself in the long mirror behind the bar and did a double take. She'd rejected some of her sister's more extravagant fashion and beauty suggestions, but still barely recognized the woman in the sleeveless, deep-blue dress, hair pulled into a tasteful upsweep and borrowed diamonds glittering at her earlobes. Because she took a larger shoe than Erika, she'd had an excuse to reject any of her sister's spike heels. But even in her own moderately high black sandals, Anna wobbled a little, because she hadn't worn them in so long.

Not since the days when she'd attended plenty of functions like this, with Richard. Though she'd enjoyed some of those occasions, the memories were tainted for her now.

She hadn't even had a glass of wine in a long time, because she preferred to stay dead-sober around the farm, but now she caught the eye of the bartender and asked for a Chablis. She sipped the drink and hoped it would quiet the butterflies in her stomach.

Anna guessed that well over two hundred people filled the vast room, softly lit by crystal chandeliers and wall sconces. No doubt they included representatives from the local chapter of the

Autism Society of America, as well as wealthy sponsors. There must have been forty of the round tables, all draped in ivory with centerpieces of pink roses.

A couple were reserved just for the *New Jersey Good Life* editors.

No getting around it. Tonight, I'm sure to run into a lot of people from my past life, which I gladly left behind. I'll be stepping back into my old identity of—

"Ann Cooper! Ohmygosh, is that really you?"

Anna recognized the bubbly voice of Jeannie Kaplish, *Good Life*'s food editor. The middle-aged woman fluttered over, trailing layers of teal-green silk that set off her curly red hair, but also made her look even shorter and rounder.

"Hi, Jeannie, how've you been?"

"Oh, hanging in there. I have to say, though, things haven't been the same since you left. How have *you* been?" Jeannie tilted her head in pity. Anna had gotten that look from too many people over the past couple years. Still, it was better than the frigid anger she felt from others.

"I'm great!" Anna took a swallow of her wine. "Do you want anything from the bar?"

The other woman gestured with her half-filled highball glass. "I'm still good. Guess we should make way for these other thirsty folks." They stepped to one side as she added, "You look gorgeous—so chic!"

Anna laughed. "Erika put me together. Even the dress is hers."

"Well, it definitely suits you. I could never go sleeveless, with my fat arms. But girl, you must work out! Do you lift weights?"

"Nope, I lift hay bales...and muck out stalls." She let Jeannie puzzle over that before explaining, "I run a horse-rescue farm, out in Warren County."

The other woman gave an uneasy chuckle. "Uh...how did you get into that?"

She probably thinks my divorce, and giving up my job, wiped me out so badly that I had to take work as a hired hand! Anna colored the truth just a little. "It's something I'd thought of doing for a long while. After I left the magazine, it seemed like the right time."

Erika joined them, and Jeannie pivoted toward her. "So good to see Ann again. She tells me she's wrangling horses these days."

Erika smoothly explained what she understood about the farm's purpose. "My daughter's also helping out there for a while, taking one of those gap years. I afraid she's having such a good time, though, that she may never go back to school!"

Clever to make it sound like a joke, Anna thought. "Don't worry. I'm working MJ so hard, come fall she'll be dying to sit down in a classroom again."

A young waitress in a tuxedo shirt and black pants offered the three of them miniature shrimp puffs. Anna snatched two, her appetite stoked by her nerves. Across the room, she spotted a certain elegant, fiftyish couple—Ian and Barb Mitchell, publishers of *Good Life*. With any luck, she could duck any conversation with *them* this evening. She knew Ian only grudgingly had agreed, under Erika's persuasion, to let Anna continue writing and editing for the magazine part-time under her maiden name. They didn't mind retaining her skills, but didn't relish the cloud that still hung over her. She did not think the Mitchells themselves ever had invested and lost any money with Richard, but maybe some of their friends had.

When Jeannie flounced off to greet someone else, Erika whispered in Anna's ear. "See the little gray-haired woman in the green brocade dress? Near the dais, talking to the very tall man? That's Lillian Gale."

"Ah," Anna whispered back, "So we have our target in sight. Time to take careful aim...or do I just throw a net over her?"

"Are you going to be serious? I'm doing this for you, y'know. Well, you and MJ. It's fine to be all idealistic, but you need a backer with deep pockets."

"You just want to make sure I can afford to repay your loan... someday," Anna teased. "You're right, of course. It just makes me uncomfortable, schmoozing someone to hit her up for money." *Too much like something Richard would do,* she finished to herself.

Erika shrugged. "If you're going to run a charity, you'll have to learn how to fundraise. You think the people who organized this dinner feel guilty about asking for money to help people with autism?"

"Point taken."

"Look, it's no big deal. She was really nice when I spoke to her about this month's profile for the magazine. I'll introduce you, and you take it from there, okay?"

Anna gulped the last of her wine. "Lead on."

Following her sister through the crowd, she brushed past a medium-tall, blond man in a gray summer suit. When he glimpsed her face, he looked so startled that she wondered if her nerves had made her break out in some kind of ugly rash.

"Ann Cooper!" He covered his reaction with a wide, fake smile. "Didn't expect to see *you* here tonight."

Inwardly, she cringed. Another person she had hoped not to run into. Zack Burgess, the former photo editor who now filled her old position at *Good Life*.

And in spite of his grin, he probably was none too thrilled to run into her, either.

CHAPTER TWENTY-ONE:

FROM THE PAST

Even though Zack was now Anna's boss, they communicated rarely and always by phone or email. She hadn't spoken with him face-to-face since she'd left the magazine.

He recovered his composure enough to wink at her. "Or should I call you 'Anna Loehmeyer'?"

In his mid-thirties, with a boyish, preppy haircut and an energy level to match, Zak always had struck Anna as ambitious. It hadn't surprised her when the Mitchells tapped him to replace her. Whether he possessed the skills to back up that go-getter impression remained open to debate, from what she'd heard.

Lightly, she answered, "That *is* the name I grew up with, and the one on the magazine's masthead these days."

"Distancing yourself, eh? Can't say I blame you."

Anna would not let herself be dragged into any discussion of Richard, especially not with this guy. "As for what brings me here, tonight, Erika invited me, and I'm happy to help support a good cause."

Meanwhile, from a couple yards away, her sister caught Anna's eye and frowned. Anna just lifted one shoulder in a half-shrug. *What can I do? Be rude to my boss?*

"Well, it's great you could make it. I'm sure lots of people will be glad to see you again." Zack bent his head toward hers confidentially. "I don't mind telling you, for months after I took over, all I heard from the staff was, 'Ann always did it this way,' 'Ann could edit a story like a brain surgeon,' 'Ann always came up with such creative layouts.' Sometimes I felt like the poor woman in that old Hitchcock movie...y'know, the one where everybody keeps talking about how her husband's late wife was so perfect?"

Rebecca, Anna thought. *Nice—he's comparing me to a dead woman, who also turned out to have been a total witch.* Beneath Zack's snarky humor, though, ran a note of anxiety. *Does he think I want my old job back? That I came here tonight to kiss up to the Mitchells?*

Good manners seemed the only way to go. "From what I've seen of the magazine lately, you're doing fine. As for me, I'm perfectly happy these days just copyediting and fact-checking. Much less stressful than when I was running the show, and I have more time for other things." A human wave swept toward one side of the room, giving Anna an excuse to break off their chat. "Oh good, the buffet's finally open!"

Lillian Gale paused near the poached salmon filets, as if wavering between them and the chicken piccata. The Loehmeyer sisters hurried to take advantage of her indecision.

The heiress greeted Erika warmly, told her she'd enjoyed talking with the magazine's writer the week before, and joked that she hoped the photo department would be able to erase some of her wrinkles. That gave Erika the opening she needed to introduce her sister.

"Anna and you have something in common. She's also very interested in horses. She used to ride in a lot of those...er...jumping shows."

The small woman with the queenly posture faced Anna with interest. "Really. Would I have seen you?"

"You might have. I did some of the B-circuit shows with my horse Ebony Duke. We took a couple of firsts, over the years."

Lillian narrowed her eyes. "A big black, wasn't he? Nice mover, as I remember. You still have him?"

Nothing wrong with her memory, Anna thought. "Unfortunately, no. He got sold in...my divorce."

"Ah, yes. Your husband was Richard Cooper, right? I did hear about that."

"I'm afraid most people have."

To Anna's surprise, the little woman broke out in a devilish grin. "At least you dumped the SOB. Good for you! Just too bad you had to sell your horse."

"That's pretty much the way I look at it. At least these days I have four others, even though none is in Duke's class. I started a small rescue farm."

While Erika drifted away, Anna shared her enthusiasm for her cause with Lillian Gale. It wasn't as hard as she'd feared, because the woman obviously loved horses, too, and understood the need for such operations.

"You know," Lillian said, "I became involved with the ASA because I have a grandson who is autistic. He's benefitted a great deal from a riding program for children with special needs, and they use a lot of rescues."

Anna nodded eagerly. "I've thought that, somewhere down the line, we might try to cooperate with one of those programs. We have two animals now who aren't up to hard work but could carry children or light adults for therapeutic riding. We also have two others who are more adoptable. One's an off-the-track Thoroughbred who's a tremendous jumper." Seeing a chance to name-drop, she went for it. "In fact, he's in training right now with Josh Buchanan."

Lillian's delicate gray eyebrows arched. "You don't say! I've never seen any of Buchanan's clinics, myself, and I've heard pros and cons from other trainers. But he does seem to get results."

Anna drew a breath and plunged ahead. "The farm is still getting off the ground, of course. Erika's niece is updating our website and I'm ready to file our paperwork as a nonprofit. The more I learn about how many abused and neglected horses are out there, the more I want to make this work."

"You do seem to have the passion." Lillian studied her more coolly now, aware she was being pitched. "I would think you'd be able to find plenty of supporters, too, through your magazine connections."

"Yes and no," Anna admitted. "A lot of the connections I made back when I was an editor aren't so receptive anymore."

"Hmm, I guess not. But none of that was your fault, was it?"

Turning back to the buffet for a moment, Lillian opted for the salmon fillet. "It's always nice to see a person who's had some hard knocks try to turn the experience into something positive. When you've filed that paperwork and got the website up, send me a link. Erika has my contact information. Can't promise anything, but I'll have a look."

Anna could hardly believe her bold attempt had paid off. "Thanks so much. I almost was afraid to ask, because...you might think..."

"That you'd be up to the same tricks as your ex? I'm sure you're smarter than that, dear." Before heading back to her table, Lillian faced Anna again with a canny gleam in her clear blue eyes. "My late husband was into plenty of financial shenanigans that I didn't find out about until after he died. Only difference was, he never got caught."

⟨⟨⟨⟩⟩⟩

When Anna climbed the steps to her own porch around ten thirty, she could see lights beyond the window curtain, and heard the AC going and the TV droning in the living room. She rang the doorbell as a warning, then used her own key to let herself in.

Walt met her at the door. "Hi, how was the party? You're still dressed up!"

"It went well, thanks." On a side chair, she set down the Bloomingdale's shopping tote that held her jeans and T-shirt. "I didn't bother to change back, because I didn't want to keep you and your mom here too late."

Dottie rose a bit stiffly from her seat on the couch, eyelids drooping. "You look very nice," she said. "Very tasteful."

MJ bounced up from the ottoman. "Ha, I figured you'd pick that dress. I always liked it. Mom calls it 'sensible,' but you know her taste."

"It served its purpose." Briefly, Anna filled them in on her conversation with Lillian Gale.

"Awesome!" gushed her niece. "Nice work, Anna."

"Well, your mom helped a lot."

Walt elbowed MJ. "Guess now you're gonna have to finish that website, eh? To impress the rich donors."

"And I'm going to have to finish and file that nonnprofit tax form." Anna's gaze took in the bowl of popcorn on the coffee table, the half-filled glass of iced tea by Dottie's seat, and the soda cans elsewhere. The TV screen showed a sober young man reading the day's headlines in front of a large number 12. "Watching the local news?"

"We just switched," Walt told her. "We had the ball game on before. Yankees won."

"MJ and I checked the horses about an hour ago," Dottie added. "They should be settled for the night."

"Thanks so much," Anna told the Pattersons. "I owe you a favor."

"Don't be silly." Dottie lifted her shoulder bag from the arm of the sofa. "S'what neighbors are for."

After Anna saw them out and shut the door, she faced her niece. MJ stood with arms crossed and lips pursed.

"You guys all got along okay?"

"Sure, as long as we followed *her* rules," MJ said. "Trying to watch TV was insane. All the cop shows were too violent, all the sitcoms and movies were too sexy. We tried HGTV for awhile, until Walt got bored and his mom started sermonizing about how wasteful it is for people to spend so much money on their houses. So, we switched to the History Channel for half an hour. Finally, Walt saw the Yankees were on..."

Anna shook her head at the girl's outraged recitation. She might never be the mother of a teenager, but she was getting a feel for the experience.

MJ finished, "In other words, don't ever, *ever* do this to me again."

"C'mon, it was only for a few hours. Just think, Walt has to live with her."

"That's only half of it. Now that Dottie knows I dye my hair green, have one small tattoo, go to rock concerts, and watch uncensored movies, she thinks I'm some kind of threat to Walt's virtue. I swear, she wouldn't leave the two of us alone together for a second. I mean, we're just friends!"

Anna kicked off her heels and sank down on the sofa. "I'm sorry, MJ. I had no idea she'd be as strict as that."

Her niece returned to the ottoman. "It was kind of flattering. Nobody ever acted worried that I'd seduce their son before, or even their boyfriend. But next time you're afraid to leave me here alone, maybe we can just borrow one of the Pattersons' dogs. Walt says they have a couple big ones to spare."

"At least a dog would let you watch whatever you wanted on TV."

The girl brightened. "There *is* something I've been dying to watch, but I didn't want to do it behind your back."

Uh-oh, Anna thought. Maybe Dottie Patterson did need to worry about MJ's influence on her son. "What would that be?"

"Not on TV, on your laptop." She got it from the hall table. "I was showing Walt what I did with the farm's website, and saw an email from Josh Buchanan with another video attached. He sent it to you, so I didn't open it, but the suspense is killing me!"

Anna felt the same. "Okay, just let me get out of this dress and into pjs."

They sat on the sofa and MJ opened the video. Again, Josh wore a wireless mic as someone recorded him lunging Murphy in a round pen. The horse went far more calmly than he ever had with Anna, and balked only a little when asked to move clockwise. Next, Josh had him trot over cavalettis—poles spaced several feet apart on the ground, to teach the horse to measure his stride. Finally, Josh added a small cross rail, so Murphy had to take the hurdle at the end.

Despite her fatigue from the long evening, Anna leaned forward to watch. For the first time, she could picture the big gray becoming a well-trained, well-coordinated jumper. But would he do the same thing with a rider on his back?

The rest of the footage answered that question.

With Murphy saddled and bridled, Josh went through a routine similar to what Anna had done with Clint's help, resting his weight on the horse gradually before he sat astride. Meanwhile, he again traded occasional comments with the woman who was shooting the video. Anna saw Murphy raise his head and pin his ears, and at her elbow MJ hissed in concern. But Josh quickly pulled the horse's head down to one side and rode him in a small circle. He then urged him forward again, and at every sign of tension he repeated the circle.

He explained via his mic, "A horse can't rear while he's circling. It distracts him and also disciplines him for acting up."

The trainer walked, trotted and cantered Murphy around the ring, with no rebellion except some snorting and head-tossing. Josh explained that until the Thoroughbred adjusted to his new role, it was best to ride him on a loose rein. "A racehorse is trained to lean into the bit when he gallops, and the harder a jockey pulls, the faster he'll go. Of course, that's the opposite from what you want on a trail ride or in a show ring."

Near the conclusion, Josh also rode Murphy over the line of cavalettis with a raised one at the end. The gray took off at a speedy canter following the jump, but his trainer quickly got him under control once more.

"Wow," said MJ, "that's great. Josh really did 'fix' him."

Before Anna could sound a note of caution, Josh did it for her. He dismounted and, stroking the horse's neck, addressed the camera in closeup. "Anyhow, that's where we're at after two weeks. If it suits your schedule, Anna, I'll bring this guy back to you Wednesday morning. He's still got a lot to learn, though, before you can adopt him out to anyone. From here on, most of it will be up to you."

CHAPTER TWENTY-TWO:

POTENTIAL

Wednesday morning found Anna once more hunched over the keyboard of her desktop computer, as she tried to wrap up the paperwork to incorporate her farm as a nonprofit.

Although she still wasn't a hundred percent happy with "Reboot Ranch," it did appear to be one of the few names not spoken for. She paid a fee to reserve it for two months while her application was considered. Anna already had researched other rescue operations to help her compose bylaws and a description of her organization. Pressed to list a board of directors, she had gotten permission from Erika, Julie and Clint to use their names.

Was that stretching the truth? Could any of the information she was providing backfire and get her in trouble somewhere down the line? She dreaded anyone saying she had accepted donations under false pretenses. That she was a con artist, just like her ex-husband.

She got up to pour herself a second cup of coffee from the little machine on top of the office's file cabinet. Maybe she was still feeling raw because of the party the other night, where people had reminded her of the scandal with Richard.

Don't they understand that he duped me, the same as all those investors? Even more so! They didn't fall in love with Richard, marry him, live with him and sleep with him, never quite understanding his complicated business dealings but trusting that he would never deliberately cheat anyone. Even the night before my horse show, when he stormed out of the house, I suspected another woman. I never imagined he was meeting with lawyers, trying to figure out how to beat a federal investigation!

Of course, Richard never put our money into any of those shaky stocks. Thank God for that. If he'd lost my trust fund, I'd never have had enough to start this farm.

Since her divorce, Anna had worked hard to put all that history behind her. Rarely did she allow herself to even wonder about Richard anymore. Through the society grapevine and gossip columns, she'd heard that he remained in Hawaii, shacked up with another, younger woman who no doubt thought the sun rose and set on him. Anna never tried to get in touch with him, and as far as she knew the reverse was also true. He wouldn't have known her address at the farm, and she'd changed her personal email address. But from what Erika said, no mysterious letters or emails for Anna had come to the magazine, either.

This opened up an even older wound. After her parents divorced, when she was twelve, her successful executive father had done a similar vanishing act. Anna knew Erika understood her pain and sympathized, since she also had suffered from the disappearance of their dad.

Anna settled back in front of the computer with her coffee. *In Richard's case, though, maybe it's for the best. Better to keep my distance from him, the way a reformed alcoholic steers clear of his old favorite watering hole.*

After the divorce, Anna had seen a therapist who'd suggested that her ex sounded like a narcissist. He'd even implied that maybe Richard put off having children because he didn't want the responsibility, or didn't want to compete with them for Anna's attention. All of that further convinced her that any contact with Richard could be bad for her mental health.

MJ stuck her head in the office door, derailing Anna's morose train of thought. "Hey, is Walt coming by today?"

"Not sure. Why?"

"With Josh bringing Murphy back, I figured he'd want to be here. Y'know how he likes to watch the horse whisperer work his magic."

"He might've forgot. Give him a call, if you want."

"I tried. Just got the Patterson family answering machine. If Walt even has a cell, he never gave me the number."

Noticing MJ's disappointment, Anna reflected that in the past month or so her niece had made quite a U-turn, from mocking Walt's countrified ways behind his back to enjoying his company. Probably good that she'd made a friend of someone from a very different background than hers. Anna worried about the outcome, though, if the two teens began to develop stronger feelings for each other. At the very least, Dottie Patterson would probably try to squelch any budding relationship.

A diesel engine droned into the barnyard, and MJ dashed to the door. "He's here!" she yelled to Anna. "Murphy, I mean. And Josh, too, of course."

By the time they went outside, Josh already had opened the back of his expensive-looking, two-horse trailer. With the extra room, he could turn Murphy around and lead him out head-first, and the gray behaved like a gentleman. The horse wore thick leg wraps, and a leather "bumper" over his ears, to protect his head in case he reared.

MJ, at Anna's side, laughed out loud. "He looks like he's going into battle."

Josh smiled at them. "With his trailering history, I didn't want to take any chances. But he was fine."

The gray did seem to have learned a new set of manners during his two weeks away. Valentine and Patches neighed to him from the paddock, and though Murphy whinnied back, he made no attempt to drag Josh in that direction, as he used to with Anna. MJ walked right up to him to stroke his neck, and the horse calmly accepted her attention.

"Let's get all this paraphernalia off and let him relax," Josh suggested. "Then I need to talk to Anna for awhile."

She tried to decide whether that sounded ominous, as she helped unwrap the horse's legs. She was able to hold Murphy with just the lead rope looped around his neck, while Josh removed the head bumper from his halter. Meanwhile, Anna spotted another change. "You pulled his mane."

"Hope you don't mind. I thought I'd see how he handled that.

We had one tense moment—he backed up on the cross-ties, and I was afraid he might try to flip—but then he chilled out."

That impressed Anna. Having the longer hairs methodically yanked out with a comb, to shorten their manes, didn't normally hurt horses, but even quiet ones sometimes objected. Murphy would have had it done before, as a racehorse, but it could have triggered bad memories.

She smoothed the flat, even, four-inch-long fringe. "He looks ready for business now."

Josh met her eyes with a serious look. "That's what we need to talk about."

A flutter in her stomach, Anna tuned the gray loose in the second paddock, where he could see and show off for his friends. "MJ, keep an eye on him for a few minutes? Josh and I are going up to the house."

Anna brought a pitcher of lemonade and two glasses out to the porch. She sat on the loveseat and Josh in the wicker chair across from her.

After a long swallow of the tangy drink, he cut to the chase. "You've got a young, healthy horse with plenty of his own opinions. I think your friend Clint might've been right, that Murphy has more issues with men, though I think I got him past some of those."

"I saw you riding him, even jumping him, on the video. I'd say you made great progress."

"But like I said then, it's just a start, and his future from here on is up to you. My main question is, what do you want for this horse?"

Anna pondered for a minute. "First of all, I want him to be safe from any more abuse. But after that, I'm inclined to go with what Murphy seems to want. His first day here, he jumped a tractor! And when I turned him loose in the field, he actually looked for piles for rock and fallen branches to jump over. I'd like to see him go to a rider who can use that talent. On the other hand, I don't want him ever to be stressed out again like he was at the racetrack."

Josh nodded and took another sip of lemonade before he went on. "It'll be a balancing act, with this guy. He's high-strung, but he also needs a challenge. I don't see him in many hunter classes..."

They both chuckled. Anna knew show hunters were judged on looks, obedience and how smoothly they cleared low-to-moderate hurdles. Show *jumpers* tackled more challenging obstacles against the clock. Their conformation, turnout and style of jumping didn't count so much, as long as they got around the course fast and clear.

"He's good-looking enough, but he still might forget his manners now and then," the trainer said. "He's got speed, though, and if he's ridden well he'll probably jump the moon."

Anna heard a caveat in the phrase *if he's ridden well*, and sensed what was coming.

"Lucky that you have the right experience," Josh went on, "and you seem to have done pretty well on your own horse. Think you can continue Murphy's training?"

Anna wrapped both hands around her frosty glass and drew a deep breath. "I don't know. The only horse I ever showed was Duke, and he came to me beautifully trained, almost push-button. I've never trained a jumper from scratch, and I've never ridden any horse with the kind of issues Murphy has. I wouldn't want to mess him up...or, frankly, have him mess me up."

She half expected Josh to give up on her. He did stare so intently that she squirmed under the scrutiny, but his tone remained level. "Well, at least you're honest. But the faster this horse progresses, the sooner you'll be able to adopt him out. He should be put into training for an hour or so every day. I don't have the time in my schedule right now to do that, and..."

"And even if you did, I couldn't afford your rates," Anna finished, with a weak smile.

"Which are about the same as those of any other decent trainer," Josh added. "So, the logical thing is for you to do most of the work yourself."

She dropped her gaze to her almost-empty glass and blinked away tears of shame. She couldn't stand the idea of letting Murphy down, just because she was afraid.

Josh broke the silence. "Anna, I know about your accident."

His gentle comment made her sit up straight. "You...how?"

"Word gets around. I heard about it from someone who competed in the same event."

Horse showing was a small world, she reminded herself. In the same state, the same general region and the same discipline, people kept tabs on their fellow competitors.

"Any injury serious enough to land you in the hospital is bound to shake your confidence," Josh said. "It's even happened to me a couple of times."

That, at least, kept Anna from feeling cowardly and neurotic. "How did you get over it?"

"The oldest cure in the world. Soon as I was able, I got back on the horse. Or, if the same one wasn't around, at least back on *a* horse."

"I've done that. Since the accident, I've ridden all three of my rescue horses—Valentine, Starbuck and Dash. But Murphy is different."

"Yes, he is. He's got a lot more potential. And maybe you do, too, Anna. You might be selling yourself short."

This guy did have a way of instilling confidence, she thought, and not just in animals. "Think so?"

Josh gave a shrug and stood up. "Before I go off and leave the two of you alone together, let's find out."

CHAPTER TWENTY-THREE:

RIDER UP!

J osh put the gray on cross-ties in the barn aisle as Anna brought her all-purpose saddle and snaffle bridle from the tack room. Meanwhile, MJ trailed her curiously.

"Is Josh going to ride Murphy?"

"No, I'm going to. At least, that's the plan."

"Oh, yeah?" The girl grinned. "Still got Dr. Kowalski on your speed dial?"

"Har-har." Though Anna knew her niece was just teasing, right now she didn't need anyone undermining her already shaky confidence.

When the Thoroughbred saw the tack from the corner of his eye, he pawed the wooden floor as if eager to be off.

Josh helped Anna center the saddle on the animal's broad, dappled back. She bridled Murphy, and at least he did not pull his frequent trick of throwing his head out of reach. As the two of them led him outside, Josh told her, "You can ride him in the round pen, to start off. No corners where he might try to spin around on you."

MJ followed them at a distance. Anna saw her touch the screen of her phone, speak into it briefly and then tuck in back into the pocket of her shorts. Was she still trying to reach Walt?

Inside the pen, Josh halted Murphy by the mounting block and handed Anna the reins. Her heart thudded when she remembered chickening out the last time she'd tried this, but she felt safer with Josh there. She started to spring into the saddle...and Murphy took a few steps forward. She pulled on the reins to halt him, but meanwhile almost lost her footing on the block.

"Good," the trainer told her. "You were ready for him."

Red-faced, Anna maneuvered the gray back into position.

"Ever watch jockeys mount in the paddock?" Josh asked. "Somebody gives 'em a leg up, and they jump on while the horse is walking away. So, this guy needs to learn to stand still. If he starts to move off, do just what you did and tell him 'Whoa.'"

More determined now, Anna kept a firmer hold and landed lightly in the saddle. Murphy kept still.

"Okay, walk him on."

With the slightest nudge from her calves, Murphy moved out in a purposeful stride, with no threat of backing up or rearing. Head high, he neighed to the horses in the other pen.

"Keep his attention," Josh called, from the center of the ring. "Collect him a little."

Anna gathered the reins, and her mount fussed for just a minute before dropping his head into a more attentive position. She felt exhilarated to be back on a young, fit and somewhat challenging animal.

Next, they trotted. As they went around several times, in each direction, Anna worked to keep Murphy's mind on his job and his head down. They did well enough for Josh to ask, "Want to try a canter?"

She glanced toward MJ, on the rail, who gave her a thumbs-up. "Sure, why not go for broke?"

She collected the horse in a half-halt, sat back and brushed her outside leg behind the girth. Murphy must have been itching for that signal, because he bolted forward. Anna saw her niece jump away from the fence as they swept past, and the rails became a blur.

She hauled on the reins until her palms burned and her arms ached. "Whoa, boy...*whoooa!*"

But it did no good. Murphy leaned on the bit so hard that he pulled her up in her stirrups like a jockey. She might have been in a car careening downhill with no brakes. The round pen felt too small, as they whipped around it a second time.

"Let go of his mouth! Let go of his mouth!"

Over the pounding hooves, Josh's shouts reached her panicked brain. Still, it took Anna another second to respond. She forced herself to unclench her grip and let the reins out an inch...then another.

Murphy slowed enough for her to sit back more. Her weight in the saddle brought him down to a more relaxed, civilized canter, then finally a fast trot.

By the time they settled back to a walk, Anna was breathing harder than the horse. She reached under her helmet's visor to wipe perspiration from her brow.

The trainer fell in step with them, and she admitted, "Sorry, I forgot. The harder you pull on a racehorse, the faster he runs, right?"

Josh nodded. "I didn't have time to completely train that out of him, so it's something you'll have to work on. All in all, though, you did great for your first ride."

"I did?"

"Sure. Every time you corrected him, he listened to you."

MJ stepped through the gate and joined them, with a nervous laugh. "At least Murphy's got over his hangup about going to the right."

"That's true." Josh grinned at Anna. "He ran away with you clockwise."

She managed a twitchy smile of her own. "Imagine how fast he might've gone in his good direction."

While she and MJ untacked the horse and hosed him off, Josh proposed a strategy. At the start of every week, he would email Anna a training schedule she should follow, to improve Murphy's obedience and prepare him for jumping. Every week or so, Josh would stop by to check her progress and discuss any problems she might be having.

"I think you should set a goal," he added. "Have him jumping a two-foot-six course by the end of August."

Anna wondered how much work it would take to get Murphy to that point. He could *jump* that high with one leg tied to his belly. Controlling his speed and strides would be the real challenge. "I appreciate your help. But what's your fee—"

The trainer waved a hand. "It's not much work on my part, and I'd like to see you place this horse. If we can get him ready to show, I might even be able to help you find a home for him." Josh glanced at the sports watch on his tanned wrist. "I'd better get moving now, but I'll send you the first week's schedule tonight."

They shook hands before he got into his SUV and pulled his trailer away down the driveway.

"Wow," said MJ. "Sounds like you and Murph have your work cut out for you. He's gotta be ready to show by August?"

"That'll take some doing, all right," Anna admitted. But tough as it sounded, for the first time she could imagine herself accomplishing it. She'd been scared today, but sitting on such a lively, powerful mount again also had reawakened the excitement she used to feel riding Duke.

I might never have had the nerve to try if Josh hadn't pushed me. I should also have thanked him for that.

Around five, MJ and her aunt had just finished feeding the horses, and were heading in for their own dinner, when the girl's cell phone rang. Walt, finally getting back to her. She let Anna go ahead inside and stayed behind on the porch.

"Sorry I missed your call," he said. "I was driving around all day. Dad threw his back out yesterday, and I had to make a bunch of deliveries for him."

This explanation soothed MJ's hurt feelings. "That's too bad. I hope he's okay."

"He oughta be. It happens once in a while, when he lifts something the wrong way. He's usually over it in a day or two."

"Sorry I left so many messages at your house. I guess you don't have a cell."

"I do, but it's an old flip phone. I just use it for emergencies, so I keep it turned off to save the battery. If you left a message on that, I might not see it for days." He paused. "I only found one message from you on the house machine. You left a few? About something important?"

"No...I just thought you'd want to be here for Murphy's big return. Josh got Anna to ride him and they really kicked up some dust."

MJ recapped the morning's events for Walt. He listened with mild interest, but not the kind of enthusiasm she'd expected. A couple of times, someone—no doubt his mother—called to him from the background. First, she must have asked who was on the phone, because Walt answered, "It's MJ." A few minutes later, she must have reminded him of some chore he needed to do, because he called back, "Sure, soon as I get off."

The girl sat down on the loveseat to resume her story. "So, Anna's going to start training Murphy herself, working from a schedule that Josh sends her. You still can watch her do that."

"Yeah, that'll be great." Again, he sounded a little flat.

"Think you can get over tomorrow?"

"I dunno. Depends on what kind of shape Dad's in."

"Oh, sure."

"That reminds me—" Walt's voice gained more energy "—with Dad laid up, I got a chance to ask him what Anna wanted me to, about the man who used to own Dash. Dad still has a news clipping from when the guy was arrested and fined. His name was Jeffers...Art Jeffers. Had a small farm about five miles from here. Dad thinks he must've moved on, though, 'cause the place looks deserted lately."

"Uh...okay. I'll tell Anna." MJ wondered why her aunt thought that information was important.

"Well, dinner's on the table, so I better go. Good luck with Murphy. Glad you got him back."

Walt's abrupt disconnect left MJ staring at the phone in her hand.

Weird. A week ago, he would have given anything to watch Josh at work and to soak up all those training tips he was giving Anna. Now, it's almost like Walt's finding excuses not to come over...and even not to stay too long on the phone with me.

Plus, I left three messages on their machine. How come he only heard one? Who erased the others?

MJ thought she knew, only too well.

Over dinner, she did pass along Walt's message to her aunt.

"Jeffers, huh?" Anna squinted in thought. "No real way to know if there's any connection to that woman from Hackettstown, since she never filled out the form or even gave me her last name."

"And maybe she just *said* she was from Hackettstown." MJ couldn't resist adding to the intrigue.

"I can do some checking online. Guess it doesn't matter all that much, though, as long as she never comes back."

After they'd eaten, Anna pushed away from the table and winced. "Wow. I thought I was in decent shape, but I worked muscles today that I haven't used in a long time."

"You'll have to get back in practice."

"Guess I will. C'mon, let's turn those guys back out before it gets too late."

Outside, MJ suggested, "Can we put Murphy and Patches out in the pasture, while it's still light? I might be able to shoot some video of them for the website."

"Well..." Anna gazed in that direction. "We cleaned out all those branches and rock piles. I guess we can let him blow off a little steam before he goes back to working for a living."

They turned Patches loose first. That way, instead of bolting off as soon as he was released, Murphy paused to touch noses with his friend.

"Just keep an eye on them," Anna said, before she went to deal with Valentine and Dash.

The Thoroughbred and the pinto pony did play a little, and MJ videoed a few minutes of Patches chasing Murphy around the field. The big gray would pretend to gallop off in terror, then circle back when he realized he'd left his friend far behind. But they soon gave up the game, and sunset found them grazing peacefully a few yards from each other.

Murphy's probably tired from his long trailer ride and all the work he did with Anna, MJ thought. *Besides, he's tamer now, isn't he, since Josh retrained him?* Part of her missed the old, rebellious Murphy, though she knew that was foolish. "Wild," unpredictable horses were exciting to watch in the movies, but dangerous in real life. If Murphy had stayed crazy, a "flipper," he would have been put down. Still, MJ hoped he wouldn't lose all of his independent spirit.

After replaying the video on her phone, she noticed a new text. The sender's name made her heart skip. Bobby Raser finally was replying to her messages? Could be that he'd been so busy, he just hadn't seen them before now.

His communication was brief. "Hi, MJ! RaserzEdge is playing next Saturday at the Broken Inn. Stacey said that's sort of near where you are. Show's at ten, hope you can make it."

He'd added a link to the website for the roadhouse, with directions. The place looked to be half an hour from Anna's farm, maybe less.

Walking back to the barn, MJ fixated on the screen of her phone long after it had gone blank. She'd heard Bobby's band play a few dances at their school, but never a real, paying gig. And this place was so close, how could she miss this chance to see them again? To see *him* again?

But, damn, ten? These days she was in bed before that time, so she could get up at five thirty to feed the horses. *Even if Anna would let me go out to a club to at that hour—a big "if"—I haven't got a car of my own here.*

She'd probably never leave the farm long enough to drive me there and pick me up after. Maybe I could borrow her truck?

MJ figured she knew the answer to that question, too.

But Anna had gone to that fundraiser and came back late. Okay, that was a business thing, but still a party. Why should she be the only one having any fun?

Just inside the barn, MJ glanced toward the office. The door stood ajar, but she could see her aunt at the desk reading something on the desktop computer. MJ mustered the courage to plead her case and stepped inside.

Anna heard her enter but kept her eyes on the screen, doom in her voice. "I just got the schedule Josh wants me to follow for next week."

"That's bad?"

"It's going to be a lot of work, a couple extra hours every day just training Murphy. I'm going to need your help, too, okay?"

"Sure." MJ's tight throat muted her response.

She'd wait for a better time to ask about going to Bobby's roadhouse gig.

CHAPTER TWENTY-FOUR:

REQUEST

"Don't stand too close," Anna told her niece. "Just be handy, in case...well, in case."

MJ nodded, feeling almost as tense as her aunt sounded. She watched from a few feet away as Anna stepped onto the mounting block, paused, and then eased into the saddle.

As before, Murphy started to walk off, but Anna stopped him. Once she was aboard, he stiffened a little, but she pushed him forward and walked him in a circle until his head came down and he seemed to relax.

"Okay, I think we're good," she called to MJ. "Go on back out."

MJ left the pen and latched the gate behind her. She and Anna had lined up four cavaletti in the middle, about three and a half feet apart, Murphy's estimated stride.

Anna trotted the gray around the fence line, using the techniques Josh had taught her to keep his attention. Meanwhile, MJ was the one whose mind wandered.

So far, she hadn't dared to ask about going to the RaserzEdge show. Anna seemed too focused on all the work she'd have to do to make Murphy a decent jumper by the end of the summer.

I'll have to ask her soon, with the gig set for Saturday! Maybe if things go well today, and she's in a good mood...

The Thoroughbred trotted a bit too fast, but MJ thought he at least seemed under control. Anna steered him toward the cavaletti, aiming for the center of the first one.

The horse didn't balk, probably because he'd been through this routine with Josh. He stepped cleanly over the first two, but thunked his front hoof on the third. Annoyed, he did a little hop over the last and broke into a canter. Anna circled him in the open to slow him back to a trot, then brought him over the poles again. The second time, he was more careful and stepped neatly over all of them.

Having taken some jumping lessons, MJ knew this drill taught a horse how to pace himself, so he wouldn't take too many or too few strides when approaching a hurdle. Murphy might be able to judge the distance fine when running free, but learning to do it with a rider became a different issue.

After a few more trots over the poles, Anna eased down to a walk. "Not bad, huh?"

"He learns fast," MJ agreed.

"I'll let him stretch his legs as a reward, see how he behaves."

She took the gray out to the rail again and let him canter. When he sped up, instead of pulling back she just circled to rebalance him.

MJ had to admire her aunt's skill...and courage. Anna might say she was rusty, but she managed to keep that twelve-hundred-pound dynamo on a fairly small circle until he slowed to a safer pace. She kept his head down, too, which MJ knew was key to controlling an excitable horse. The pair cruised around the last couple of times on a looser rein, and Murphy remained obedient. Anna wore a wide smile as she walked him to cool out.

MJ stepped back through the gate. "You did great!"

"Thanks. I'd say we're off to a decent start." After a few minutes, her aunt hopped off and patted the gray's perspiring neck. Leading him back toward the barn, she explained, "Tomorrow we're supposed add a couple more cavaletti. If he does okay, I can raise the last one six inches, as a foot-high jump. By the weekend, I'd like to have him jumping about eighteen inches with no knocks."

"I'll bet you won't have many problems. Everything he did wrong today, you fixed. I think he likes you." Though MJ meant the compliment, she laid it on a little thick. "Anna, speaking of the weekend..."

She pitched her request the way she'd practiced it in her mind. Some friends from her high school who had a band were playing Saturday night at a place on the highway, not far. Other kids from school would be going there to hear them.

"It'd be a great chance to see those people again and catch up," MJ added. "I"ve really missed them this summer."

In the barn aisle, Anna slipped off Murphy's bridle and replaced it with his halter. "What time would this be?"

"Oh...not too late. They should be done by...ten-thirty, eleven?"

"Where are they playing?"

MJ had thought this one through, too. "It's a restaurant called the Broken Inn."

Anna clipped cross-ties to the gray's halter. "I've heard of it. It's a roadhouse—with a bar. How old are these kids?"

"The guys in the band are seniors. They graduated this year. It's legal for them to play if they don't drink onstage."

Anna stripped off Murphy's saddle and asked her niece to hang it up in the tack room. When MJ came back, her aunt was squatting with the horse's right front foot between her knees, digging dirt out of the hoof with a pick.

"How would you be getting out to this place?" she asked.

"Well, I dunno." MJ pretended she hadn't considered the question before. "I've got my license, y'know. Maybe I could borrow your truck?"

Anna's throaty chuckle made it clear she wasn't deceived. "O-h-h, no. That's our only means of transportation. Besides, there's a lot of dark, twisty road between here and the Broken Inn."

"I'm a good driver!"

"From what Erika tells me, you haven't driven much. And a pickup handles differently from a car. Sorry, honey."

MJ opened her mouth to protest, but a rumble in the barnyard interrupted them.

"Oh, good," said Anna, "Walt's here. Just in time, we're almost out of eggs."

As MJ watched him hop down from the cab of the family

truck, she reflected it had been longer than usual since his last visit. Even a couple of days since their last, awkward phone conversation. Unloading the supplies and helping to bring them up to the house, Walt still acted a bit oddly. Too polite, with none of his usual wisecracks.

He set two egg cartons and basket of freshly picked strawberries on the porch. Meanwhile, Anna led the gray horse from the barn and turned him back out in his paddock.

MJ told Walt, "You missed her riding Murphy, again."

"Oh, yeah?" He turned to Anna. "How'd it go?"

"Not half bad, for our first time without Josh's supervision." She explained about the training schedule she was supposed to follow.

"Sounds stiff."

"It does leave me and MJ less time for our usual chores. We might be able to use your help a little more often. For pay, of course."

Walt waved away Anna's last suggestion. "Ah, don't worry about that. We're neighbors."

MJ noticed that he concentrated on chatting with her aunt. *It's like he doesn't even want to make eye contact with me anymore.*

Anna told him, "Poor Dash has been neglected lately. Could you do a little work with him, when you've got the time?" She threw a glance in MJ's direction. "Since it's not too hot today, maybe the two of you could even go on another trail ride."

Walt's expression brightened, MJ thought, before turning guarded once more. "I'd like to...but my dad's still not a hundred percent. Once I finish these deliveries, I gotta get home an' do a bunch of chores he usually takes care of."

Anna bought this excuse. "I'm sorry he's still having trouble. Did he see a doctor?"

"Oh, sure. He said Dad wrenched his back, just needs more rest. 'Course, by now he's getting fidgety. He's not a guy who can lie around too long just reading or watching TV." Walt shifted on his feet, and even though MJ took a stance right alongside her aunt, he still didn't look at her. "Anyhow, I oughta be getting back. Next time I'll come earlier, Anna. Maybe I can finally see you riding

Murphy."

Adding just a quick, "'Bye, MJ!" he hopped into his truck and drove away.

"A shame Sam Patterson is still laid up," Anna said, carrying the eggs into the house. "I was hoping Walt would have some free time to help us between now and August." She glanced up with a twinkle in her green eyes. "Say, he can't do many chores at night. Maybe he could drive you out to hear that band on Saturday."

This blindsided MJ, and for a second she almost considered the idea. But no, it would be a disaster! Walt would never fit in with her school friends—they might even make fun of him. And she sure didn't want him hanging around while she tried to reconnect with Bobby.

"Why?" she half-teased Anna. "Because he's so moral, he'd keep me out of trouble?"

"Because he's about your age and can drive, and you might have fun together. But about him keeping you out of trouble... yeah, the thought did occur to me."

MJ set the basket of berries on the kitchen counter. "Forget it. His mama doesn't want him hanging around with me. Why d'you think he ran off so fast when you said we could go for a trail ride?" A sudden image made her grimace. "Can you image what she'd say if I asked him to take me out to a *bar,* to see a rock band?"

"You said it was a restaurant."

"It is...but that's how she'd look at it."

Anna straightened and studied her niece. "If she is trying to keep Walt away from you, MJ, that is too bad. And unfair. Want me to talk to Mrs. Patterson?"

The girl shook her head. Anna meant well, but sometimes she was clueless! "No, please. It's no big deal."

MJ retreated to her room and closed the door, trusting that her aunt wouldn't follow to ask any more questions. She didn't care what uptight Mrs. Patterson thought about her, or Walt, either.

And I'll find some other way to get out to see RaserzEdge this weekend!

CHAPTER TWENTY-FIVE:

GRIEF

The lean black man stood over the crude grave, topped with withered daylilies and the twig cross. He pulled off his rumpled sun hat and bowed his graying head. He stayed that way in silence for so long, Anna wondered if he was saying an actual prayer. Seeing him grieve Starbuck's death revived all her feelings of guilt.

"Poor dude was only 'bout eight years old. Wouldna thought that, wouldja, the way he looked when I first brought him here?" Clint finally glanced up at Anna. "You took good care of him, though, and got him back into pretty fair shape."

"And then I screwed up, big time," she admitted. "I'm so sorry, Clint. I worried, when I didn't hear back from his adopters, that something might be wrong. I should've gone to check on him sooner, but I was afraid to leave the farm unattended for that long."

He settled his hat back on his head. "You can't be in two places at once. It's a problem."

"At least these days I have MJ to fill in for me. By now, she knows enough to take charge in an emergency."

"The kid who risked her neck closin' the gate, that day Murphy was runnin' loose? And then got kicked by yer pony?"

"She's learned a lot since then," Anna insisted.

As they walked back toward the barn, Clint said, "I thought you were hopin' MJ might decide to make up her grades and go on to college. Won't be much help to you if she does that."

In his low-key way, Clint tended to act as her conscience, Anna realized. She'd almost started hoping MJ would stay on at the farm, even though that might not be the best thing for her niece's future. "Guess I'll cross that bridge when, and if, I come to it."

"Ever thought of reachin' out to some of the other groups around here? There's a Standardbred rescue in the next county. Good outfit—I almost brought Starbuck to them, but at the time they were full up. An' there's a place not too far south that's more of a sanctuary. They don't adopt out, just take animals that're on their last legs and let 'em live out their days in peace. Maybe you could work out some kinda deal with them."

A horsefly lighted on Anna's upper arm, and she swatted it away. "I don't know... From what I've heard and read, every place has its own way of operating. I don't want to always have to consult with somebody else before I make a decision. I'd rather go my own way, at least until I get this place off the ground." When Clint threw her a sidelong glance, she laughed. "I know. Sounds like I'm talking about my divorce, right?"

"Lady, I'd never pass judgment. After what that guy put you through? I'm just wonderin' if you got some better plan in mind."

"I'm working on one. That's what I wanted to show you today."

She trotted Murphy over four cavaletti and let him take the fifth one as a little jump. He no longer even tried to gallop afterward, but yielded to her steady hold on the reins and kept to his trot. Anna's heart swelled. He was starting to listen to her, the same as he had with Josh!

Clint watched from outside the fence, eyes shaded by his floppy hat. When she pulled up near him, he gave a slow nod. "You might make a solid citizen outa this boy yet."

"Starting to look that way, isn't it?" Anna let the gray walk on a loose rein.

Clint slipped through the gate, fell in step alongside them, and rubbed Murphy's shoulder. "Last time I saw him, he'da never let me do this. Woulda et me alive."

"I remember. Sometimes I still feel like I'm sitting on a powder keg, but he hasn't done anything really dangerous since Josh brought him back. He can get over-excited, but no more than I'd expect from any ex-racehorse."

Clint glanced around at the paddocks and the big field beyond. "Well, it's quiet here. People treat him right. The other horses are laid-back. He got everything the way he likes it, no stress."

Anna heard an odd note in her friend's voice. "You say that like it's a bad thing."

"Oh, no. Probably just what he needs, for now."

"But?"

"This Josh guy wants to put him in a show by the end of summer?" Clint shook his head. "That's gonna be a lot of excitement. Bunch of people millin' around, strange horses, loudspeakers. Our Murphy might think he's back at the track."

Anna frowned. "Are you trying to scare me?"

"Just prepare you. Before you get on him in a show ring, better make sure he can handle all that to-do. Otherwise...best-case, he comes up alongside another horse in the ring and tries to race 'im. Worst case..."

"Yeah, we both know what that would be." She'd hoped to impress Clint with the horse's progress, and it annoyed her that he still harped on the dangers. "Don't worry. I have no intention of taking him to a show until both of us are ready."

Clint looked up at her with grave, dark eyes. "That's good."

Anna halted her horse and hopped off. "Josh said if Murphy's ready to show by then, he might be able to help find someone who'll adopt him."

"All the more reason, then, not to mess up."

"Well, that's my problem, isn't it?"

"Mine, too, now that you put me on—whatchucall it? Your board of directors."

His tone made it clear he was having fun with this idea.

"Don't make me regret that."

The big grin again, complete with the flash of gold toward the back. "If the rest of us don't like how you're runnin' things here, we just might fire you! Be kinda sad. Anna's Horse Rescue with no Anna."

"It's not even Anna's Horse Recue anymore. Another board member renamed it. What do you think of 'Reboot Ranch'?"

Anna had to admit, the name didn't look so bad the way MJ had redesigned it. She'd used all lower-case letters, but enlarged the r's so they looked like upside-down English riding boots, and expanded the name to "Reboot Ranch Rescue."

Sitting at the office computer, the girl explained, "I thought that'd make it less Western, y'know?"

"Reboot, like a computer, huh?" Clint chuckled. "Clever."

"Oh well," Anna pretended to accept defeat, "that makes two board members voting for the new name. And the third one is MJ's mother, so we know whose side she'll take."

The girl lit up. "So, you're gonna use it?"

"Got a confession to make—I already put it on the 501(c)(3) application."

"Awesome." MJ glanced at Clint. "Lemme show you what else I added."

She clicked on a link that brought up an embedded video. When she opened it, Murphy and Patches chased each other around the big pasture, just before sunset. The scene lasted only a couple of minutes, but Anna fought back tears over the sense of joy and freedom expressed by the playing horses.

Clint scratched his head in wonder. "You took that movie? An' then you put it on the computer?"

"Shot it with my cell phone and just downloaded it," MJ told him, proudly. "It's not hard."

"More'n I'd know how to do." He turned to Anna. "Better hang onto *this* board member. She got real skills."

"She has, hasn't she?"

After Clint drove off, MJ told her aunt, "If you like the site this way, I can launch it tonight. We can still tweak things down the road, but at least the farm will have a web presence in the meantime. And you'll have something to show that Lillian lady."

"That would be great." Anna had to marvel at the amount of work MJ had put into the project and how much she had improved the site. "I should pay you something for this, honey. If you hadn't been able to do these upgrades, I would've had to hire a pro."

MJ smiled, a bit slyly. "Aw, you don't have to give me money. But if you do want to repay me..."

Uh-oh, Anna thought. "Does this have something to do with that concert Saturday night?"

"I got a ride! My friend Stacey is going, so she can come by and pick me up. She just turned eighteen, so she has her license."

Anna started to waver, then caught herself. "That's still not old enough to drink."

"I won't drink, I promise. We're just going to hear the band."

"I trust you, MJ, but I've never met this Stacey. I don't know anything about her."

"My *mom* knows her. Stacey and I have been friends for years."

"Okay." Anna shrugged. "Then maybe that's the best way to settle it."

"You mean I can go? Great!"

"I mean, I'll ask Erika. If it's okay with her, it'll be okay with me."

This apparently was not the answer her niece had hoped for. With a pout, MJ threw her hands in the air and tramped out of the office.

Jeez, Anna thought, *sweet to sour in seconds flat. Nothing like those teenage mood swings!*

CHAPTER TWENTY-SIX:

DILEMMA

etreating to the privacy of the front porch, MJ slumped on the old rattan loveseat and pondered her latest dilemma. If Anna called Erika, might she still get permission to go to the roadhouse?

Mom's not nuts about Stacey. She's lectured me before about how I should "make other friends" because Stacey "isn't the best influence" on me. Like it's that easy for me to make friends. And like I want to hang out with those preppy snobs or spoiled suburban Barbie dolls in our town, anyway.

At this point, though, even MJ was having second thoughts. Stacey probably *would* try to drink at the bar, maybe with a fake ID. If by any chance they had an accident, even a fender-bender, MJ knew she'd be in huge trouble with both her mom and Anna.

I could offer to drive home...but Stacey might have her old Corvette, a stick-shift. I've never driven one of those.

Pulling out her phone, MJ texted her friend: *Don't think my aunt will let me go. She's worried we'll drink and said she doesn't know you.*

After sending the message, MJ lay back on the loveseat's faded floral cushions and stared morosely at the porch's beadboard ceiling. Bobby would be playing a professional gig less than half an hour away, and she'd have to miss it. Would she ever see him again? If he went out of state to college, maybe not!

She shut her eyes to better envision his crooked grin and his dark eyes peering from under that sweep of bleached-platinum bangs. No other guy in school had the nerve to wear his hair like that, but Bobby was so cool that nobody bugged him about it. He played great guitar, had a band, and had plenty of girls chasing him, so it was okay. He even got away with being good at nerdy subjects like English Lit—MJ knew, because they had that class together. When Mr. Robitz called on him, sometimes Bobby would give a funny answer, but never so wise-ass that it got him in trouble. He always knew where to draw the line.

Bobby managed to be popular while still being himself, a knack MJ had never developed. Plus, he looked hot in skinny jeans.

I always figured someday I'd get up the nerve to tell him how I felt about him. I thought I'd always have time.

On the cushion next to her, the phone vibrated. Stacey had replied: *Okay, tell her my mom's driving us.*

MJ's heart bounded, and she wrote back, *Really?*

Sure, why not.

Awesome, you're the best!

Stacey did not respond to this, so MJ assumed it was settled.

That wouldn't be so bad. Stacey's mother liked rock, too, so it wasn't a big surprise that she'd agreed to take them. It was a solution even Erika might accept.

MJ heard a truck pull into the barnyard, but didn't turn to look. Must be the hay delivery—it was due today. A minute later she heard voices, Anna talking with somebody. Still bearing a slight grudge, MJ did not volunteer to help unload the shipment.

She closed her eyes and lay back again, this time tingling with excitement. *I might get to see Bobby, after all!* Then her eagerness turned to panic. *Ugh, my hair looks disgusting. The cut's grown out, and all my clothes have gotten baggy since I lost weight. Not much chance to go shopping before Saturday, or even to borrow anything from Mom.*

On the other hand, maybe Bobby will notice I'm a little thinner. He might even be interested in the rescue farm, and think it's cool that I'm taking a risk for something I believe in. Maybe I'll have the nerve to flirt with him more than I did before.

The noisy roadhouse might not be the best place for them to get re-acquainted, but the band had to take a break sometimes.

If she could just get a minute or two alone with him, someplace where they could talk...

A warm tongue bathed her cheek in a sloppy kiss.

She shot upright with a shriek. From somewhere on the porch, she heard Walt's hysterical laughter. Just a few inches away, a pair of soulful brown eyes stared into hers. A tawny paw landed in her lap.

"Sorry, MJ," Walt gasped, wiping his eyes with his hand. "Meet Delilah."

The girl felt herself blush, even though Walt couldn't know that he and the dog had interrupted her romantic daydream. She patted the mutt's golden-brown head.

"What a relief," she cracked. "It was just a dog, not you."

Now it was Walt's turn to redden. That would teach him.

Anna jogged up the porch steps to join them. "What happened, MJ? Did the dog scare you?"

"Nah, just startled me. I was napping."

"Oh, good. I thought maybe...Erika's terrified of dogs."

"Don't I know it. She'd never let us get one."

Stooping to ruffle the fur around Delilah's neck, Walt smiled. "Well, here's your chance, if you want. My folks thought maybe you could use a dog around this place. We've already got four others. Delilah showed up a few months ago as a stray and we took her in, but we'd be happy to loan her to you. And if she works out..."

To MJ's surprise, the mongrel already seemed to have taken to her. Delilah was a good size, maybe a cross between a retriever and a shepherd. Her silky coat was light tan with a darker nose and paws. Almost ignoring Walt now, she leaned against MJ's legs and grinned up at her, panting from the day's heat.

"Hmm." Anna didn't sound too sure.

"She's real friendly, but she's also a good watchdog. Barks every time somebody comes near our house or barn," Walt said. "We taught her to sit and stay and fetch. And she behaves around other animals, so she won't stir up your horses."

"You make a good sales pitch."

"And, if you act now—" He shifted to the upbeat tone of a TV huckster—"I'll throw in her leash, her dog bed and a week's supply of food. Got 'em all in the truck."

"Guess it's worth a try," Anna relented.

Walt glanced back toward MJ. "My mom figured Delilah can keep you company, and give you some protection, in case Anna has to go away again at night."

He brought in the dog's supplies, then gave his usual excuse about having a lot of errands to finish for his dad and drove off. He told Delilah to "Stay," and though she watched him leave with a wagging tail, she didn't try to follow.

This time, even Anna seemed to find Walt's behavior abrupt. As she and her niece brought the dog's supplies into the house, she commented, "Guess Mr. Patterson is still having back trouble."

"Does sound that way, doesn't it?" MJ, in the kitchen, tore open a bag of the dry dog food and poured some into a dish for Delilah, who chowed down.

"You're skeptical?"

"Isn't it obvious, what he did? Or, I should say, what *they* did? Now, if you go away, our new watchdog can 'protect' me at night. No need for Walt to be here after dark, ever."

Anna leaned against the kitchen doorway, arms folded across her chest. "I didn't think of it like that because it seemed so spontaneous, but...you could be right. Wow, seems like Dottie will go to any lengths to keep you two apart, doesn't it?

"Ah, who cares." MJ knelt to ruffle Delilah's fur and whispered into her floppy, fringed ear. "I'd rather have you for company, anyway."

Anna saw through her niece's performance and ached with sympathy. She reminded herself that MJ used to spend most of every day in school with people her own age, and probably got together with them in the summer, too. At home, she also had her younger brother.

For the past month-and-a-half, though, she's been stuck out here with mostly me and the horses for company. I thought she and Walt could at least be friends, and that seems to be all MJ wants, too. But it must be frustrating to have even that option taken away from her.

As if reading her mind, her niece piped up, "Stacey said her mom can drive the two of us to the club on Saturday! Is that better?"

Anna considered. Would it be so terrible to let the girl have one night out with her pals, as long as there was an adult along to keep an eye on them? "Well...I don't know Stacey's mom, either."

"Oh, c'mon. She's *your* age." MJ half-smiled, to show this was a tease.

"There are lots of irresponsible people my age. I'll still have to clear it with Erika."

Leaving her niece to bond with the new dog, Anna took her cell phone out on the porch and speed-dialed her sister. Got voice mail. Not wanting to explain the whole situation in a recording, she just asked Erika to call her back—"Today, if possible."

She saw then that she had a text from Josh. He wanted to come by Saturday morning to check on her progress with Murphy.

Ye gods, we're supposed to be jumping a foot and a half by that time, aren't we? I'd better step things up, in more ways than one.

She wasn't concerned about whether either she or the horse could handle that beginner's height. It was the other details that Josh might pick apart. But having worked with several riding instructors over the years, some of them pretty tough, Anna figured she could take any criticism Mr. Natural Horsemanship might dole out.

The issues Clint had mentioned troubled her more. Maybe this would be a good opportunity to discuss those with Josh, too.

While Anna and MJ brought the horses in for their evening feed, Delilah watched from a distance. True to Walt's promise, the dog did not bother the horses or get underfoot. Once in awhile she would chase a barn cat, but just in play; it always outran her or climbed beyond her reach.

Tonight, Anna also noticed Valentine coughing more than usual. That worried her, though the mare always suffered more from her heaves during the hottest, most humid part of the summer. Anna added two scoops of an herbal powder mixture to Val's senior feed, hoping it would help. Julie had warned they might have to put the mare on a stronger steroid one day, but Anna hoped to postpone that as long as possible.

Tired from the strenuous day, she cut up cheese and hardboiled eggs, and tossed the bits with fresh greens, for a hearty dinner salad. Between bites, MJ mentioned again that she planned to launch the farm's website that evening. "I was going to invite Walt to the big occasion, too, but he moved so fast today, I didn't get the chance."

Anna sympathized again. "I know, that stinks. But we can make it an occasion, anyway."

After they'd turned the horses out for the night, she brought a bottle of sparkling cider, and some cupcakes she'd ordered with her last grocery delivery, into the barn office. MJ already sat at the computer, the dog sprawled on the floor near her feet.

At least we shouldn't have to worry about Delilah getting lonesome for the Pattersons and running back to their place, Anna thought.

MJ asked, "Have you got an email or a Twitter list? People you want to tell about the website updates?"

"I do...though both could be out of date. And I'm sure there are some new names I'll want to add."

"Like that Lillian lady."

"Definitely her. Erika did give me her card."

Anna poured the cider into plastic glasses for both of them. With a mouse-click, MJ launched the revamped site, and they toasted.

"Too bad it's not champagne," the girl teased.

"You wish. Even if you were legal, we're on a cider budget."

"For now. Soon, you'll be able to just sit back and watch the donations roll in!"

"Let's hope people donate money and supplies, not just more horses. We can barely feed the ones we've got now."

MJ's reference to alcohol reminded Anna that she hadn't heard back from her sister yet, and she checked her phone messages. Found only an email from Erika's assistant, about a freelance article for the next issue of *Good Life* that needed serious editing. She added that if Anna had any questions about it, Erika would be back in the office on Monday.

MJ must have seen her frown. "Something wrong?"

"That's funny. I got a message that makes it sound like your mom's away through the weekend. Did you know about that?"

"First I heard of it." The girl sounded sincere. "But she does that sometimes. Lets Carl stay over with one of his buds and takes off for a few days. Y'know, spur-of-the-moment."

Anna knew her sister had an impetuous side, but this sounded unusual. "I never realized she did stuff like that."

"She didn't used to, but..." MJ curled her lip. "She's probably off with her new boyfriend, Burt. The real estate 'mogul.'"

For once, Anna shared her niece's irritation.

Nice work, Sis. Your underage daughter wants to meet her pals at a roadhouse on Saturday, and I need your input. You picked a swell time to disappear!

CHAPTER TWENTY-SEVEN:

LAME!

Saturday afternoon, Murphy was hopping over a one-and-a-half-foot obstacle in the round pen like it was a twig. He cleared it with so much room to spare that Anna felt him asking, *C'mon, lady, this all you got?*

Outside the pen, eyes shaded by his baseball cap, Josh looked satisfied. "He's got no problem with that height, for sure. And you have his speed under control."

Anna slowed her mount and patted his neck. "Yeah, we're getting more in sync."

The trainer turned his gaze out toward the pasture where Valentine, Dash and Patches grazed peacefully. "Got another big, open space around here somewhere?"

"There's another fenced field at the back of the property. Maybe half an acre. It's all gone to weeds, but I do keep it cut down."

"Let's take him back there." Josh opened the gate of the round pen so she could ride out. "Time to start working in something more the size of a show ring."

He led the way on foot and Anna followed, staying alert. As Murphy passed his buddies, he neighed to them and got more bounce in his step. She collected the reins a little, never having ridden him in the open before. By the time they reached the dead-looking field beyond the pasture, the gray's ears were pricked and his muscles vibrated.

Hope he doesn't decide to dump me out here, Anna thought.

This ground looks hard.

Once they stepped inside, Josh grasped the reins just under Murphy's chin. "I'll lead you around first, make sure nothing spooks him."

"Thanks," Anna said.

No doubt hearing the tension in her voice, Josh glanced up. The day had turned overcast and he'd taken off his sunglasses; thin creases fanned from his warm gray eyes. "Relax. If you stay calm, he will, too."

Anna knew that. Act nervous on a high-strung horse, and you convinced him there really was some predator out there to be afraid of.

Josh led Murphy all along the fence line to the right. Because a horse's brain sees his surroundings as completely new when coming from a different direction, they then turned and walked counterclockwise.

Near the gate again, Josh backed off. "It's nice and level out here, and I don't see any rocks or branches to give him trouble. Just start with a collected walk on a big circle."

Anna kept a supple feel of the horse's mouth. Though he still moved with a spring in his step, he behaved, and after a few minutes Josh asked her for a trot. That took just the lightest squeeze from Anna's calves.

"Nice," Josh said. "He's a got great movement, long and low. Okay, let's canter. If he gets strong, circle a little tighter until he calms down."

The gray responded to Anna's signal with a leap forward, but she was ready. She sat deep in the saddle, and when he started to lean on the bit she spiraled in from the original circle to rate his speed. Before long, he mellowed out enough for her to let him go wide again. They moved together in smooth, powerful strides—

Suddenly, his right shoulder dropped. Adrenaline shocked Anna's heart. Her legs clamped to the horse's sides and she grabbed mane...

...Flashed back on her old accident.

No, no!

The jolt threw her almost onto Murphy's neck, but she hung

on. With a feisty snort, he got his front feet back under him. He stood still, breathing as hard as Anna from the scare. But at least he hadn't gone all the way down, and she hadn't fallen.

Josh ran over, some color drained from his lean, tanned face. "You okay?"

"I am. Better check him, though." She hopped off and landed on wobbly legs; leaned against the horse to steady herself.

"Maybe he threw a shoe?" Josh ran his hand down the gray's left foreleg to lift it. "No, but the heel's bleeding a little. Like he cut it on something."

"Damn." Anna knew the heel was the back part of the sole, just behind the tough, shock-absorbing frog. A cut there would be painful and could get infected.

How could that have happened? Feeling negligent, she scanned the nearby ground for anything that might have caused the problem.

Josh left them for a minute to do a more thorough search. "Here's the culprit." He held up a curved piece of light-brown glass, the same shade as the dry weeds. "Looks like part of a beer bottle. He probably tripped over one and broke it at the same time."

"Where on earth did that come from?" Anna read Josh's frown as a mild accusation, and hurried to explain, "I don't like beer, so I never even keep it around."

"Not even for guests?"

Thinking of MJ, Clint, Walt and Erika, she answered almost primly. "None of my 'guests' would ever come out here without me along."

"Did you hire any hands who might've been tippling on the job?"

"None working around this field. And I went over it with the riding mower just a couple of weeks ago. If the bottle was here then, I would've seen it, so it must have been dumped recently." Almost over the trauma of her near-fall, Anna shuddered from a fresh chill. "Some stranger must have been on my property!"

Josh squinted into the sunset glow beyond the western trees. "The fence at that far end sags almost to the ground, and the road runs just beyond those woods. Wouldn't be hard for someone to park on the shoulder and sneak in."

Anna stared at him. "Now you're scaring me."

"Sorry, I didn't mean to." He seemed to grasp her agitation for the first time. "Are you sure you're all right?"

"I'll be okay. It was just...that's the closest I've come to falling since..."

"Your last accident. Of course." He reached out a hand as if to comfort her, but stopped himself.

Anna broke the awkward pause. "I'm probably making too much of this."

"Probably. One beer bottle...might've been just a kid." Josh studied Murphy again. "We'll fix him up back at the barn. Before we leave, though, we'd better find the rest of that bottle."

They combed the grass and collected several more shards. Anna also made another discovery—her cell phone. It must have slipped out of her breeches pocket when she'd lurched forward onto the horse's neck. And whether from the fall or getting stepped on, the screen was cracked.

She tried to power it on, without success. *Great.*

Anna shoved the useless thing back into her pants and joined Josh and Murphy. She and the trainer matched up the bits of glass to form a whole bottle.

"That's good, anyway," Josh said. "There shouldn't be any left in the field or stuck in Murphy's foot. I'll keep an eye on him, though, while you lead him back."

MJ sent Patches into her stall for her evening meal, then glanced at the big, round clock on the barn wall. With Delilah trailing her, she'd finished feeding all of the horses...except, of course, for Murphy. Where had Anna taken him? An hour ago, she and the gray had been working under Josh's direction in the round pen.

I stepped into the barn office for a minute, and by the time I came out they'd all disappeared. She could've told me they were going someplace else.

MJ wouldn't have cared, except Stacey and her mom would be picking her up at eight. MJ had suggested that, so Anna wouldn't gripe about her going out too late. *If I don't get home until eleven, or later...like Stacey sometimes says, easier to ask forgiveness than permission.*

The girl chewed her lip with impatience. After all this barn work, she needed time to shower and to do something with her impossible hair. At least she'd persuaded her aunt to give her some old, black breeches, now too big for Anna but fitting MJ just fine. Wearing those as stretch pants with her own short, black boots, and a long T-shirt as a tunic, she could pull off a slightly punk look for the evening.

Through the open barn door, MJ watched the sky turn cobalt blue. A couple of bats swooped from the hayloft window across the barnyard. They had creeped MJ out at first, until her aunt explained that they did not bother people and ate mosquitoes.

I still have enough time to get ready...but where is Anna? I hope nothing's wrong! Half of the sentiment was selfish—she didn't want anything to stop her from getting to the roadhouse that night.

Her aunt, Josh and Murphy came trudging back over the slight rise in the dirt road. They must have been somewhere out beyond the pasture, farther than MJ had ever explored. Josh frowned as he walked; Anna carried her helmet and a few strands hung loose from her ponytail. Even Murphy looked subdued, head low and steps a little uneven.

MJ jogged out to meet them. "I was worried about you guys. Everything all right?" She faced Anna. "Did he throw you, or—"

Her aunt smiled. "No, poor Murphy's not to blame this time. But we did have a little accident."

Josh showed her his handkerchief, filled with big shards of amber glass, and explained what had happened. "We'll need your help, MJ. Murphy has to stay in a clean stall for the night. *Really* clean, so the cut doesn't get infected."

His stern tone gave the girl a sense of what it must be like to work with him in training a horse. "I just changed his bedding this morning."

"We use shavings," Anna told him, as they all entered the barn. "Is that okay?"

He nodded. "Better than straw. No sharp pieces to stick him while he's healing."

They cross-tied the gray in the barn aisle and stripped off his tack. Josh felt the horse's left front leg for heat or swelling but found none. While her aunt cleaned out all of Murphy's hooves, MJ filled a bucket with fresh water; Anna sponged the injured foot. The Thoroughbred shifted his weight and occasionally clicked his teeth, but on the cross-ties he couldn't put up too much resistance. Delilah stayed out of the way and watched with a tilted head.

"You have Betadine?" Josh asked Anna.

"I know where it is," MJ volunteered. As she started for the tack room, Josh called after her, "Cotton balls and some gauze, too, if you've got it. And duct tape."

The girl halted. "Duct tape?"

"Check the tool box," Anna told her.

Without much trouble, MJ located everything and hurried back with her arms full. Josh used the sponge to dab the antiseptic, a kind of horse iodine, onto the sole of Murphy's foot. He and Anna then cooperated to pack the hoof with cotton balls, wrap it in gauze and finish off with a makeshift bootie of duct tape.

MJ stood by Murphy's head and soothed him during all of this. Whether he felt outnumbered or just confused, he stopped trying to pull his foot away.

At last, the three sweaty and stained humans rested. "That should hold him, at least for the night," Josh said, patting the gray's shoulder. "Put the poor guy in his stall and give him his dinner."

MJ thought it was odd for Josh to be telling them what to do with their own horse on their own property, until she remembered people hired him for just that purpose. When he gave directions, it seemed natural to follow them, and he seemed to know how to handle an emergency. Maybe, dealing with so many problem horses, he saw a lot of them.

The drama had distracted MJ from her clock-watching, but another glance at the time sent her into a panic. *Less than an hour until Stacey and her mom get here! I've got to shower, fix my hair, do my makeup—*

While Anna dropped a couple of big flakes into Murphy's hay rack, Josh's cell phone rang. He sidled away to answer it, but MJ heard him tell someone, "Yeah, sorry about that. We ran into a complication here, but I'm leaving now. See you soon." Tucking the phone back into his jeans pocket, he told Anna, "I hate to leave you two alone to deal with this. Especially since it was my idea to go work in that field."

She shook her head ruefully. "I'll have to check better before we go out there again."

"And we will." Josh grasped her shoulder with one hand, looked into her eyes and spoke gently. "Murphy will be fine, I'm sure. I'll give you a call tomorrow, okay? Meanwhile, phone your vet."

"Thanks for your help."

MJ watched their exchange with interest. As Josh left the barn, she wondered, *Did those two just have, like, a moment?*

Anna still seemed a bit dazed as she watched him drive off. Then she smoothed her messy hair, pulled out her cell phone and grimaced. "Oh, right...this broke when Murphy stumbled! I'll have to call from the office."

Alarmed, MJ whipped out her own cell. "Here, use mine. I've got Julie on speed-dial, too."

With a nod, Anna punched the number for the vet.

MJ leaned against the closed door of Murphy's stall and let out a breath. Earlier, she'd seen the blinking light and read her mother's mobile number on the office machine. She hoped to keep her aunt from picking up that message for as long as possible.

If Anna's cell is broken, maybe Mom hasn't connected with her yet. With any luck, by the time she does, I'll be on my way to the Broken Inn.

CHAPTER TWENTY-EIGHT:

ESCAPE

O ver the phone, the vet confirmed that Anna had done everything necessary for Murphy at the moment.

"I gave him a tetanus booster right after you got him," Julie recalled, "which should help. I'll stop by tomorrow to X-ray the foot for any glass, but if there were no shards missing from the bottle he should be safe. Just keep him quiet and keep checking his leg for heat."

"I will," Anna said. "Yeah, Josh took charge and helped us deal with the situation. I might have figured it out on my own, but I would've had to check a book or two first."

Julie laughed. "I'd better watch that Buchanan doesn't cut into my practice."

When MJ came through the barn door, Anna gave her back her phone and passed along the news to her.

"That's a relief, huh?" The girl seemed distracted. "Anyway, I put the other horses out for the night, so I'm going up to the house now to shower and change."

"Okay." Anna saw by the barn clock that it was twenty to eight. "Gosh, I don't even know what to make for dinner, and I'm so-o-o tired. Maybe I'll just heat up some leftovers."

"Sure, why not?" MJ tossed off on her way out, Delilah trailing her as usual.

Only a minute later did Anna wonder why her niece needed to shower and change just for dinner. *That's right, tonight she's supposed to go hear that band! How on earth does she even have the energy, after how hard we both worked today? Boy, to be seventeen again.*

Anna supposed it would be okay, and the girl did deserve some reward for helping out during their mini-crisis. But why hadn't Erika ever called back? Earlier that day, Anna had left a second message, spelling out her concerns about MJ going to the roadhouse, so Erika would understand the urgency. And still, no response! Was her sister that wrapped up in her romantic-getaway weekend, or...

Anna reached again for her cell, then remembered it was broken. *So, if she did call me back this afternoon, I wouldn't know, would I?*

But she could still get through on...

Anna crossed to the barn office, saw the light blinking on the desk phone, and played the message, left hours earlier.

"Sis, your reception out there stinks. Today I couldn't get through to your cell at all! Though I have to take some of the blame. Burt and I are in the Catskills, and we haven't been too conscientious about checking our messages." She giggled. "Anyhow, glad you checked with me about MJ's plans. If she's so intense about going to hear this band, it's got to be Bobby Raser playing. He went to her school and she idolizes him. But I don't trust that Stacey. I doubt her mother is driving them, either. She probably just made that up. So, tell MJ I said no! If she doesn't like it, she can call and bitch to me."

Anna stared at the answering machine. She hadn't expected her sister to nix MJ's plans outright. *I'll have to act fast to stop her. This late in the game, it's going to get ugly.*

She was deciding how to break the bad news to her niece when a steady pounding began in the barn. Anna guessed the problem even before she reached Murphy's stall. All of his buddies had been turned out for the night, and he'd just realized he was alone inside. The door to his box stall shuddered as he struck it again and again.

"No, honey, stop!" Anna pleaded. "You'll hurt your sore foot." She couldn't see which foreleg he was striking with, but either way he could do himself more harm.

When Murphy saw her coming through the upper bars of his stall he stopped kicking, but neighed to the horses out in the paddock. Valentine whinnied back and Patches answered with her high, pony squeal.

Frantic, Anna searched for a solution. Valentine usually ate her meals in the stall next to Murphy's, but if kept indoors all night she might get an attack of heaves.

Anna went outside, haltered the half-blind pony and brought her into the barn, where Murphy had started to kick again.

"Here's Patches!" she called out, like a mother trying to calm a wailing toddler with a favorite toy. "She'll stay in here with you tonight, okay?"

Once the pony occupied the next stall, the two animals touched noses through the side bars. Anna gave Patches hay and water for the night.

At last, Murphy seemed to relax. *Another crisis averted, for now.*

MJ poked her head through the open barn door. She'd gelled her hair into spikes and wore more makeup than Anna had ever seen on her before. "Okay, I'm leaving!"

"Hold on." Ann started after her.

"Can't. Stacey's mom is parked out by the gate. I don't wanna hold them up."

Maybe the mother really is driving? But...

"MJ—"

The girl walked backwards as she talked, the dog still trotting after her. "Don't worry, I'll get dinner at the restaurant."

"Come back!"

MJ thought her aunt was talking to the dog...or pretended to think that. "Go back, Delilah, stay with Anna."

At least the mongrel obeyed, halting in the middle of the barnyard.

MJ, on the other hand, sprinted toward the main gate, and Anna didn't have the wind left to chase her. From a distance, she saw her niece hop into a low-slung, silver car with someone female at the wheel. Never having met either Stacey or her mother, Anna couldn't say who was driving, but it looked like just one person.

The car made a flashy U-turn and sped off down the dirt road.

Anna fumed. *Yeah, Erika was right. The kid played me like a violin...or maybe an electric guitar.*

Six of them crowded around a long, rustic table near the door to the kitchen. MJ realized that, far from getting star treatment, at a roadhouse the band was part of "the help," and better tables were kept open for real customers.

She sat across from Bobby, but so far she'd barely gotten to say two words to him. The first set by RaserzEdge had been amazing—they'd gotten even sharper, she thought, since the last time she'd heard them at school. She wanted to tell Bobby that, but she would've had to interrupt the steady barrage of inside jokes and reminiscences from everyone else.

Lorne, the lead guitarist, hung out at the bar hitting on a twenty-something woman he'd just met, but the rest of them lined up on either side of the table. On the bench along the wall, Bobby sat at one end, with Stacey squashed between him and his burly, square-jawed drummer, Mike. On the opposite side, Mike's sleek, exotic girlfriend Kayla faced him. Then came Gary, the somewhat nerdy keyboard guy, and finally MJ. It almost looked as if Gary was paired up with Stacey and MJ with Bobby, but that sure wasn't the way it was playing out.

Since MJ last saw her, Stacey had punched up her hair color to almost magenta, and smoky makeup encircled her blue eyes. Now she grabbed Bobby's arm, as if she'd just remembered something urgent. "Hey, that guy who came up to you at the club in the Village, and said he was some kind of agent? Anything ever happen with that?"

Bobby tossed his head, flipping the platinum bangs. "Nah, he was just blowin' smoke. When I asked him some questions about actual contracts, he backed off fast."

Stacey pouted. "That's awful. All you guys need is one good break, somebody to recognize how talented you are. Besides us, of course."

Bobby grinned in appreciation, and MJ brooded. *I should be saying those kinds of things to him, so why aren't I? Is it because they all seem so cozy together and I still feel like an outsider?*

She was already P.O.'d at Stacey for lying about who would be at the wheel that night. If Anna found out, she'd be furious.

But Stacey doesn't care. Now she's flirting up a storm with Bobby, and how can I hope to compete?

MJ knew she even looked wrong. Oh, her clothes blended well enough with the other clientele at the Broken Inn, but Stacey and Kayla both were dressed to party, showing a bit of cleavage and lots of leg. No doubt they'd gotten their nice, even tans from lying on the beach or maybe in salon beds. Most of MJ's summer color was on her arms and the back of her neck, from pushing a wheelbarrow or leading horses back and forth to the paddocks.

The waitress set down big plates of chicken wings and nachos to share, and the salty, greasy aromas intoxicated MJ. How long had it been since she'd had food like this? At least there were some vegetarian options, in the mozzarella sticks and the salsa and avocado dips. MJ wanted to gorge herself, but Stacey and Kayla were just picking, as if too fascinated with Bobby and Mike to even notice the food.

Bobby moved on from the subject of the bogus agent. "I did get a call last week from a guy who sounds a lot more legit. He couldn't make it here tonight, but he promised he'd come to our next gig and check us out." Bobby then turned his full attention on MJ. "And I have you to thank! He said he heard about us somewhere, went to our website and was very impressed. He told me it had a lot of good information and looked real professional."

The encouragement finally loosened MJ's tongue. "Wow, that's great. I'm so glad it helped."

"Maybe you oughta think about doing that." He dipped a tortilla chip into the common bowl of salsa. "I mean, for a living. People make good money designing websites."

"I have thought about it. In fact, I just finished updating a site for the farm where I'm working this summer."

"You're working on a *farm*?" Kayla scrunched her nose.

MJ half-expected the reaction, since Stacey had the same attitude, and kept her cool. "My aunt does horse rescue. She takes horses other people don't want and tries to get them back in shape to be adopted. So, having a good website is important. We need to ask for donations and—"

"They've got one horse that killed somebody!" Stacey announced.

"That's not true." MJ was losing patience with her supposed best friend. "Murphy did hurt one jockey, but he's working out okay for us. My aunt Anna is teaching him to jump—"

Lorne popped back to the table, and everyone ribbed him about striking out with the older woman at the bar. She hadn't believed him when he swore he was twenty-one.

MJ heard Gary's voice from her other side. "So, what is it with girls and horses, anyhow?"

She faced him. He was odder-looking than his three bandmates, with rather bulgy eyes and a Mohawk haircut that flopped rather than standing up straight. But right now, he was the only person paying any attention to her, so she wanted to be polite. "What do you mean?"

"A lotta young girls seem to go horse-crazy. I heard it's kind of a Freudian thing." He narrowed his eyes in what was probably meant as a seductive expression.

MJ had heard this kind of BS before, and would not have bothered to reply, but Lorne leaned on her end of the table so she couldn't slip away without making a scene. Since she didn't care what Gary thought of her, she decided to be totally honest.

"I'm not good at most sports," she admitted. "I'm too short for basketball, too clumsy for tennis, and too slow for soccer. When I play on a team, people laugh at me. But when I get on a horse, suddenly I'm tall, strong and graceful. I can run faster and jump higher than any track star. And even though I've fallen off a couple times, no horse has ever laughed at me."

When MJ finished her explanation, everyone else had gone quiet, looking at her. If she'd felt awkward before, now she wanted to crawl under the table.

Gary at least broke the tension. "Well, I gotta give you props. I'd never go near one of those things. They're too damn big."

Some of the others chuckled in agreement.

"And they *smell*." Stacey glanced at Bobby for corroboration. "Don't they?"

He didn't answer, but continued to study MJ for another minute. Then he got swept back into the general conversation, mostly about disastrous dude-ranch and trail-riding experiences.

MJ tuned them all out, wondering how soon she could escape from this train wreck of an evening.

A few minutes later, Stacey excused herself to go to "the girls' room," and Bobby changed places to let her out of the booth. All at once, MJ found herself in the situation she'd been hoping for all evening—across the table from him with no competition.

Before she could think of a good conversation starter, he lowered his voice and told her, "That was awesome, what you said just now. About how riding makes you feel."

"Oh, gee...thanks." MJ made a face. "Gary was asking me silly stuff—like whether it was a turn-on—so I just wanted to set him straight. I didn't mean for the whole table to hear."

Bobby shook his head. "He's a good drummer, but with girls he can be kind of a douche. So, I heard you didn't get into the college you wanted."

"I'm taking a year off to make up my mind. After what happened to my Dad, I'm in no hurry to get on that whole nine-to-five track."

"I hear that." He gazed into her eyes as if he did understand. *Maybe he feels the same way about his music—that he wouldn't want to give it up for a straight job.*

It was the kind of moment MJ had dreamed of, but it didn't last long. Lorne bent down and slapped Bobby on the shoulder. "We're on again in ten minutes. You said you wanted to get that stuff from the van?"

"Oh...yeah." Looking a bit torn, Bobby told MJ, "Sorry, I gotta go."

"Sure."

MJ watched him and Lorne head for the rear exit and reassured herself that at least Bobby didn't think she was an idiot. Her appetite came back and she helped herself to two more mozzarella sticks. Mike flagged down their waitress and ordered more.

As time dragged on, MJ started to wonder what kind of equipment the guys were bringing in, that was taking so long. Was it just a coverup, did they have beer or something in the van? She wasn't interested in drinking, but damn, she'd been having almost a heart-to-heart with Bobby when Lorne had pulled him away. This might be their last chance to really connect.

"'Scuse me," she told Mike and Kayla. "I have to make a run outside, too."

"Su-u-ure you do." Gary winked, and the other two also smiled knowingly.

CHAPTER TWENTY-NINE:

SURPRISE

After the air conditioning inside the restaurant, the humidity of the July night outside dropped over MJ like a hot, damp towel. She found the parking lot jammed with cars, more than when she'd arrived with Stacey a couple hours ago. How many of these people, she wondered, came just to hear RaserzEdge? If they'd become that big an attraction, she hoped they were getting decent pay.

When she and Stacey had first arrived, they'd spotted the group's van at the rear of the lot. Now, in the dark, MJ had trouble re-orienting herself. The lot's half-dozen pole lights were hardly bright enough for her to tell a blue car from a black one. Still, a silver minivan with the band's name and razorblade logo on the side shouldn't be hard to find.

Crickets cheeped in the nearby woods and fireflies winked among the rows of cars. A few people drifted out from the roadhouse and lingered to talk near their vehicles. As MJ searched, she suddenly wondered how she'd explain why she'd come out here. She didn't want to drink anything and give her aunt even more reason to be angry. *Maybe I'll just offer to help the guys bring in the equipment?* Even if that sounded lame, it would give her a chance to talk some more with Bobby.

At last she spotted the van at the farthest corner of the lot. The roadhouse owner probably made the band park there to leave the better spaces for customers. She saw Lorne starting back toward the restaurant with an extra mic stand. He didn't notice her and she hesitated to call to him. If Bobby was still out there by himself, that would be ideal.

MJ stepped up her pace, threading between the tightly parked cars. As she neared the van she saw a dark gap in the silver side—the panel doors were open. Lorne wouldn't leave their stuff unguarded like that, so Bobby must still be nearby.

She rounded the front of a bulky truck and saw two figures sitting in the gap between the open doors. They didn't notice her, though; they were wrapped in a tight clinch, making out like crazy. One of Stacey's hands rested on the black denim of Bobby's thigh, and both of his hands massaged her back through her flimsy cotton top.

The taste of the salsa dip rose again, sourly, in MJ's throat. She tried to back around the pickup truck without drawing attention, but she knocked an empty beer can from the cab's hood and it clanked to the gravel.

Bobby and Stacey both looked up, like startled rabbits.

That's it—this night officially cannot get any worse. MJ swallowed hard and spoke through a pinched throat. "Uh...the guys said you're due back on stage."

Bobby at least had the grace to act embarrassed. "Oh, er, sure. Thanks."

Stacey just let out a tinkling laugh. MJ pictured delicate horns poking through her mop of magenta hair, and a tail with a spade-shaped tip curling out the back of her shorts.

MJ stalked back to the roadhouse, almost tripping over the gravel. The last thing she wanted was to return to that table by the kitchen door.

No way can I spend another minute sitting across from Stacey, and I sure as hell can't ride back to the farm with her. But what other choice do I have? Call Anna to come pick me up?

She ducked into the ladies' room and hid in a stall for a minute to release a few tears. Then she drew a deep breath, emerged and patched her makeup in the tarnished mirror. She pulled out her cell phone, checked the time. *Ten-thirty already!*

She also checked for phone messages and saw Anna's office number.

Even if she believes Stacey's mother drove us to the club, she'll still be mad that I'm out so late. I'd rather deal with her yelling at me, though, than watch Stacey paw Bobby for another hour.

MJ started to punch her aunt's number, but two tipsy women half-stumbled into the bathroom, gossiping at full volume. For privacy, she took her phone out to the hall between the back door and the kitchen, which was quieter and still gave her a glimpse of the restaurant.

Before she could dial again, she spotted an unlikely figure standing near the long table she had vacated, chatting with Mike, Kayla and Gary. This was too big a coincidence—she had to find out what was up. She stuffed her phone back in her purse, straightened her spine and crossed the room.

"Here she is now," Mike announced.

The standing guy swung around and smiled at her, showing a crooked front tooth.

"Walt? What are you doing here?"

"Good to see you, too," he tossed back. "I was on the phone with your aunt, and she said you came here with some friends to see this band. Sounded like fun, so I thought I'd drop by."

The explanation only baffled MJ more. Early-to-bed, early-to-rise Walt—not old enough to drink, and too moral to use a fake I.D.—had "dropped by" a roadhouse at ten-thirty at night to see a rock band he knew nothing about? Just because he heard she'd be there? After the way he had behaved toward her over the past week or so, MJ decided he couldn't be lovesick.

Anna must have sent him to round her up, like a stray calf, and drag her home. Ordinarily MJ might have been angry. But as she noticed Stacey sashaying back toward their table, she started to view Walt as a temporary knight in shining armor.

"Well, I'm so glad you did!" She introduced him to Mike, Gary, Kayla and Stacey. When the two guys rejoined Lorne and Bobby onstage, leaving plenty of room at the table, MJ invited Walt to sit. She passed the nachos his way and ordered him a Coke.

Kayla and Stacey eyeballed her as if she'd grown another head, but MJ didn't care. They were in the country, so why be surprised to meet a guy their age with a boring barbershop haircut, dressed in a plaid shirt and jeans actually faded from hard work?

When they asked Walt how he knew MJ, he explained that he helped out at her aunt's farm.

"He also exercises one of our horses," MJ jumped in. "He's a good Western rider. He took me out and showed me around the trails in the woods."

Stacey smirked as if this implied something more than horseback riding.

"You're a good rider, too, MJ," Walt told her. "You just aren't used to Western."

She told the story about accidentally putting Dash into a spin. "It took me awhile to get the hang of things, for sure. Another time, when the pony kicked me, Walt found me sitting in the stall and called the vet!" She laughed. "Can you believe I had a vet X-ray my leg?"

"Just lucky we didn't have to put you down," Walt added, in a grave tone.

By now even Stacey and Kayla were grinning. Whether with her or at her, MJ didn't care. She felt more relaxed, more herself, than at any other time that evening.

She also realized something else. RaserzEdge had started their set awhile ago, and though they still sounded good, she'd hardly paid them any attention.

Feeling cocky, MJ decided to probe Walt's reasons for coming to the roadhouse. "How come Anna called you tonight? Anything wrong?"

"She was having some trouble with Murphy. I guess he got hurt earlier today."

"I know. She and Josh bandaged his foot."

"He was kicking the stall and Anna was afraid he'd hurt himself worse. I think she's got things under control, but..."

Not even sure whether this story was true, MJ figured it gave her the out she needed. "Oh, man, if I knew that I wouldn't have left her alone. Maybe I should go back and make sure everything's okay?"

Walt locked eyes with her. "That might be a good idea."

They waved the waitress over again and settled up. "Tell the guys I'm sorry I couldn't stay," MJ told Stacey and Kayla, on her way out. They looked dumbstruck when she left with Walt.

As they pulled out of the parking lot in his truck, MJ needled him, "Aren't you afraid you'll go to hell? Saying you just dropped by to see the band! Anna sent you after me, didn't she?"

Walt's mouth twisted. "I didn't want to embarrass you in front of your friends. Your aunt figured maybe they tricked you—told you there'd be an adult driving—and that you might be stuck without a safe ride home."

Anna's even smarter than I thought. "That's exactly what happened. And Stacey's lied to me about more than just that. So, don't worry about embarrassing me—I may never talk to her again. I can't believe I ever thought she was my friend."

"Sounds pretty rough."

"Nah, I'm over it already." MJ rubbed a finger beneath one eye, hoping she'd wiped away all of the smudged mascara. "I'm still wondering, though, about you."

"Huh? Me?"

"Are *you* still my friend? You acted like it tonight, but the last couple weeks, even when you came to the farm, you kept avoiding me. Even Dash is missing out on his exercise because you're so afraid to hang around."

"Sorry about that. I've been—"

"C'mon, don't say you're too busy. Your dad must be feeling better by now, and you have brothers and sisters to help out. I know it's because of your mom. She doesn't want you spending time with a...a heathen like me."

Walt laughed out loud. "I don't think even Mom would use that word."

"She'd probably use worse. Maybe not curse words, but..." Another thought occurred to MJ. "She has no idea, does she, that you came out here tonight?"

"I told her your aunt called and asked for help with a lame horse that was kicking his stall. That was the truth."

"But not the whole truth. And now you're going to tell her you were helping Anna until eleven at night?" MJ faced the road ahead with a grin. "Yeah, you're going to hell."

His reply was quiet and firm. "I'm almost eighteen. I can make my own decisions about who I hang out with." After a beat, he added, "Maybe next week, you and me can go for another trail ride?"

"Sure, that'd be cool."

They drove through the open gate, up the road to the farm, and slowed near the house. The porch light was on and MJ could see Anna silhouetted in the rocker. *Guess she was pretty sure Walt wouldn't come back without me.*

Parking, he also spotted her aunt. "At least she doesn't have a shotgun across her lap! Want me to come along for moral support?"

"No, thanks, you've done your part. I'm a big girl, I can take my medicine. Better get home now, before your mom thinks Murphy trampled you." MJ hopped from the truck cab with a wink. "And don't worry—I'll make sure Anna backs up your alibi."

CHAPTER THIRTY:

MYSTERY DONOR

D r. Julie Adams fastened Velcro straps to secure the foam bootie over Murphy's foot, then straightened up. "With that," she told Anna, "you should be able to turn him out in his usual paddock. The wound's clean, so he should heal fast."

"Great." Anna patted the horse's dappled-gray shoulder. "He was *not* happy about being stuck here in the barn, even with the pony for company."

The vet studied her. "Kept you up all night, did he?"

Anna laughed. "Do I look that bad? Murphy can't take all the blame. My niece went out to a club on the highway with some friends, and came home way later than she was supposed to."

"Ah, you're finding out what it's like to raise a teenager!"

"Yeah, it's giving me a whole new understanding of my sister's point of view."

Arriving home after eleven the night before, MJ had claimed she didn't know Stacey would be driving until she reached the car. At that point, she didn't want to "chicken out," she said, and after all her friend did have a valid license.

"But once the band finished their first set, I saw she was sneaking out to their van to drink," the girl went on. "The show was running late and I knew she wouldn't want to leave 'til the end. Honestly, I had my phone out ready to call you when Walt showed up."

Anna had remained skeptical. "Your mom told me you really like this guy in the band."

"Yeah, well...Besides lying to me about who'd be driving, Stacey also was putting the moves on Bobby. She acted like a jerk all night. Believe me, I was glad to have somebody else give me a ride home. And Walt was cool about it, let them think it was just a coincidence that he came by."

Reading between the lines, Anna sensed her niece's disappointment in the way the evening had ended.

She told Julie now, "I think MJ learned her lesson, so there was no point in punishing her any further. Anyhow, Erika called this morning and really lit into the poor kid, I guess."

"My two broke a few rules at that age, but they turned out fine." With a smile, Julie packed up her medical kit. "And no harm done as far as the horse goes. Good thing Buchanan was here when Murphy stepped on that bottle."

"He did hang around longer than he'd planned, to help us out." Anna freed the gray horse from his cross-ties, and she and Julie walked him out to the paddock. "It got so late, Josh called somebody to apologize for getting hung up here. Wife, I guess?"

Julie sent her a sidelong glance. "Not that I've heard. And I imagine if Josh Buchanan got married, word would've spread fast through the grapevine."

"Why, because he's so well-known?"

"After he got divorced, about four years ago, every eligible female in the local horsey set started flinging herself at Josh. A few not-so-eligible ones, too."

Anna hated to picture herself as one of a long line of man-hungry ladies, but covered her discomfort with a chuckle. "I know what you mean. When I took lessons at various stables—all English riding—we'd joke that any male trainer who was straight and remotely good-looking had to beat the women back with a riding crop." Opening the paddock gate, she reconsidered how that sounded. "Not me, of course. I was married. Happily, I thought."

"And I don't mean to imply nothin' about Josh, either. From what I hear, he put one cute little thing in her place but good. Told her he doesn't get mixed up with other men's wives. Like I said, word gets around, the bad and the good."

Anna turned Murphy loose in his paddock. He trotted into

the center and proclaimed his return to his buddies with a loud whinny. *He'll convince them all that wearing one blue bootie is the latest style.*

MJ popped out of the barn office, shadowed as usual by Delilah. Anna noted that her niece appeared no worse off after her escapade of the night before.

"Our new website is getting hits!" the girl announced. "But we got a couple of emails I didn't know how to deal with, Anna, so you'll need to look at them. One guy wants to sponsor a horse. And some rescue group in New York State asked if we can take in a couple of—" MJ checked a scrap of paper in her hand—"PMU foals. What's that?"

Anna exchanged frowns with Julie, who looked ready to answer the question.

"No, you have places to go and patients to see," Anna told the vet. "I can handle this. Part of raising a teenager, right? Explaining some ugly facts of life?"

After Julie drove off, MJ faced her aunt, hands on hips. "You're going to tell me about the birds and the bees? Hate to break it to you, but you're a little late."

"Oh, I'm sure you know all about sex." Since her niece was so awkward around boys, though, Anna suspected most of the girl's knowledge was still just theoretical. "But how much do you know about menopause?" When MJ made a face, Anna explained, "There are drugs women can take for hot flashes and other change-of-life problems, and some are made from pregnant mares' urine."

Her niece's face twisted further. "Gross!"

Leaning against the paddock gate, Anna went on. "Labs extract the estrogen from horse pee because it's 'natural.' But that means a lot of mares have to be kept pregnant. They're confined in narrow stalls, with equipment attached to collect the urine, twenty-four/seven."

MJ gaped as if listening to a horror story. "What a terrible life!"

"Yeah, they develop all kinds of health problems. And that's just half of it. The mares eventually give birth to foals, of course. And while other farms breed to get good racehorses or show horses, PMU foals are just a byproduct. Nobody needs or wants them. A farm might keep a couple of fillies to add to the assembly line, once they're old enough. But the rest—including all the colts—usually get sent to slaughter."

"The babies? Man, that's awful." The girl cocked her head at her aunt. "How do you know all this?"

"Once I decided to get into the rescue business, I did a lot of research." Anna could empathize with MJ's shock. She'd found out more than she really wanted to know, and had seen many grisly images online and in pamphlets, over the past two years.

"Can't somebody stop it?"

"It's not against the law, but humane groups have been protesting the industry for decades. Last I heard, there aren't too many PMU farms left here in the U.S. But, like the slaughterhouses, a lot have moved to Canada."

Under this gloomy cloud, they walked together back to the barn. MJ said, "The lady who left the message made it sound like they had a lot of these foals. More than she had room to keep."

"Maybe her group bought them at auction or brought some over the border." Anna felt conflicted. She wanted to help, but now might not be the best time. Foals could be a lot of extra work—and expense. "I was kind of afraid of this, when we updated the website. People want to send us horses, but not many want to send us money."

MJ reminded her, "There's that guy who wants to sponsor a horse."

"Yeah, I really should get back to him." Anna stepped into the hay-scented shade of the barn.

"And if Josh can find you someone to adopt Murphy—"

"That can't happen until he's sound enough to start jumping again. Which reminds me, I've got a job for you."

"Oh?"

"Know the big field where Murphy stepped on the bottle? I need you to search every inch and make sure there's nothing else up there that shouldn't be." Anna glanced at her watch. "You should be done before lunchtime."

The girl's dark eyes narrowed. "Seriously?"

"Hey, you've got it coming for the way you made me worry last night." Anna plucked a rake from a wall rack and handed it to her niece. "Take some work gloves, too, and that big plastic tub."

MJ knew better than to protest. She equipped herself and trudged off toward the distant field.

Left alone in the office, Anna checked the new emails her niece had mentioned. One came from a Jeb Andrews, who specified that he wanted to "sponsor a rescue horse." He included his phone number.

Funny, Anna thought. Their new website had requested donations for feed, bedding, supplements and medical care, but said nothing about sponsoring a particular animal. There was a simple online form to fill out, requesting just the donor's name, email and credit card information, so the donation could be made electronically. But she understood why the guy might want to talk to her first, to get a sense of whether her operation was legit.

She called him from her office and was surprised when Andrews picked up on the second ring. "Why, hello!" he answered in a hearty tone. "Thanks for getting back to me so fast."

"Thanks for your interest in Reboot Ranch." Anna realized it was the first time she had used the new name of the rescue with an outsider. "How did you come across our website?"

"Oh, I'm a horse guy myself and I do a lot of business online. I just stumbled onto it, but you seem to be doing some good stuff. How long you been at it?"

They chatted awhile about the evolution of the farm and Anna's hopes to expand the operation. "I understand you want to make a donation," she said.

"Yeah. At some farms like yours, a person can sponsor a particular horse—donate a certain amount every month to his upkeep. You have any arrangements like that?"

"Not so far, but I don't see any reason why it couldn't be done. We only have a few horses to choose from..."

"Just the ones on the website, eh?" He paused. "I'd like to sponsor one that has a good chance of being adopted. Y'know, once he's better."

Anna reflected that the ones who might never be re-homed,

Valentine and Patches, might need his charity more. But she supposed that, like the customer, the donor was always right. "Our best candidate for adoption is Murphy, the gray Thoroughbred. But Dash is coming along well, too. He still has a few medical issues."

"That's the buckskin, right? Looks like a nice animal. Maybe I'll sponsor him, then."

When Andrews proposed sending two hundred dollars a month for Dash's care, Anna's heart leaped—that would go a long way toward the horse's upkeep. "That would be terrific, thank you!"

"No problem." Andrews chuckled. "So, what do I get for my money?"

"Excuse me?" It didn't seem like the kind of question anyone would usually ask when donating to a charity.

"Do you list your donors on the website? Send me a newsletter?"

She exhaled in relief. "We can start a list, with you as the first. And we can email you every month with news of the farm and about Dash in particular."

"Great, I'd like that. And y'know, I don't live so far away. Maybe sometime I can stop by and see the horses for myself."

Again, she grew cautious. "Of course, you'd be welcome. Just call ahead to make sure someone is here to show you around."

"I understand. Well, it's been fine talking to you, Anna. You take care, and keep up the good work."

After he clicked off, she studied the phone handset for a second longer. A strange call, she thought, but a lucrative one. Was this guy so loaded that he just called up charities and made spontaneous pledges?

Maybe it was a prank, and he has no intention at all of—

A delicate *plink* sound called her attention to her computer, where the screen still displayed the farm's Welcome page. She clicked an icon to bring up Donations.

The two hundred bucks from Jeb Andrews already had come through.

What the heck! Whether this guy is eccentric or not, Dash's expenses are pretty well covered for the next month. Don't they say never to look a gift horse in the mouth?

CHAPTER THIRTY-ONE:

FRUSTRATION

Anna also returned the call from the New York organization trying to place the PMU colts. She connected with a volunteer named Francie who sounded thrilled that Anna had even responded.

"We'll keep them another month or so, anyway," Francie said. "The farms wean them young, and we'll geld them before we send them anywhere. But even though we've got a pretty big facility here, we're getting overwhelmed. We rescued six of these foals at an auction and we can't keep all of them."

Anna started to weaken. If the colts would be several months old and already gelded, they wouldn't require as much care as if they were babies. A lot of training, though. She explained to Francie that Reboot Ranch was a small operation just getting off the ground. "I probably can find stalls for them, though. We have one horse we're hoping to adopt out by the end of the summer..."

"Perfect timing! And we can help out with their care, at least while you're getting them settled. We've gotten donations for this PMU project, and we could allocate a portion for upkeep of these two boys."

"That would help, since we're still soliciting funds, ourselves."

Anna finally agreed to consider taking the colts, which Francie described as Quarter Horse-Belgian crosses. After Anna hung up, she realized this might be her first cooperative arrangement with another rescue group.

But how am I going to train two strong, spunky yearlings to be riding horses? I've only done that from scratch with Starbuck, who was older, and at least had been tacked up and hitched to a sulky.

The knock on her office doorjamb sounded a bit formal for MJ. "Don't tell me you finished with that big field already?" Anna spun half around in her desk chair to see Josh in the doorway. "Oh, hi! I...I wasn't expecting you."

"Sorry. I tried to call from the road, but your line was busy. I was in the area and thought I'd visit our patient." He nodded in the direction of the paddocks. "Looks like he's doing well."

"Seems to be. Dr. Adams put him in that boot just to be on the safe side."

"Oh, is Julie your vet? She's terrific."

"She's been a lifesaver, sometimes literally."

The two of them went out to look the Thoroughbred over. "Doesn't seem to be favoring the foot at all," the trainer observed. "When did Julie say you could take the boot off?"

"Tomorrow. But he should still take it easy for a few days, no galloping or jumping. I guess that will put me behind schedule in terms of getting him ready to show." Anna broached a worrying subject. "Clint, the friend who brought Murphy to me, raised some issues last time he visited. He said if we go to a horse show, Murphy may think he's back at the track. He might try to race the other horses, or get so stressed that he..."

Josh finished the thought. "That he flips on you? I don't think that's likely, after the de-sensitizing work I did with him. Still, I can see why you'd be concerned."

"Anything more we can do to make sure he behaves?"

"A couple things. And now, while he's taking it easy, might be the perfect time for you to try them."

Anna felt her stomach drop at the word "you." It reminded her that, in the end, the horse's re-education was her responsibility.

"Ride him in the ring with someone else," Josh suggested. "Another good rider, who can handle a problem if it comes up."

Anna thought briefly of MJ. She wasn't sure if her niece was that experienced, and anyhow, the only horse on the farm the girl could ride well was Valentine. Anna imagined Murphy trying to cozy up to the chestnut mare, with poor MJ caught in between,

210

and shuddered.

"Our neighbor Walt is pretty expert," Anna said. "He's ridden our Quarter Horse."

"Sounds good. You two try working together a few times. Ride alongside each other, then opposite. Just walk and trot, nice and easy. You've handled Murphy enough by now that you should be able to keep control."

Anna hoped so. At least it would be in a pretty safe, enclosed situation, and Walt would know how to get out of their way if the Thoroughbred acted up.

"Also, take him out to another show before the real thing. Bring him to the grounds, unload him and walk him around. If he seems okay, saddle him, get on him and maybe go around the warmup ring a couple of times."

That sounded doable, and Anna breathed a little easier.

Just then, Delilah came trotting up from the distant field, wearing her doggie grin. Behind her trudged MJ, who dragged the big plastic tub by its rope handle. She wiped her brow and announced to Anna and Josh, "Well, *that* sure was a lot of fun."

Since Anna had intended the chore as a mild punishment, she expressed no sympathy. She let the girl air her gripes to Josh about the rigors of her cleanup detail.

"An important job, though," the trainer told her, with subtle psychology. "Now that Murphy's on the mend, Anna will be schooling him out there, and we don't want any more accidents. You didn't find any more beer bottles?"

"No, just a couple other disgusting things." Still wearing work gloves, MJ rummaged through the weeds in the tub and picked out a small, round tin. "This is so scratched up, I can hardly read the label. 'Skoal'? What's that?"

"Chewing tobacco," Josh told her. "Let me see."

MJ handed over the tin with her favorite sarcastic comment. "Seriously?"

"Maybe left by the beer-drinker. But it's empty and rusted. Could be it was out there a long time."

Anna relaxed a bit. After all, she'd been here just a year and a half, and the farm had sat vacant for a while before that. She might have overlooked the flat, greenish tin the last time she'd mowed.

"Even worse, Delilah found this dead animal. Looks like a big, white rat." MJ lifted it out of the tub by its hairless tail, with even more distaste than she'd handled the tin. The creature was stiff but still mostly intact.

"It's a 'possum." Anna figured her niece had never seen one before.

Josh brushed back some of the dirty-white fur on the animal's side, and his thick brows drew together. "It's been shot."

The perspiration trickling between Anna's shoulderblades turned to icewater. "Maybe some kid with a BB gun?"

"The hole looks bigger than that." Josh set the dead creature back in the tub with peculiar care, and turned his gaze down the road toward the field. "Some people hunt them, but this one hasn't been dead very long. Besides, opossums are nocturnal. So that means..."

Anna finished the thought for him. "Somebody's been prowling around my field at night. With a gun."

"I wouldn't worry about it," Walt told her the next morning, while they tacked up Dash and Murphy in the barn. "That 'possum could've been shot somewhere else, and just crawled into your field."

Anna peered at him down the aisle. "Trying hard to make me feel better, aren't you?"

"No, think about it. If somebody was hunting it for food, he wouldn't have left it behind." Walt pulled up the rope cinch on Dash's saddle. "How well do you know your neighbors?"

"Not very. I've talked to the Pasquales, who have the dairy farm. I never met the guy who lives in that crappy old house north of me."

"Mr. Deavers? No surprise—he keeps to himself. But he's been known to shoot foxes to keep 'em away from his hens. Even killed a couple dogs and cats over the years. I'll bet he shot that 'possum and it ran onto your property just before it died."

This explanation soothed Anna's nerves, on edge since the previous evening. "Guess I'm still learning to think like a farmer."

They led their mounts out to the barnyard, side-by-side. Although Murphy had never been turned out with Dash, they occupied paddocks close enough to see and smell each other and seemed relaxed together.

"It was real brave of you to take on this whole place by yourself," Walt told Anna.

"A little crazy, too," she admitted. "I'd been around a few different stables and saw how the owners ran them, so I figured I could handle it, as long as I only kept a few horses." She opened the gate to the round pen. "But still, it was more work than I ever expected. That's why I appreciate the help I've gotten from you, and now MJ."

Inside the pen, they both mounted. Anna told Walt, "We'll walk alongside you at first. Start clockwise, in his bad direction."

Murphy was just out of his boot and his lay-up had left him with energy to burn. It didn't surprised Anna that he tried to jog instead of walk and even aimed a nip in Dash's direction. Although the buckskin laid back his ears in warning, he stayed calm. Anna realized Murphy would have been ponied, or escorted to the track, by a similar "bombproof" horse. But she wasn't going to let him bully Dash, and tightened her rein to tug his head away. Before long, the two were walking quietly together.

MJ strolled down from the house with Delilah and hung by the fence to watch.

"Okay," Anna told Walt, "Let's kick it up a notch."

They started trotting, and she soon saw the effect Clint had warned her about. Easy enough to control when ridden alone, Murphy now seemed determined to "beat" Dash and leaned on the bit.

"Walt, I'm going to circle him to the inside. You stay on the rail." Anna used her weight as much as her reins to turn the gray in a wide arc, then brought him back alongside the buckskin at a safe distance. She repeated the move a few times, until they were trotting in sync with the other, steadier pair.

Thank God for Walt and Dash—two level-headed guys.

When they came down to a walk again, MJ called out, "At this show, will you have to keep pace like that with another horse?"

Anna laughed. "No, but we will have to warm up in a ring with others. I want him to get used to that idea."

She and Walt tried both gaits going counter-clockwise with better results. Anna was feeling confident until he asked, "Should we also ride in opposite directions?"

Rats, she thought. "You're right. We'll pass left-to-left."

This exercise did not go as well. Murphy apparently wasn't used to having another horse ridden toward him, and a couple of close passes at the trot resulted in ear-pinning by both animals. As Anna had hoped, though, Walt read her horse's body language and at the first sign of trouble steered Dash out of harm's way.

As they walked together to cool down, Walt grinned at her. "That wasn't *too* bad."

"Better than I expected. Now I'm not as worried that he'll bolt or pick a fight when he gets next to a strange horse."

"Ah," Walt said. "But Dash isn't a strange horse, is he?"

He was right, Anna realized. If Murphy behaved like this with a pal he saw every day—! "C'mon, what happened to boosting my confidence?"

They were leading their mounts from the pen when MJ intercepted Walt. "Hey, as long as you've got Dash saddled, want to go for that trail ride?"

He paused. "Aw, gee...Wish I could, but I got something else to do this afternoon."

A wary look crept into the girl's eyes. "We don't have to be gone long."

"Yeah, but I've gotta get cleaned up, change my clothes...It's a thing with my church group. I'm one of the organizers, so I gotta be there. Sorry!"

MJ's rounded features hardened. "No problem."

"Honest, we'll go for that ride soon, okay?"

"Whatever." With a flip of her hand, she paced back toward the house.

Walt continued to the barn with Anna. "I don't think she believes me."

"She's probably just frustrated. She left all her friends behind to work out here with me for the summer, and maybe didn't realize how much she was giving up. I guess Saturday night at the roadhouse didn't go too well, either." Anna would not mention the girl's unrequited crush on Bobby Raser, in case Walt didn't know about that. "She probably feels her whole gang is moving on without her. And right now, you're the only person around here who's her own age."

"Yeah, I figured that out, too. But I'm not trying to avoid her—not this time—and I *will* make it up to her."

They sponged down and brushed their mounts and turned them out. Then Walt headed home. Up at the house, Anna found her niece on the porch, brooding.

"After the talk we had Saturday, I thought he was done lying to me," MJ complained.

"I think he was telling the truth. After all, he must be busy some of the time." Anna clapped her niece on the shoulder. "Let's have lunch. I bought a frozen pizza. It's a margherita, the kind you like."

While they ate, MJ seemed to gain more perspective. "I guess I got ticked off because the two of you were riding all morning, while I just did chores. I know you were training Murphy, but…I never get to ride much at all."

Anna supposed she'd feel the same way in MJ's shoes. "Why don't you take Valentine out in the pen for a while. She's been doing okay lately."

MJ nodded, though Anna knew it must sound boring compared to a trail ride with Walt.

Later, while feeding Delilah on the front porch, Anna watched her niece work with Valentine. At a walk, the girl put the chestnut mare into a training-level dressage frame and did some smooth figure-eights. MJ also tried some leg yields, walking forward and sideways at the same time, with Val's legs crossing neatly. The kid might not be up to dealing with Dash's spins or Murphy's tantrums, but she was a good rider.

Anna wandered down to the pen to tell her, "You two look great."

"Thanks." MJ lifted the brim of her helmet to let her scalp breathe. "It's sure hot, though. I think it's bothering Val, too. Maybe I could take her on the trail, where it's shady?"

Anna saw the mare's nostrils flaring and her sides were heaving a little. "Are you sure you know the way?"

"When I went out with Walt, the trail looked pretty clear."

"But that was a month ago. I haven't been out to clean it up and it could be overgrown by now."

"I won't go far. If I hit a spot that's hard to get through, or something, I'll come back."

Valentine knows the way home, anyhow, Anna thought. She opened the gate for them. "Okay, but just walk!"

"Yes, ma'am." Leaving the pen, MJ rubbed the mare's thin neck.

Delilah watched them head for the woods with a wagging tail, but when ordered to stay she obeyed. That reminded Anna of what Walt had said, about the neighbor who shot not only wild animals, but dogs and cats.

Something else to worry about. But at least MJ's headed in the opposite direction from Old Man Deavers' place.

CHAPTER THIRTY-TWO:

Harsh Words

Enveloped by shady woods, MJ felt not only cooler but freer. Much as she liked her aunt, living out here with Anna had turned out to be not so different from being at home under her mom's watchful eye. If anything, Anna seemed even more "watchful."

Sure, 'cause I'm not her kid. If I get in trouble or get hurt, she figures my mom will say she wasn't looking out for me.

Still, the girl relished being on her own for awhile. And aside maybe from Delilah, who'd become her confidant over the past week or so, MJ figured she couldn't ask for a better non-human companion than Valentine. She was starting to understand why her aunt kept saying the chestnut mare was special. Just riding Val in the pen and asking for a few beginner dressage moves, MJ had noticed how quickly the horse responded and how eager she was to please, in spite of her health problems. Val's long-limbed, deep-chested conformation showed she was a Thoroughbred like Murphy. But maybe because she was older, or had never raced, she was much calmer and gentler.

It's a shame she's so sick. She would've made a great lesson horse, or maybe even a show horse for a beginner. Hard to believe she was almost on the truck to a slaughterhouse when Anna saved her.

MJ scratched the chestnut near the roots of her mane, as she'd seen her aunt do with horses. "You were lucky Anna came along that day, huh?"

Valentine stretched her neck, asking for more rein. MJ gave her some slack, trusting her completely. *She must be cooler out here, too. She's not coughing as much and her sides have stopped that awful heaving.*

The girl lost herself for a while in the steady rhythm of her mount's walk, the squeak of the English saddle, the twittering of different birds, and the whisper of a breeze through the trees. She might not have appreciated those quiet things as much if Walt had been with her.

That thought reminded MJ of the disaster that was her social life. She'd heard nothing from either Stacey or Bobby since Saturday night. Not that she'd really expected or wanted to. Even if one or both of them apologized, what difference would it make?

While I was away, Stacey saw her chance to hook up with Bobby and took it. And why would he turn her down? She's hotter than me, she's been around more, she knows how to get a guy interested. Bobby probably had no idea I'd even care—he figured he and I were just friends. After all, I was the one who took off to spend the summer at some farm in the middle of nowhere.

A startling thought occurred to MJ. *What if they don't even think I mind, because they figure I'm dating Walt? Wouldn't that be a kick in the head!*

Valentine slowed to step over the same thick log, fallen across the trail, that MJ and Walt had ridden over two weeks ago. "I just hope he's not back to avoiding me," she muttered to the horse. "Anna thought he really did have something else to do this afternoon. With his church group, he said. He has to keep reminding me that I'm not as holy as he is." She felt a tear start down her cheek. "What the hell, Val? Why do I keep losing people I care about? Starting with Dad. Now I've lost two friends from school, and even Walt's keeping his distance. At this point, I might actually start missing Mom and Carl!"

The last cranky statement made MJ smile to herself. She wiped her cheek and straightened in her saddle. She'd be okay. She could get along without them all if she had to.

Meanwhile, her mount slowed as if confused, and MJ wondered if they'd lost the trail. As Anna had warned, it was badly overgrown out here. Since they'd passed the fallen log, nothing else looked familiar.

But then, it's all trees and bushes and rocks. What is there to recognize?

Val planted her feet and pricked her ears.

"What's up, girl? Did we make a wrong turn?"

The mare sidestepped left, neck arched and ears pointed at something only she could see...or smell. MJ gathered up the reins.

Damn, I forgot that something out here spooked the horses last time. "Easy, it's okay."

A rustling, now, and a glimpse of something deep in the trees. Something big ...and alive.

Not like a deer, though, or even a bear. Something black and white—?

The mare spun, almost dumping MJ, and took off at a gallop. She headed back toward the farm, but raced over the uneven trail at top speed. Small branches tore at MJ's clothes, and one overhanging tree limb bounced hard off her helmet.

She saw the fallen log ahead and didn't have time to stop. She rose a little in her stirrups, as she'd been taught, and pressed her hands into Val's neck. The mare jumped the log, and the effort made her slow to a canter.

MJ sat back in the saddle and pulled. "Who-o-a, girl!"

Not a racehorse like Murphy, Val obeyed. She came down to a trot and finally a walk. MJ gasped in relief.

Well, I can't say I haven't done any real riding since I got here. Not after that gallop!

Their problems were far from over, though. Valentine's sides worked like a bellows now, and she hung her head to give several racking coughs. When MJ hopped off, to ease the strain, she saw mare's nostrils had grown huge and worked desperately to pull air into her lungs. Even her big, dark eyes had gone dull with misery.

"Oh no!" The girl groaned. "You poor thing, what did I do to you?"

At her computer in the office, Anna found a brief email from

Josh and clicked on the web links he'd included. Two amateur-level horse shows, each within about twenty miles. The soonest was set for the coming weekend. A flutter rose in her chest again. Did she have the nerve to take Murphy?

Not alone. I'll call Clint and see if he's free to go with me.

Delilah, who had been dozing near Anna's feet, sat up and cocked her silky ears toward the door. Then she bounded outside with a happy bark. MJ must be back.

Anna followed, but even from the barn doorway could see something was wrong. Why was her niece walking and leading Valentine? Had the girl fallen off? At least she didn't seem hurt. But the mare—

Hurrying toward the two of them, Anna could hear Valentine's labored breathing and see her nostrils straining for air. "What happened?"

MJ looked pale. "She...she ran away with me."

That sounded preposterous to Anna, not only because Valentine was so well-behaved but because she rarely could muster that kind of energy. Besides, MJ's stammer also sounded like she might be making up an excuse. "You expect me to believe that?"

"It's true! Sh-she spooked at something in the woods. Galloped halfway back here before I could stop her."

Anna saw the horse's coppery coat was dark with sweat. Val dropped her head, stretched her neck and gave several coughs that shook her whole, thin frame. Her sides just behind the rib cage slammed inward, to force the bad air out of her lungs.

Hot tears sprang into Anna's eyes. "Oh, God...Get her into the barn, into the shade. We have to cool her off!"

They stripped off her tack, then Anna hosed the sweat from Val's body and MJ sponged the mare's head. But none of this seemed to help her labored breathing.

Anna pointed toward the office and told her niece, "Call Julie." She dashed to the tack room for a bottle of medicine and a big, plastic syringe she kept on hand for emergencies.

By the time she returned with these, MJ told her, "Julie isn't far away. She'll come as soon as she can."

Anna heard the strain in the girl's voice but felt little sympathy.

She loaded medicine into the syringe and struggled to make Val raise her head. She worked the tip sideways into the horse's mouth, between the front and back teeth, and pushed the plunger. When the mare resisted, though, some of the liquid dribbled away.

Standing clear during this process, MJ asked, "What's that?"

"Cough medicine. It might help until Julie gets here."

The girl almost whispered, "Is Val going to be all right?"

"I don't know. I haven't seen her this sick in a long time." Setting the empty syringe aside, Anna rested one hand on the suffering horse's back and closed her eyes.

Behind the lids, she traveled back to that day almost two years ago, at the auction barn. Once more, she stood outside the kill pen, searching in vain for Duke. Sagged against the railing and started to weep. Felt a soft muzzle against her cheek and heard the same harsh breathing as now. Found Valentine standing there, marked for death but still reaching out to offer comfort...

MJ stammered again. "Maybe...maybe I shouldn't have taken her out on the trail—"

Anna turned on her niece. "Maybe you shouldn't have *galloped* her."

The girl took a step back. "I didn't. Not on purpose!"

"Valentine doesn't spook and she doesn't run away with people. You were bored because you had to ride by yourself and just walk. You thought it wouldn't hurt to go a little faster. Well, it did hurt!" Facing the horse again, Anna added quietly, "You'd better *hope* she's all right."

MJ's mouth dropped open, but Anna didn't care. It was one thing to lie about who was driving, so she could sneak out with her friends. But this!

Maybe her mother and her therapist were right. Maybe MJ does have a problem with "impulse control."

Still avoiding her niece's gaze, Anna rested a hand on the neck of the suffering horse and felt the racing pulse. *What if she doesn't recover this time? What if we have to—*

A door slammed out in the yard. Anna knew it must be Julie's truck and breathed a prayer of thanks. Seconds later, Doc Adams hustled in with her regular medical bag and something else, like a squarish oxygen mask. MJ skittered to one side to let her by.

"Don't have to ask where the patient is," Julie said. "I could hear her from outside. Poor sweetie."

"I gave her the cough medicine, but it didn't help," Anna said.

"This ought to. Let's just hope she'll put up with it."

The vet soothed Valentine and slid the transparent mask over her nose, while Ann fastened the strap behind the horse's ears. Next, Julie connected a tube a few inches long to the front of the mask, then stuck something into the end that looked like an asthmatic's inhaler. She pumped this, releasing a puff into the mask. Waited a minute and did it again.

"Sometimes the horse is afraid to breathe, at first, with this weird thing on its face," she explained.

Anna rubbed the mare's neck to relax her. After another pump or two, Val finally took a deep breath.

"I can only give her six pumps at a time," Julie said, "so let's hope that does the trick."

Leaving the mask in place, she and Anna watched until the mare's breathing eased closer to normal. Julie took out a stethoscope and listened to the lungs and heart. "She's still pretty distressed. Turn her out on the grass tonight, not in that dusty paddock. And I think we'd better put her on that stronger steroid, at least for the rest of the summer. She was going to need it sooner or later."

Thanks to MJ, it's sooner. Still, now that it looked as if Valentine would survive the attack, Anna realized she'd been pretty hard on her niece. *Maybe I should apologize.*

But when she glanced down the aisle, the girl was gone.

Julie removed the mask from the horse's face. Anna asked her, "Did MJ leave?"

"Yeah. She took off right after I put this thing on Val and started doing the puffs." The vet frowned sadly. "I guess that really shook her up. She looked scared to death."

Anna turned Val out in the big pasture with Dash for company. Weary from another long and stressful day, she trudged up the road to the house.

She found MJ where she half-expected to, slumped on the porch loveseat with Delilah lying near her feet. Petting the dog and dodging Anna's eyes, the girl said, "I saw Julie leave. Is Valentine okay?"

"For now. The mask helped. I have to start her on dexamethasone, though, to help keep her lungs open. She'll have to get that every day with her feed."

"Sorry I left, but I figured I'd just be in the way. I didn't want to screw up anything else."

Anna couldn't miss the hurt in MJ's voice, and sat in the rocker across from her. "I'm sorry I snapped at you like that. I was just so worried about Val. You know she means a lot to me."

"I do know." The girl finally locked eyes with her aunt. "But I did *not* gallop her on purpose."

Anna drew a deep breath. "Okay, tell me what happened."

"I *might* have gone off the trail, by accident, 'cause, like you said, it was overgrown. Anyway, I ended up in a spot I didn't recognize. Suddenly Val acted nervous, like there was something behind the trees. She saw it first, I guess—or heard it. Then I did, too. Something big."

"A bear?"

"I dunno. I just got glimpse, but... it looked black-and-white."

For a second, Anna thought of a paint horse. But would Val go crazy over that? Then everything fell into place, and chagrin washed over her. "A cow."

"Seriously?"

"You might've crossed onto the Pasquales' property. Sometimes their cows knock down part of the fence and get loose."

"A *cow*." MJ's mouth twisted to hold back a laugh.

"Valentine has a phobia about them. I'd forgotten. When I first brought her here, I rode her all over the property to check how far it extended. But she wouldn't go near the Pasquales' pasture. Those big Holstein dairy cows freaked her out. She planted her feet and trembled until I turned her back toward home."

"So, now you believe me." MJ's voice turned frosty. "But you wouldn't have, if I didn't see the cow. If I just said I heard a rustling, or that I didn't have any idea what spooked her, you'd still think I was lying."

"MJ, you have to admit, you did lie to me about Stacey's mother driving you to the roadhouse."

"Stacey lied to *me* about that...Oh, what's the use!"

Anna crossed to the loveseat and put a hand on the girl's stiff shoulder. "I'm sorry I doubted you."

"You didn't even ask if *I* was all right. She scared the heck out of me."

"I apologize for that, too. Frankly, I could see you were okay, but I thought Val might be...I didn't know if we could save her." Anna hugged her niece, though she still felt resistance. "Anyway, we're both tired and stressed. Let's give the other horses their supper and then have our own, okay?"

MJ helped with feeding the animals, but during their own dinner she made little conversation. It wasn't exactly the silent treatment or a typical teenaged snit—she remained polite but cool. And as soon as they'd cleaned up the dishes, she retreated to her room and closed the door.

She's still ticked off at me, Anna thought. *Are only teenagers allowed to have emotional outbursts? Can't an adult "lose it" once in a while, too?*

Anna was about to knock on the girl's door when the main house/barn extension rang. She picked it up in the living room and heard Walt's voice.

"How're you guys doing?" he asked. "Julie was just here to check on one of our dogs, and she said you had a problem with your mare. Sounded pretty serious."

Anna didn't want to go into the misunderstanding between her and her niece, so she gave him the simplest explanation. "Cows are Kryptonite to Valentine—the one thing that spooks her. She bolted for home before MJ could stop her, which didn't help her breathing problem. She was in bad shape by the time the two of them got back here, so Julie had to do some triage."

"Oh man, that's rough. She's better now?"

"For the time being." Anna filled him in on the vet's directions for the future.

"Now I really feel bad that I couldn't go riding with MJ."

"You were committed to something at your church, right?"

"Not at the church, exactly. It was the annual picnic for our youth group, and I was on the committee."

She pictured him spending the summer day socializing with other church-going teens, all more acceptable to his mother than MJ would be. Well, that certainly was his prerogative. "Sounds fun."

"It was, but we did serious stuff, too. We played some sports, but we also broke up into groups to talk about different things. I led a discussion on community service."

Anna heard the pride in his voice. "Good for you."

"It could be good for you, too!" Walt said. "I told my bunch about your farm. How you're taking in horses that need help, and you want to do more but you're short-handed. Three or four of them want to volunteer. "

Now Anna understood his enthusiasm. "Gee, that sounds great, but—"

"These are kids the same ages as me and MJ, so they can do pretty hard work. And they either live on farms or at least know about horses, so they won't make dumb mistakes."

"Like getting kicked by the pony?"

He laughed. "Anyway, if you can use the help, these kids are psyched. And it'll be their community service project for our youth group."

The kid had the makings of a salesman, Anna thought. Or a preacher? "Walt, you're terrific. I'll bet you've had this idea up your sleeve for a while."

"Didn't want to say anything until I knew if it would work out. You're interested?"

"Sure. Bring them over whenever you want and I can at least show them around. Thanks!"

Only after Anna hung up did she notice MJ standing in the hall doorway, the dog again near her feet.

"That was Walt. I didn't see you, or I'd have asked if you wanted to talk to him."

"What was *he* calling about?"

Anna decided not to bring up Valentine's problems again, and cut to the good news. "First, he absolutely was at a function for his church youth group this afternoon."

The girl rolled her eyes. "I don't even care anymore."

"You might care about this—he's got some kids from the group who want to help us here on the farm. If that works out, maybe they also can handle some of the stall cleaning, manure moving and other boring jobs. Then you can do more interesting stuff, like exercising and training the horses."

MJ showed little reaction. "I guess it's good that you can get some more people to help out here, 'cause I've decided...I need a break."

Anna heard fatigue in her voice and sympathized. "Sure you do. You've been working hard for months, and—"

"I mean, I need to go home for a while. See my mom and my brother. Get some fresh clothes. And a haircut."

"Oh. Okay." This took Anna by surprise, but it was a reasonable request.

"I was just on the phone with Mom. She's picking me up tomorrow morning."

The girl's flat tone chilled Anna. "How long do you think—"

"I don't know."

With a shrug, MJ slouched back down the hall to her room. Delilah padded quietly after her.

CHAPTER THIRTY-THREE:

HOME

MJ parked her mother's big suitcase and her own canvas duffle in the foyer of their house. She'd been away less than three months, but it seemed longer. The two-story entry, with its glossy porcelain floor tiles and curving staircase, felt bigger than she remembered. And every surface gleamed, thanks to the housekeeper who came twice a week.

Her mother must have noticed MJ's bemused expression, because she chuckled. "Back to civilization, eh?"

"Yeah. Even central air."

Erika closed the front door behind them, sealing in the welcome chill. "I don't know how Anna can live like she does. When I think of the beautiful home she had with Richard...Such a shame he ruined it all for both of them." She started for the kitchen. "I need a cold drink after that long drive. Want a soda?"

"Have any iced tea?" When her mother threw her a quizzical glance, MJ explained, "I kind of got into it, at the farm. Anna doesn't buy much soda."

Erika found two cold bottles of diet tea and set one on the granite-topped island in front of her daughter. "No wonder you needed a break. Does Anna stomp the tea leaves herself?"

MJ grinned. "You're thinking of wine, Mom."

They seemed to be getting along better today than in a long while. Definitely better than that day in early June when Erika drove her out to the farm. *At least she has to admit that I stuck it out at Anna's for nearly the whole summer,* MJ thought.

Erika opened her own bottle and took a swig. "What do you want for lunch? I've got pasta salad, leftover takeout pizza..."

MJ groaned with pleasure. "Oh, the pizza! We can't get delivery, only frozen."

Erika took the box from the refrigerator and transferred half a pie, studded with mushrooms, onto a platter that she stuck in the microwave. "Not that I'd want you to undo all of your hard work." She scanned her daughter head-to-toe. "I'm sure you've been watching what you eat. You look great, honey!"

"Thanks." MJ didn't bother to explain that, for the most part, she'd eaten whatever she wanted, and as much as she wanted, while at the farm. Her efforts had not involved strenuous dieting—just, literally, hard work. With pride, she added, "None of the pants I brought to Anna's fit me anymore."

"Well, that's easily solved. Tomorrow we go to the mall. And I made an appointment for you at The Coolest Cut, like you wanted."

MJ ran her fingers through her now-shapeless dark mop. "Did you tell them it's an emergency?"

Her mother laughed. "I'm sure when they see you, they'll scramble to repair the damage. It's for two o'clock Monday, the soonest they had open."

"I was just kidding. No real rush."

Erika studied her, and looked about to speak when the microwave chimed. She set the platter on the island for them to split the half-pizza. For a minute they ate in comfortable silence.

"Not that I doubt you need clothes and a haircut," her mother said, "or missed me and your brother. But what really happened between you and Anna? You said she thought you rode the horse too fast, so that it got sick, and she was mad at you for that. But when I picked you up this morning, she seemed sorry to see you leave. So, who's really mad at who?"

MJ sighed. "I just needed to get away from there for a while. I feel like I'm always messing up. I mean, I was only there a little over a week when I got kicked by the pony."

"Well, her stupid pony kicking you wasn't your fault!"

"It kind of was—I got careless. Plus, Anna's still upset because I sort of sneaked out to the roadhouse. I guess when I got to the car and saw Stacey was driving, I could have refused to go."

Erika reached across to squeeze her daughter's hand. "Yes, you could have. But I'm sure at that point you were psyched about having a night out, and seeing the band, so it was hard to resist. At your age, I might've done the same thing."

"Really?" MJ actually didn't have much trouble picturing that.

"Anna's being over-conscientious because she doesn't want you to get in trouble, or get hurt, on her watch. And maybe because she never had kids of her own."

MJ remembered her aunt's explosion over Valentine's coughing attack. Never before had she heard that nasty edge in Anna's voice, and she never wanted to hear it again. "Maybe that's a good thing!"

A sharp inhale made her look up; Erika wore a pained expression. "Oh, MJ. Don't ever, *ever* say that to her."

"I wouldn't, but...why?"

Her mother glanced away, as if trying to decide whether to explain. The big digital clock on the stove gave her an out. "Yikes, I almost forgot! I have to pick up Carl from his soccer game." She hopped down from the counter stool and grabbed her purse. "You'll be okay here 'til I get back?"

"Guess so. I did grow up here."

"Smartass. I've got a Southwest pasta salad for dinner, with lime and avocado, from Whole Foods. Oh, and tomorrow night Burt's taking us all to dinner at Villa Antonella. He wants to hear all about your adventures this summer."

Erika was out the door before MJ could mutter, "Yeah, I'll bet."

Left alone in the echoing house, she hauled her bags upstairs. Already she missed Delilah's cheerful, adoring presence to keep her company. *I could at least bitch to her about having to go out to dinner with my mom's new boyfriend.*

In her bedroom, MJ stepped into another time warp. She barely remembered faux-painting these walls hot pink two years ago, and replacing her childhood furniture with this Victorian-style, all-black set. She'd even changed out the ceiling light fixture for a chandelier draped with black beads, and the shelf above her computer desk displayed a collection of skull and gargoyle knickknacks.

At the time, her mother had bemoaned this orgy of bad taste, while her dad laughed it off. MJ had overheard him telling Erika it was just a phase their daughter would outgrow. Maybe he'd been right, MJ thought now, and maybe she already had outgrown it. Since his death, the skulls and other gloomy touches didn't feel like so much fun anymore.

What bothered her more, though, were two other reminders of her former life. An electronic frame on her desk featured a color selfie of her with Stacey, cheek-to-cheek and grinning. And on the wall next to her bed hung a RaserzEdge poster, the band's logo printed large above the date of one of their school concerts.

MJ picked up the frame and punched a series of buttons to delete the photo from its internal memory. Then she ripped the poster free of its thumbtacks, rolled it up and stuffed it into her wire-mesh wastebasket.

Those were two ghosts from her recent past that she didn't intend to live with for another second.

MJ had met Burt Preston once before, when he'd come to pick her mother up for a date. She thought she'd resented him then, but tonight it was worse. This time he sat across the table from her and Carl, at Erika's side. *Where Dad should have been.*

Not that Burt had anything else in common with her late father. He was tall, sandy-haired, handsome, well-dressed, and looked like he worked out. Her dad had been medium-height, with dark hair and a roundish face—like MJ's—and visited the bakery more than the gym. She knew Burt was a real estate developer, and Erika had met him through one of her co-workers at *Good Life*.

Maybe he played sports, too. The way he chatted with Carl about soccer sounded like Burt knew something about the game, and even about her brother's skills on the field.

Great, let him bond with Carl. I don't care how good-looking or successful this guy is, he's never going to replace our dad.

His full name had been Martin Joel Klein, and because of that she'd been named Martha Joan. When she was little her parents tended to call her Marty, since her father rarely went by that nickname. At about age thirteen, though, she began to insist on "MJ." Much later, in therapy, she remembered getting the idea from her father's monogram, MJK, on the leather portfolio he carried to work.

After his death, she'd sneaked out—with a fake ID supplied by Stacey—and had her upper arm tattooed with the same three initials, framed by a thorny heart. MJ hadn't realized that it might look like an ego trip instead of a tribute to her father. Erika understood, though, which was why she hadn't yelled about it too much.

Tonight Burt and Erika conferred over the wine list, their heads almost touching in a cozy way that killed MJ's appetite. When the waiter came, Burt ordered something in what she figured was correct Italian pronunciation, though he seemed to lay it on thick.

MJ tried to hide behind the huge, hard-cover menu. All the names of the dishes were in Italian. The small print did explain what was in them, but tonight nothing appealed to her.

"So, MJ," Burt began in a positive tone, "your mom says you're interning this summer at your aunt's...riding stable?"

She wondered if Erika had added that spin or if Burt had just misunderstood. "It's a horse rescue farm."

His eyes clouded with confusion. "What's that mean? You rescue horses—from what?"

MJ thought for a second. "People."

Next to her, Carl snickered. Her mother, across from them, told her, "MJ, don't be flip."

She hadn't meant to be, and shrugged. "A lot of people who have horses don't treat them very well. They abuse or neglect them. If a horse gets lame or sick, or the person just can't afford to keep it, they'll send it to auction."

Burt tilted his head the way Delilah sometimes did, MJ thought, only on him it was less appealing. "What's so bad about that? Sounds like a way to get some of their money back."

"A lot of the bidders are killer buyers, who pick up horses

cheap for the slaughterhouses. Aunt Anna's horse, who won ribbons at a lot of shows, went to an auction and ended up going to slaughter. She didn't find out until it was too late and she was really upset. That's why she started the farm."

Erika closed her eyes and waved a French-manicured hand. "Please, this is not dinner table conversation."

"He asked," MJ said.

The waiter came back with the wine and, as he was pouring, Burt's cell phone buzzed. He exchanged a few businesslike words with someone before pocketing it again. Her father, MJ recalled, had never taken calls during dinner, whether they were eating out or at home.

As if in imitation, Carl pulled out his own cell. Erika warned, "Not at the table."

"I just want to show Burt the website MJ designed for the farm." He passed his phone over.

Burt studied it for a few minutes, fingers brushing the screen to browse through the links, then looked at MJ again. "You did this?"

"Anna already had a basic site set up. I just added a few bells and whistles."

"She shot that video of the gray horse and the pony," Carl added.

MJ saw a chance to get back to her original point. "The gray is Murphy. Isn't he beautiful? He was a racehorse but he stopped wanting to run. He would've gone to slaughter if Anna hadn't taken him. Now she's retraining him to be a jumper."

"Very nice design work." Burt handed the phone back to Carl.

The waiter stopped by again, ready to take their orders, but Burt told him everyone was still deciding. MJ figured she'd better make up her mind, appetite or not.

"I can see why finding homes for those horses would be a problem," Burt went on, while scanning his own menu. "Around here, I see horse farms for sale all the time. My company bought a couple, just last year, to build luxury estates."

Erika spoke up. "Burt's building Fox Chase, that big community we passed on the highway tonight. He took me through one of the model homes, and they're amazing."

"In the old days," Burt said, "people needed horses to get around, pull carts and plow fields. Now, what are they used for? Racing, but the tracks are struggling to survive because nobody goes. And horse shows, I guess."

"Anna never won much money, for all her ribbons," Erika agreed.

"That's my point. Probably not many horses earn enough to pay for their own oats. I guess people still ride for fun, but it must be an expensive hobby." He smiled at MJ. "I'd think kids of your generation are too busy with their electronics, and with other sports, to be much interested in horseback riding."

MJ had to admit, grudgingly, that a lot of what Burt said was true. He was missing something important, though, and she struggled to express it. "It's not like any other hobby or sport. You're on this big animal that doesn't speak your language, but you communicate without words. Once you can ride pretty well, it's like the two of you are one creature. On a trail ride, for instance, you're in the horse's head. You see the woods, feel the breeze, and hear the sounds the way he does." Getting worked up again, the way she had at the roadhouse, she steadied her emotions. "You might be right, that not so many people my age ride horses. But maybe they should. It gets you back to nature."

She wasn't sure she'd converted Burt, but at least he took awhile to respond. "Well, MJ, the horses are lucky they have people like you and your aunt to go to bat for them."

The waiter came again. MJ ordered kale lasagna, Erika a salmon-pesto dish, and Carl chicken cacciatore.

Burt said, "And I'll have the *vitello scallopini.*"

While they handed back their menus, Carl sent MJ a sly look. Even though the girl didn't return it, their mother frowned.

Burt also noticed. "What? Oh, that's right, there's some problem with veal, too, isn't there?"

"Don't!" Erika begged him.

The calves are taken from their mothers right after birth, MJ thought. *Shut up in small crates so they never go outside and get too weak to stand, all to make the meat tender. Then they're*

233

killed when they're just a few months old.

Definitely not "dinner table conversation."

Burt might've had a cocktail or two even before he'd started on the wine. For whatever reason, he was in a "make my day" frame of mind.

"No," he told Erika, "I can see your daughter has some strong opinions, and she seems very well-informed. Tell me, MJ, what's wrong with eating veal?"

CHAPTER THIRTY-FOUR:

MENDING FENCES

Anna centered the Havana-brown jump saddle, which gleamed like new and smelled of polish, on top of the white fleece pad, then fastened the girth around Murphy's rib cage. He'd put on some healthy weight since coming to her farm, partly because he'd calmed down from his racetrack days.

She'd just buckled the throat latch on the dark brown bridle when Josh strode into the barn, a few minutes late.

A wide grin split his sun-weathered face. "Doesn't our boy look professional today!"

"It's Duke's show tack," Anna told him. "I think it suits him, don't you?"

"Very well—sets off his dapples. I'm glad to see you're thinking ahead. How'd things go last weekend?"

Anna had been dreading that question. "We didn't get to the 'practice' show, I'm afraid. Clint wasn't free to come with me, and MJ left unexpectedly, so I had no one to watch the farm."

Josh narrowed his eyes, as if she might be making excuses. "Left 'unexpectedly'?"

"We had an argument." Briefly, Anna explained. "Now she's mad because she feels like I accused her of hurting Valentine."

She led the gray horse from the barn, with Josh on the other side. The opaque, white sky threatened rain soon, and meanwhile blanketed them with humidity. It was overcast enough that Josh had pocketed his sunglasses.

He gave her a leg up, and walked with her and Murphy up to

the practice field.

"Funny thing about horses," he said. "They bring out strong feelings in people. For such big animals, they're pretty fragile, and of course they're expensive to keep. So, we get protective of them, like they're somewhere between pets and children. I've never known a stable that didn't have occasional blowups between the management and the instructors or the boarders over how the horses were being trained or taken care of."

Anna admitted she'd observed the same thing. "When I saw Val suffering, I did get a bit hysterical. But MJ also is young and a little spoiled. This is the first 'job' she's ever had. She doesn't realize that sometimes you screw up and the boss snarls at you. At least I apologized, which is more than most of my bosses ever did."

"Is she coming back?"

"I'm getting a little worried about that. Last I heard from my sister, they made plans to go clothes shopping and to the beauty salon. MJ could decide she's tired of roughing it out here."

Josh smiled with a twist. "'How you gonna keep 'em down on the farm, after they've seen the mall'? Got to be hard for you, though, if you're back to doing everything by yourself."

"Walt Patterson found me a couple new volunteers who pitched in the last few days. One of them used the riding mower on the back field, and they helped me carry all the jumps up there. So, it's set up the way you wanted, or as close as I could manage."

When they got there, Josh surveyed the results. Anna and her helpers had built eight hurdles; she'd tried to pace out the correct distances between the obstacles and to angle them as Josh had instructed by email. The course was an easy one, most of the jumps only two feet high.

He nodded approval. "Okay, warm him up, then take them in the order I gave you."

Anna trotted and then cantered Murphy around the whole field. Their practice sessions over the past week had helped them get more in sync. She was even starting to enjoy that surge of raw power when the gray picked up speed. Duke, for all his size, had an easy, measured way of going that she could collect whenever she wanted. Murphy's strides were so long and swift that she needed to keep her wits about her, or he'd arrive at a jump too soon.

Anna rose in a two-point seat, gripping with just her lower legs, and sent him toward the first hurdle—a rising oxer with two crossbars, the second slightly higher. Murphy pricked his ears and gunned his engines without even a nudge from her legs. When he rose, she reached her hands forward to let him stretch his neck. As he landed, she fought the urge to collect him too quickly, and just used her weight to steer him. He made a wide arc but headed eagerly toward the next, a stack of striped rails.

The low jumps posed no real challenges and he skipped over them with horsey glee. He also changed leads at the far end of the field like a pro. Luckily, Anna thought, that was part of a racehorse's basic training. She began to recapture the excitement of competing on Duke, the thrill of moving in harmony with a talented mount.

She had made the next-to-last hurdle a few inches higher than the rest, about two-foot-four. It woke Murphy up a little and he gave it a more powerful spring. Then he cruised easily over the last upright and did his own victory lap around the fenceline. She gave him his head as a reward, something she'd been afraid to do just a week earlier.

They trotted back to the gate and found Josh grinning. "Wasn't taking any chances with the triple-bar, was he? I think he cleared it by an extra six inches."

Anna scratched the crest of her horse's neck. "He can do more, that's for sure."

"You okay? You look flushed. I know it's a muggy day..."

"I'm fine." Despite her protest, she felt tears rising. "I just... didn't realize how much I've missed this. I've exercised the other horses, but it's been so long since I've *really* ridden."

Josh placed his broad hand over hers, on the front of the saddle. There was nothing flirtatious, just the silent reassurance that he understood and shared her passion. Anna found that more moving than any overt come-on.

Then he withdrew his touch, with the air of someone used to keeping a professional distance. "Sounds like you're ready to go back in the ring. Glad to hear it—I found you a show for the middle of August. The Green Jumper class has fences two-foot-three to two-six. I think he can handle that, don't you?"

"Easily." She rode back to the barn, with Josh on foot, the same as they had come. "We haven't practiced for time at all, though."

"Well, he's got speed, and you already know how to ride for it. He's the 'green' one, not you. But don't make yourself crazy over that part, Anna. Just get him around clear, if you can." The trainer paused. "I told you before, I have somebody who might be interested in adopting him. She'll be coming to the August show. She won't expect Murphy to be perfect, but she does want to see if he has talent and can behave under pressure."

"'She'?" Anna thought of the female voice on Josh's videos.

"Might as well play it safe—we know Murph is partial to women. She's a serious jump rider and she's looking for a young horse to bring along. This could be his shot at a real future."

In the barnyard, Anna vaulted off. "Do you think that's best for him? I do want to find him a home, but if someone is planning to campaign him as a jumper, that's a lot of pressure. Can he handle it?"

"Only one way to find out." Josh's gray eyes turned flinty. "You've *got* to trailer him to that show this weekend. It's your last chance before August to see how he handles a mob scene. If your friend Clint can't go along, bring Walt or one of his helpers. Promise me?"

Anna swallowed hard, but knew he was right. "I promise."

Driving MJ to the hair salon on Tuesday, her mother still had not gotten over the fiasco of Saturday's dinner at the restaurant.

"You know I like Burt," she fumed. "Why did you have to get into all that gross talk about horses going to slaughter and crippled baby calves in crates? I mean, right *after* he ordered a veal dish?"

MJ shrugged, unwilling to accept the blame. "He wanted to know. Whad'ya expect me to do, lie?"

"I expected you to make polite conversation, like a normal

person! It's like you went out of your way to ruin a nice evening. I apologized to him, but you should, too."

"No way. I didn't do anything wrong." *So, he hardly touched his* vitello *after it came. Maybe I made him think, for a change.*

"Martha Joan, you're almost eighteen years old. You're not a child anymore. You can't keep acting out and expecting other people to make excuses for you." Turning onto the busy main street of their town, Erika slowed to thread her way between the other SUVs and luxury sedans. "I thought the whole purpose of spending summer on the farm was so you could figure out what you want to do with your life."

"Not the *whole* purpose," MJ objected. "And maybe I still haven't figured it out."

Erika steered into a pay parking lot, as crowded as the street, and searched for a space. "Maybe you should go back to seeing Dr. Mayer."

MJ groaned, remembering her three boring sessions with that old, bald guy who kept asking her how stuff made her feel. "I don't need a shrink. I'm not crazy."

"Of course you aren't. But sometimes after people go through a...shock, it's hard for them to get their life back on track without help." Her mother's tone mellowed. "Just because you got rejected by a couple of colleges, it isn't the end of the world. We'll go back over the catalogs and find some that aren't so...well, choosy. There are online classes you can take to boost your grades, so schools will be more likely to accept you."

MJ hated the thought of going back to all that studying, though she supposed she'd have to at some point. "Maybe."

Her mother seized on this ray of hope. "Tell you what. Find a college, get accepted, and you can have my little red hatchback. Carl's got his eye on it, but he won't be driving for a couple more years. And if you commute, you'll need a car."

While MJ contemplated this bribe, her phone rang. She read Anna's number on the screen. *Great—the last thing I need right now is two "moms" nagging me.* She silenced it.

Erika beat another driver into one of the scarce parking spaces. In fact, there was no hurry, MJ thought, since she was a few minutes early for her hair appointment. When the two of them got out of the car and started walking down the long block to the salon, she changed the subject.

"A couple days ago, when I said maybe it was good that Anna never had children, you got upset and told me never to mention that to her. Why?"

Her mother paused, as if she didn't want to have this conversation on a busy suburban sidewalk. Up ahead, a white wrought-iron bench stood empty in front of an antiques shop. Erika led her daughter to it, and they sat.

"I don't suppose it's any deep, dark secret," she began, quietly, "but I don't know if Anna ever told anyone except me... and of course, Richard. When she had that accident at the horse show, she was about two months pregnant. In the hospital, she lost the baby."

MJ sat back in shock. "Oh, wow." She remembered her aunt's fall, the end of one pole smacking her in the stomach. She'd never questioned why Anna spent a couple of days in the hospital recovering, and hadn't suspected such a tragic complication.

"Of course, right afterward Richard was arrested," Erika continued. "That was the first Anna even heard about the crooked stuff he'd been up to. Then came the legal battles, the divorce, selling their house, Anna giving up her job..."

"Her whole life fell apart, didn't it?"

Erika nodded. "All in about a year's time. I guess it's no wonder she went a little nutty, going off to live by herself in the country and save broken-down horses."

In Anna's place, I might have done the same thing, MJ thought. *Heck, with my life going down the tubes, I did do the same thing!* "She could still have another kid, though, couldn't she?"

"Maybe not. Things can happen when a woman loses a baby that way. Anyhow, she won't meet anyone suitable, stuck out in the middle of nowhere." With a sad half-smile, Erika checked her new Cartier tank watch, which MJ knew was a gift from Burt. "If that answers your questions, we'd better get to your appointment."

240

It seemed far more than three months, to MJ, since her last visit to The Coolest Cut. The smell of hair chemicals, the background of alt-rock music, and the many reflective surfaces aroused in her the usual blend of excitement and self-consciousness.

Erika took a seat in the waiting area and opened a copy of *Elle*. As a fashion editor, she seemed totally at ease in places like this. MJ, on the other hand, had come to associate them with high hopes never quite fulfilled. Too many mirrors, and she didn't much like what she saw in them.

But maybe some of that was because I kept trying to impress Bobby, and to be the kind of girl he'd want to be seen with. Maybe it'll be easier, now that I don't care any more.

Her usual stylist, Alicia, gave her a big hello and a hug. She was a good advertisement for her craft, her bright-orange hair a short, sleek cap and her makeup heavily but expertly applied. She complimented MJ on her weight loss—"You got cheekbones, girl!"—and they both joked about how long and messy the teen's locks had grown.

"I should be in an eighties heavy-metal band," MJ said.

"Not quite that bad. Just let me finish the color on my last client. Have a seat by your mom and I'll be with you in a flash."

MJ settled into a beige padded-leather chair that cradled her like the palm of a giant hand. She didn't feel like looking through any of the fashion magazines, filled with crazy clothes she couldn't imagine anyone wearing in the real world. She stole glances at the other customers, with their heads in progress, and tried to guess what they'd look like when finished.

Then she remembered Anna's phone call. *I should check her message—it might be important.* Guilt shot through MJ at the idea that something might have gone wrong at the farm in her absence.

At least Anna didn't sound upset. "Hope you're having a good time at home and enjoying your break. I just want to say again how sorry I am that I accused you of mistreating Valentine. I was so worried, I wasn't thinking straight! I should've known you wouldn't be so irresponsible, and I just hope you'll forgive me."

Anna took a breath, on the recording, as if to let that message sink in. "Anyway, I've got some exciting news...and a problem. Lillian Gale called—y'know, the rich lady I met at the fundraiser? She wants to visit the farm this Saturday. Only problem is, I absolutely have to take Murphy to a show that day, to see how he handles all the excitement. Josh wants us to enter one for real next month."

Man, that's right. She was supposed to take him to one of those "practice" shows last weekend. I guess she had to skip it because I wasn't there.

"I don't know what your plans are for coming back," Anna went on, "but can you at least help me out this Saturday? I could ask Walt or one of his friends to watch the place, but they can't show Lillian around. They don't know the horses or the background of the farm like you do. Besides, Delilah misses you. Give me a call, please."

The recording ended and MJ gazed down at the silent phone. Now she felt like a jerk for messing up Murphy's chance to get used to a horse-show environment, and not even giving Anna any idea when she might return. *Of course, I didn't know, myself.*

"MJ." Her mother tapped her arm. Alicia was waving her over.

Once her hair was washed, the girl sat at the stylist's station, a crinkly silver cape fastened around her neck. "Are we doing color today?" Alicia asked.

MJ frowned into the full-length, black-framed mirror and recalled how bad her green streaks had looked growing out. "I think I'm over that. Just a cut."

"The short spikes again?"

"I dunno." She needed gel to make that work, which got messy with the barnyard dust. "Maybe just something that's easy to deal with."

"How about a short, layered bob with side bangs? I can still make it a little edgy."

"Go for it."

The stylist began parting MJ's wet hair into precise sections. "Oh, and I'm supposed to tell you that there's a special today on manicures. A full set of wraps is half price. Any interest?"

The girl glanced down at her hands with their short, unpolished nails. After a few days at home, she finally had been able to scrub the last traces of grime from the nailbeds. She imagined snapping off a set of expensive, artificial tips the first time she tried to swing a manure fork or tighten a girth.

"Sorry, they wouldn't do me much good." She smiled into the mirror. "I work on a horse farm."

CHAPTER THIRTY-FIVE:

BARN MANAGER

Anna had almost persuaded Murphy to put his left forefoot on the ramp leading into the trailer—with less of the old drama—when the big cream-color SUV came jouncing down the driveway and jerked to a dusty stop in the barnyard. The Thoroughbred sprang backward, almost stepping on Clint, and the lead rope ripped through Anna's hands, burning her palms.

"Easy, boy!" she soothed. At least the horse quieted more quickly than he would have in the past. And she couldn't feel anything but happy to have her niece back on the job. She'd asked only for weekend help, but MJ had put no time limit on her return.

Erika slid out of the driver's side of her vehicle, oblivious to the disturbance she'd created. "Hi, Sis. Sorry we're a little late."

Delilah charged out of the barn and MJ squatted to cuddle the mongrel. Erika's expression showed that, although she'd never be fond of dogs, she could see she'd lost this round.

Anna hugged her niece. "Cute haircut!"

"Yes, isn't it?" Erika sounded relieved by her daughter's transformation.

MJ said, "I was afraid you guys might've left by now."

"Oh, not much chance of that." Anna fed Murphy another piece of carrot—she'd been bribing him all morning. "Good thing we don't have to be at this show at any particular time."

She introduced her sister to Clint, who explained. "We spent good half-hour just wrappin' this boy's legs, and the last fifteen minutes tryin' to get him in the trailer."

MJ encouraged both her mother and the dog to stay out from underfoot while Anna and Clint finally loaded Murphy. They let him stand on the trailer for while before fastening the divider. Noticing he was enclosed, the gray whinnied to his friends in the paddocks, but beyond that didn't rebel.

Anna and Clint fist-bumped.

Clint latched the trailer's back doors. "I think Murph likes your rig better than mine."

Anna thought the same thing. Her larger, slant-load model should give the horse a more comfortable trip, too, even though they weren't traveling far. "We ought to get going while our luck holds out."

Clint climbed into the passenger side of the truck cab, while Anna gave her niece a few last-minute instructions.

"Mrs. Gale is due about eleven," she told MJ.

"Anything I can do?" Erika asked, cheerily. "That doesn't involve shoveling manure?"

Anna assessed her sister's turnout, a snug yoga T-shirt and leggings with new-looking sneakers. Aware of sounding like MJ, she asked, "Seriously?"

"Yep, I'm here to serve today. After all, I introduced you to Lillian, so I figure I can be the liaison. Besides, I'm also a board member, aren't I?"

"You are, indeed." Anna didn't have time, though, to think of how Erika might be useful around the farm without putting herself in harm's way. "Until Lillian gets here, MJ can tell you what to do... and not to do. She's now my barn manager."

Mother and daughter exchanged surprised glances. Then a few sudden, metallic booms made Erika jump back from the trailer.

"Natives are getting restless, we'd better roll." Anna jumped behind the wheel of the truck. When she started the engine, Delilah darted back to MJ's side.

"Good luck," the girl called out.

Pulling away, Anna overheard her sister ask, "Why? I thought they weren't competing today."

Anna shook her head with a smile. At least today she could concentrate on dealing with Murphy, confident that she'd left the farm in experienced, capable hands.

MJ's.

○✕✕✕○

She turned up a gravel road and followed hand-printed signs that read "Horse Show Today." She drove slowly to avoid crowding the occasional person in breeches and boots who was riding or leading a mount. Most were young and female. Girls dominated English riding sports to such a degree that Anna almost felt sorry for the rare boy among them—his pals probably questioned his masculinity.

Well, it didn't hurt Josh Buchanan, did it? He makes a good living, and from what Julie says he also has more than enough offers of female companionship. Then Anna shook off such distracting thoughts. At present, she needed to focus on other things.

In an open field opposite the riding stable, she found maybe two dozen horse trailers parked every which way. Even driving around them posed a challenge.

"How about next to that big silver one?" Clint suggested. "We oughta fit there."

"Yeah, but just. I want to leave enough room to back our boy out safely. Remember when you first brought him to my farm?"

He responded with a wary laugh. "How could I forget? My head's still a funny shape from bein' squashed in that emergency door."

Anna parked in an open area well away from the serious competitors. The slanted partition of this trailer left a space next to Murphy, so she stepped inside and grasped his lead line; Clint swung open the divider and the horse backed out. They tied him to the trailer's hitching ring, with enough slack for him to graze and look around.

Clint told Anna, "I'll keep an eye on him while you go check in."

She crossed the parking area to the stable yard and found the registration tent. There, she paid a nominal "ring free" and got a wearable number that would let her use the schooling area with the day's competitors.

Wending her way back among the trailers, Anna could spot the entries of limited means. Their rigs resembled her own, and a harried mom or dad helped a pre-teen kid in breeches and a polo shirt locate her hardhat and dust off her boots. Their mounts looked crossbred with less-than-ideal conformation—though, in her time, Anna had seen some of those perform pretty darn well. But here and there, she passed a more luxurious, multi-horse trailer where a professional trainer barked instructions to more seasoned riders. Tethered to these rigs stood tall, elegant Thoroughbreds or warmbloods, their coats burnished and manes and tails expertly trimmed or braided.

When she reached her own trailer, where the gray horse still stood, Anna told Clint, "I'll lunge him first."

"Out here?"

"Not much choice." She realized it wasn't ideal—she'd always lunged Murphy in an enclosed space before. But with the practice rings occupied by real entries, she'd have to do it in the open.

She followed her usual routine of leading him around in a large circle first, then playing out the line while she moved to the center. As soon as Murphy had his head he cantered, and she decided not to correct him as long as he didn't get too crazy. Before long, she was able to bring him down to an easy trot. When she tried to change his direction, though, he resisted as in the old days.

Clint noticed. "You want the lunge whip?"

He got it from the trailer and, carrying it upright, started toward Anna.

Murphy pointed his ears, snorted and backed several steps. Then he reared, ripping the line through Anna's gloved hands and pawing the sky.

Her heart stopped. She imagined herself clinging to his back.

No time to jump off before—

"Whoa, son, whoa." Dropping the whip, Clint grabbed the line just in front of Anna's hands, to help her bring the horse down. He kept his voice low and easy. "Chill out, man. Nobody gonna beat on you."

The gray settled, but he still eyed the whip where it lay on the ground.

"God, I thought he was over that," Anna gasped, heart still pounding. "I carry a lunge whip at home, in the round pen, and he doesn't freak out that way."

"Ah, but you're a lady," Clint reminded her. "It was me carrying it that got him upset. Some dude must've whupped him, back at the track."

This notion helped Anna regard the big Thoroughbred with more sympathy than fear. After that, she did get him to circle clockwise a few times, by just pointing the whip low.

"I'm going to lead him around the place," she told Clint. "Can you walk on the other side, just in case?"

As they strolled toward the show grounds, Anna tried to see the spectacle through Murphy's eyes. He'd been around unfamiliar horses and people at racetracks, but probably not so many trailers. He'd gotten used to Delilah, but a yappy Jack Russell still might set him off. He walked with head high, eyes wide, and nostrils working as he took in the kaleidoscope of new sights, sounds, and smells. Anna wished she could just appreciate his sense of excitement, without worrying that he might do something crazy.

"Whad'ya think, Murph?" she asked him, with a neck-pat. "Your first horse show!"

"Mine, too," Clint noted.

"Is it really?"

"Sure. Spent all my time at tracks and at the auctions. Some horses I rescued might've gone on to horse shows, I guess, but I never seen 'em."

"Well, you'll come to Murphy's debut next month! Put it on your calendar." The reminder that this goal meant something not just to her, MJ, and Josh, but also to Clint, bolstered Anna's determination.

Near the stable yard, a little girl trotted by on a placid chestnut pony and Murphy pricked his ears. Anna tensed, but the big gray just looked intrigued. *Probably reminds him of Patches.*

Josh's desensitizing techniques no doubt helped the horse tolerate the striped canopy fluttering over the refreshment stand.

248

But when a harried-looking woman in   show clothes bounded out of a Port-a-John, letting the door squeal and slam behind her, Murphy leaped sideways. Clint's quick reflexes just saved him from being stepped on, and he called the woman a name under his breath. Anna recalled that, at his age, he didn't need any more Thoroughbreds crashing into him.

They stopped just outside one of the jumper rings and wiped their brows.

"Who'd have thought just walking a horse around show grounds could be such hard work?" Anna tugged a few bills from the hip pocked of her breeches and handed them to Clint. "I'll stay here for awhile so he can watch the others jump. Can you grab us some water?"

Just a short break, she thought, as her helper headed off. *Then I'll tack up and try riding in the warm-up ring with the real entries. That'll be the acid test—"where the rubber meets the road."*

Or where the seat of my pants meets the ground?

CHAPTER THIRTY-SIX:

TEAMWORK

MJ cheerfully shoveled a few balls of fresh manure from the barn aisle into a wheelbarrow, while Erika stood by holding her nose. "And to think I always had to nag you, at home, to clean up your room."

The girl was tempted to make her mother push the load all the way across the yard and empty it into the big pile out back. But she figured she had enough other ways to test Erika's mettle this morning.

Returning with the wheelbarrow empty, MJ announced, "Okay, before the rich lady gets here, we need to groom the horses. I'll work on Dash, and you can do Valentine."

Erika cast a worried gaze toward the occupied paddocks. "Isn't she the one that freaked out and ran away with you?"

"Yeah, but only because she's scared of cows. We don't have cows on this farm, so you should be fine."

MJ led the mare into the barn, parked her on cross-ties, and handed her mother a kind of oval scrub brush with rubber teeth. "This is a currycomb. Just use it on her body, but not her face, legs or belly, and not too hard. Rub in circles like this to bring out the dirt." She demonstrated. "After that, go over her with the body brush. It's softer, so you can also use it on her face and legs. Follow the grain of her coat with that."

"Looks like the kind of brush they use to shine men's shoes."

"Well, it'll also shine up Valentine. Though her coat's always kind of dull, poor thing, because of the heaves." MJ reflected that, at least on her new medicine, the mare was doing better.

Delilah, rebuffed by Erika more than once, watched the human drama while sprawled in a shady corner of the barn. The grooming process eventually finished, they took the horses back out to the main paddock. MJ insisted that her mother also lead Val. "Always walk on a horse's left side."

"Yes, boss!" came the huffy reply. But before turning the mare loose, Erika stroked her long face and whispered, "Thanks for putting up with me. You're a good sport."

MJ hid a smile. Valentine had melted another heart.

They'd just refilled the water trough in the paddock when a big, shiny black sedan cruised into the barnyard. Intimidated, MJ suddenly was grateful for her mother's presence. After all, Erika dealt with New Jersey's rich and famous for a living.

A tall, powerfully built man in a snow-white polo shirt, dark jeans and a billed cap emerged from the driver's side. He opened the rear door and offered his hand to Lillian Gale. Once out of the car, though, she didn't appear to need much help. Her wavy silver hair and fine wrinkles showed her age, but in slim, faded jeans and a fitted blue T-shirt, she had the figure and posture of a much younger woman. She crossed the barnyard with an athletic step.

MJ and Erika removed their work gloves to shake hands with her, and the girl watched her mother shift into full social-butterfly mode. "Lillian, lovely to see you again! I can't tell you how we appreciate you taking the time to come all the way out here."

"No trouble. It's a pretty drive." The visitor grinned at Erika's disheveled appearance. "I see they put you to work today."

"My daughter. And she's an ogre of a boss."

MJ winked. "I learned from Anna."

"My sister was terribly sorry she couldn't be here to greet you," Erika went on. "She had to take one of the horses to a show. Something about getting him used to the routine."

MJ jumped in to explain all about Murphy, his re-education as a jumper and their goal of putting him in his first show by the end of the month.

Lillian pursed her lips. "Pretty ambitious. I hope your trainer isn't rushing him."

MJ knew her aunt had the same concerns. "Josh said somebody might be interesting in adopting Murphy if he does well, so Anna's giving it her best shot."

Fanning herself with one hand, Erika suggested, "Lillian, we can talk up on the porch, if you'd like some iced tea."

"Thank you, maybe later. First I'd like to see the horses and your barn." Wearing sensible, low boots, Lillian started for the main paddock.

Meanwhile, Delilah trotted out from the barn, tail wagging. Lillian crouched to pet her and endure a few wet kisses.

I'd like this lady even if she didn't have big bucks, MJ thought.

She also noticed that the driver now leaned against the side of the car, beefy arms folded, and watched over Lillian. Even his dark, wrap-around shades suggested to MJ that he was more than just a chauffeur. He looked ready to protect their guest from any possible threat that might arise.

Lillian rested her hand on the paddock gate. "Okay if I go in?"

"Sure." MJ accompanied her to make introductions. "This is Valentine. She was the first horse Anna adopted. Did she ever tell you that story?" When their guest shook her head, MJ related the bittersweet tale of how her aunt got to the auction barn too late to save Duke, but came home with the mare, instead. "That's how Anna decided to start this place."

The older woman's clear blue eyes radiated empathy. She reached into her well-worn Coach purse and pulled out a bag of peppermints. "Can Valentine have one of these?"

Before MJ could answer, the mare stretched her nose forward, sniffing, and the two women laughed. Lillian tore the plastic off and the mare lipped up the candy politely.

Dash and Patches soon ambled over to join the party. MJ told Lillian what she knew about the buckskin's abusive background. "Dash already has a sponsor, a guy who saw his picture on the web and is paying for his upkeep."

Lillian patted both animals, at ease even when Dash nuzzled her leather shoulderbag in search of more candies. Then she turned to beam at Patches. "I have to confess, this is the one I've most looked forward to meeting."

That surprised MJ, because the pony with the missing eye didn't attract many fans. "Patches?"

"I saw her on the website, chasing Murphy around the field. It was the loveliest thing, watching them play together."

Erika told her, from beyond the fence, "MJ shot that video. She did a lot of work on the website."

Lillian eyed the girl with greater respect. "Did you? You have kept busy out here this summer." She went back to ruffling the Shetland's thick, wiry mane, staying where the animal could see her.

"My aunt found Patches at an auction, too." MJ told how the pony had stumbled coming into the ring and the "killers" had scoffed that she didn't have enough meat on her to be worth buying. "Our vet treated her for some problems and now she's in pretty good shape. She might never get adopted, but that's okay, because she and Murphy are best buds."

Lillian fed Patches the three remaining peppermints. "She reminds me of my first pony, Charley. He was brown-and-white, too, just a bit taller. Tossed me a couple of times in the beginning, but later on we'd go tearing around my parents' farm, jumping everything that got in our way. My father would say I was going to break my neck, but it was so much fun."

"He sounds great." MJ smiled.

As the older woman stroked Patches, a catch came into her voice. "After he got old, and I got too big to ride him anymore, I came home from school one day and he was just...gone. My folks told me they sent him to a retirement farm. Of course, I figured out later that's what adults tell kids when they put an animal down. I just hope they euthanized Charley. I'd hate to think of *him* ending up at one of those horrible auctions."

MJ could identify; she still wondered about her favorite pony from summer camp. "Even if he did, maybe somebody like Anna came along and rescued him."

Lillian shook her head sadly. "I doubt it. There weren't many farms like this around back in those days. I see a lot more now, but we also need them more now."

"That's what Anna figures." MJ decided it wouldn't hurt to

nudge their guest back around to the idea of making a donation.

Out of peppermints, the little woman stuffed the empty plastic bag into her purse. "Maybe now you can show me around the barn? Then I might be ready for that iced tea."

Erika let them out of the paddock gate. "It's almost lunchtime. I can make us sandwiches, too."

"Oh, no, I don't want to put you out."

"It's no trouble. By the time we're done, maybe Anna will be back. She said she'd only be gone a couple hours."

MJ wondered how things were going at the horse show. She knew it was important for her to be taking Lillian around the farm, and that Clint was a better person to help her aunt handle an ex-racehorse in such a stressful situation. But she still wished she could be there to see how the Thoroughbred coped with the excitement.

I just hope he's not giving Anna too much trouble.

Aboard Murphy, Anna paused outside the schooling ring, by now filled with hectic activity. The spectacle made her chest tighten.

Oh, man, it all comes back to me now. The fun and excitement of showing, but also the stress.

With Duke, it was mostly fun. Today, the stress might win out.

She figured the oval ring to be about one hundred by two hundred feet. More riders crowded in there now than when she'd been watching a half-hour earlier, and they had to weave around each other. Most worked along the rail, but three practice hurdles had been set up down the center, and once in awhile someone would cut in to take the jumps. Here again, Anna saw a mix of teens and younger kids on smaller and quieter mounts, plus a few adults on bigger, livelier animals.

"Ready?" Clint asked her.

She nodded, and as he opened the way for her she called out, "Gate."

The more experienced riders veered to give her a clear path. Clint stayed outside and shut the barrier behind her.

Anna felt Murphy's breathing quicken at the sight of so many strange horses zipping around him at different angles and different speeds. She made him walk on the rail, in the same direction as most of the others, and used her seat and hands to lower his head and keep his attention. After a minute, she decided to let him burn off some energy by trotting. That went okay, and at least he didn't try to race every horse that passed.

This isn't so bad, just like an equitation class. I think our practice session with Walt and Dash helped a little.

Anna heard fast hoofbeats behind her, and a voice shouted, "Rail!" She barely had time to leg-yield away from the fence before a big, bay warmblood cantered past, the rider's boot almost brushing hers.

Murphy tossed his head, then bolted after them.

Anna hauled back on the reins, but her ex-racer just bore down on the bit harder, scattering the other riders in their path.

Josh's voice echoed in her mind: *"Let go of his mouth."*

She forced herself to ease up on the reins and sit back. Meanwhile, she searched for an open space. *There, past the chestnut pony.* She circled Murphy until he slowed to a manageable canter.

Somebody outside the fence muttered, "...Needs to get that lunatic under control!"

Anna felt herself flush—first with embarrassment, then with annoyance.

Yes, Murphy had overreacted, but it wasn't all his fault. You didn't cut between another rider and the rail with so little warning! That boneheaded move could have spooked any horse.

To settle the Thoroughbred, she tried to calm her own breathing. Pretty soon they were going with the flow again, even changing direction when the majority of the others did so.

She could have relaxed more if a certain male trainer had not kept barking orders like a drill sergeant at one of the riders. After another trip around the ring, Anna realized he was working with the woman who had nearly banged into her. *Maybe she's just rattled. It's hard to ride well when your coach is screaming at you, especially in public.*

Now and then, Anna would find herself stuck behind a pony

and had to circle to avoid clipping its heels. Murphy's stride was so big that she kept making evasive moves to avoid the slower animals. When she passed the loudmouth coach, a sturdy blond guy in a yellow polo shirt, he sniped to someone near him, "All those circles—she thinks she's on a merry-go-round!"

Again her anger flared, but Anna sized up the stranger as generally obnoxious and resolved to ignore him.

A few riders left the practice ring to compete in their classes, and Anna felt confident enough to take Murphy down the line of jumps. The Thoroughbred seemed happy with this part of their session, and cruised over the crossbar, the triple bar and the oxer, all set low to accommodate beginners. He turned smoothly afterward and Anna's heart lifted. They were a team now, moving almost as one.

She took advantage of the thinner crowd to canter him around the whole ring, do a flying lead change at the center and approach the jumps from the opposite direction. Just as they bore down on the last of the obstacles, though, the little girl on the chestnut pony trotted right into their path.

"Oxer!" Anna shouted in horror, sure they would crash into the child. The girl saw them coming and kicked her pony to speed him up. At the same time, Anna slewed Murphy to the right of the jump, just avoiding disaster. A young woman who might have been the little girl's mother called to her over to the rail, and shot Anna a dirty look.

Anna pulled her mount down to a walk, heart hammering. She no longer worried much about how Murphy would perform in the show ring, where they'd be alone. The warm-up was a bigger challenge! She gave him a long rein and he stretched his neck, just as she and Josh had taught him to. Still, Anna knew she'd never get past the blond guy without hearing another comment.

Sure enough, he glared as she rode by. "Before you bring a horse to a show, you're supposed to teach it some manners!"

Anna bit her tongue to keep from telling him that the same applied to some people. *With a jerk like that, though, no point in sinking to his level.* The truth was, two other riders had made careless mistakes, and she and Murphy had coped about as well as possible.

A couple yards farther along, she reached Clint. He leaned over the fence and half-whispered, "Want me t' go clock that guy for ya?"

Anna laughed to picture him taking a swing at the younger, tough-looking trainer. "No, thanks. But I'm glad I don't have to actually show in a class after this. My nerves are already shot."

Clint let her out the gate and she hopped off. Both she and Murphy were dripping with sweat, and not just from the heat.

Anna said, "We'd better get him back to the trailer and give him some water."

"Before we go, I'll grab you another bottle, too," Clint offered.

She glanced wistfully toward the distant blue canopy of the refreshment table. "After that fiasco, I wish they sold something stronger!"

CHAPTER THIRTY-SEVEN:

POLICE

Anna seldom drank before dinnertime, but she savored her glass of wine. Of the group gathered on her front porch, only Lillian Gale had agreed to join her, though Anna felt sure her visitor must be used to a better grade of Chablis. Erika, Clint and Lillian's driver Jorge all had to get behind the wheel soon, and of course MJ still was under age.

As they finished up the sandwiches Erika had made, Anna explained about her problems at the horse show. Finally, Clint interrupted her tale of woe.

"You're just in a funk because that jackass in the yellow shirt gave you a hard time. Hey, if jockeys listened to all the people who talk trash to them after they lost a race, they'd never go back on the track again."

Lillian, a regal presence even while seated on the faded cushions of the rattan loveseat, smiled at Anna. "He's right, you know. That trainer might have thought you'd be competing against his student. He could just have been trying to psyche you out."

The slang expression sounded funny coming from the ladylike heiress, but Anna already had the impression Lillian was no hothouse flower. "Funny, I never thought of that."

MJ also brightened. "Sure, I bet he was trying to rattle you. Maybe the other rider was in on it, too."

Erika sipped her iced tea. "Doesn't sound very sportsmanlike."

"Oh, these little local shows..." Lillian waved a hand. "People get away with all kinds of nonsense. He couldn't pull that stuff on the A circuit. Of course, at that level the tricks get more underhanded...and more serious."

Anna mulled this. Should she really hand Murphy over to someone who wanted to compete at the top, most cutthroat levels? Would he be at risk of someone playing even dirtier tricks on him? Though the day's experiences had shaken her up, they also had bonded her more closely with the gray horse. They had faced some tough challenges, but through teamwork they'd come through okay.

"When do we go to a show for real?" Clint asked her.

"Two weeks."

Erika offered, "At least now you'll know what to expect, right?"

Clint said he should be on his way. Anna gave him a hug and thanked him for his help.

Lillian dusted a few breadcrumbs from her jeans and stood up. "I've enjoyed my visit here so much, I've stayed longer than I'd planned. But before I leave, Anna, can we have a closer look at this wonder horse of yours?"

"Of course."

As they strolled toward the pasture Lillian told Anna, "Your niece gave me a very thorough tour. She told me the stories behind all of the horses. Even why you started the farm."

Anna glanced away. "Well, I'm sure you already knew all about what happened with Richard."

"Yes, but not that you had to give up your horse, and later found out he went to slaughter. That must have been awful."

"It was." After a shrug, Anna gestured toward the surrounding property. "I'm trying to make something good come out of it."

"You're very brave, to take on so much with so little help. At least MJ seems very capable, for her age."

"She's grown up a lot since she came out here. But I guess I have, too."

They reached the pasture where Murphy grazed in contentment, a few yards from Patches. Lillian studied the gray from a distance with her expert eye. "He certainly has the ideal conformation for a jumper. If he really loves the game, that's even more important."

"He's smart, too. I really think he just needs to mature a little."

"Murphy has enough admirers, though. My heart belongs to Patches." Lillian told Anna how much the little Shetland resembled her own first pony. "I'll bet she'd be good company for a couple of Thoroughbreds I've got at my place, but I can't take her away from you as long as Murphy needs her. Maybe after he's adopted?"

That got Anna's attention. "Sure, that would be great."

"In the meantime, maybe I can sponsor her. MJ said you already have an arrangement like that for the buckskin—someone who's paying his keep."

"You'll be getting a bargain." Anna laughed. "Patches doesn't eat half as much."

Back in the barnyard, they found Jorge, MJ and Erika near the fence of one of the paddocks. It was the one closest to the driveway, where Anna kept some of the large farm equipment. The three of them peered intently at something.

When MJ saw her aunt coming, she called out, "Anna, have you been using the electric fence lately?"

"Sure, I turn it on every night."

"Has it actually been turning on?"

"I...think so." Anna tried to remember if she'd even listened for the faint hum of electricity, the last few nights. She flipped the switch out of habit, so she might not have paid attention.

Jorge spoke up, for practically the first time since he'd driven Lillian onto the property, in a faint Spanish accent. "The wire has been cut."

Anna hurried to check for herself. The yellow-coated cable had seen better days, and it wasn't completely severed, but broken through far enough that it could easily short out and lose its charge. When Jorge flipped the switch, Anna heard no current, and he demonstrated further by wrapping his whole, large hand around the wire. Either he had a high pain threshold, or the charge around the paddocks had been neutralized.

"Could a horse have chewed through it?" Erika asked.

"I don't keep any of them in this section," Anna explained. "And they respect the wires in their own paddocks. They don't want to risk a zap."

"Maybe somebody was goofing around," said MJ, a little too offhandedly. "You said Walt brought some new kids to the farm last week. Maybe one of them did it as a gag. Thought if he cut the wire the horses would get loose on us.'

"Not very funny," said Jorge, in a grave baritone.

"Or maybe one of them thought the wire was cruel, and did it as some kind of protest?" Lillian suggested.

Anna wondered. Any of those explanations could be valid...or this could be just the latest sign that someone was sneaking onto her property to cause trouble.

"You're probably right, Lillian," she said. "They're kind of idealistic kids, so one of them might have done something like that. Anyway, it's no big deal. I can splice it before we close up tonight."

Soon after, Anna and MJ watched all their guests drive off. The girl pressed a hand to her chest and told her aunt, "I was *so* afraid you'd mention the other weird stuff that's happened around here. Mom would have insisted I go back home with her."

"True. Though I'm probably selfish and irresponsible for letting you stay here, when you might be in danger."

MJ picked up her bags and started for the house. "Hey, strength in numbers, right? Somebody's got to take care of you. No offense to Delilah."

Anna held the screen door for the girl to carry her suitcases inside. "No offense to either of you, MJ, but I'm through messing around. This time, I'm calling the cops."

The black cruiser with the light bar on top, and POLICE printed on the side, did not roll into their barnyard until almost sundown. MJ supposed since it wasn't an emergency they didn't feel the need to hurry.

Just one guy got out of the car, only a couple of inches taller than Anna but almost twice as wide. Not fat, exactly...was that what they called barrel-chested? *Barrel-chested and bald.* He wore a gray short-sleeved shirt and black pants with a gold stripe down the side. From his belt hung a gun holster and a smaller leather case for something else. *Radio? Taser?* Closer up, MJ could read his brass name tag: Lt. John Mertz.

When Anna showed him the frayed wire, MJ could tell from his questions that he thought she was blowing it out of proportion. Couldn't one of the horses have done it, while the current was off? Maybe a bird with sharp beak? Anyway, it was easy enough to fix, right?

He didn't act much more interested when she told him about the mysterious vehicle that had come up their driveway one night and the strange boot prints near the horses' paddock. Though he made notes in a small pad, he asked, "But nobody approached the house? Probably just someone who got lost, realized they were at the wrong farm and didn't want to bother you."

He almost had MJ convinced there was nothing to worry about. Anna persisted, though, telling him about the recent debris she'd found in the weedy field and the dead opossum with the gunshot wound. Still with an air of humoring her, the cop accompanied them up to the practice field, Delilah tagging along. A dry spell over the past few weeks had turned the grass a dull beige, and even the trees had faded to a dustier shade of green. To his credit, Lt. Mertz walked to the far end of the field to check out the area where the split-rail fence had collapsed and just a strip of woods separated Anna's property from the road.

Meanwhile, she pointed out, "If someone is hunting on my land, they could end up shooting one of our horses—or one of us! Isn't there something you can do to stop them?"

"Not much," the cop answered flatly. "First off, your land isn't even posted."

"What does that mean?" MJ asked.

He closed his pad and regarded them both with a tolerant air. "I mean you don't have any signs that say 'No Hunting' or even 'No Trespassing,' so a hunter can legally follow wounded game onto your property. And as for people just cutting across your land, they do that all the time out here, especially with an open field like this. It might be annoying, but it's not illegal."

Anna looked startled. "Isn't there some way to keep them

out?"

"Fix the gaps in these fences, and maybe put a wire mesh over the rails so people can't just duck through. Even then, they're not so high that somebody couldn't climb over. Unless you wanna run the electricity around the whole perimeter." With a tight smile, Lieutenant Mertz added, "Cost you plenty, though, to do that."

Anna's face fell, and not until they started back to the barn did she speak again. "So...signs. That would help?"

He nodded. "Then if you caught someone trespassing, you could press charges, because they were told not to. Of course, you might want to be careful about ticking off your neighbors. From what you say, nobody's threatened you and none of your animals have been hurt."

"One of our horses cut his foot on the broken bottle," MJ reminded him.

"But that was an accident. If you get a feud going with somebody who lives nearby, he could start making trouble for you on purpose."

MJ thought of the dog-shooting rumors about Old Man Deavers, and called Delilah closer to her side. Before Mertz left, Anna requested that an officer at least cruise by the farm once in awhile on their rounds, especially at night. The bald man said he'd try to arrange that, though with no uptick in concern that MJ could see.

Her aunt returned to the house with a discouraged slump to her shoulders. MJ tried to cheer her. "Maybe it is all just a bunch of coincidences. If it's normal out here to cut through somebody's field, at least it doesn't mean some serial killer is hanging around and spying on us."

Anna climbed the porch steps and opened the screen door. "But if someone did want to hurt us, we don't have much protection. Even Delilah's not bulletproof, and I wouldn't want to put her to the test."

"He said if we could *catch* someone trespassing..." MJ remembered. "What about security cameras?"

"Where would we put them? And how many? Like electric fencing, that could cost a lot of money. At least a few signs, I probably can afford." In the living room, Anna sank down on the old sofa. "Trouble is, I want this to be a welcoming place where people can visit, see the work we're doing, meet the horses and consider adopting them. I don't want to turn it into a...a compound with scary signs, electrified fences and cameras tracking their every move."

MJ finally asked a question she'd been mulling for a while. "Could you...maybe...get a gun?"

Anna threw her a skewed smile. "When I first moved out here, I had people suggest that. I think most of the Pattersons know how to shoot, and Sam, the dad, even offered to teach me. They were thinking mostly about me fending off bears and coyotes, which turned out not to be a problem—they're happy to stay in the woods. But I hate guns and especially the idea of having one around the house. What if I made a mistake and shot an innocent person?"

With an evil grin, her niece plopped down next to her on the sofa. "Like, what if you had a gun the day I brought Valentine back from that trail ride, and you got so mad at me?"

Her aunt laughed and gave her a hug, "Oh, I don't think I actually would've *shot* you. But seriously, what about the night someone drove onto our property, and I couldn't see who it was? I wouldn't have wanted to decide, out there in the dark, whether he was dangerous or not." Anna sighed. "Anyhow, even to get a simple hunting rifle, I'd have to get a special ID card, go through a background check...it would take months. And after all that, I'd still have to learn how to shoot the thing well."

MJ hadn't realized it was so complicated. Bad guys on TV seemed to have no problem getting guns. But then, they didn't have to obey the law.

"First," her aunt said, "let's try fixing the fence and posting the property. If it's just a hunter, or kids sneaking into the field to drink, maybe that'll discourage them."

Her more hopeful tone reassured MJ. "Yeah, guess there's no point in getting too paranoid. Like the cop said, nobody's hurt us or the horses."

"So far," Anna agreed, soberly. "I just don't want to wait until somebody does."

CHAPTER THIRTY-EIGHT:

BOUNDARIES

The next day, Anna drove her truck to the nearest farm-supply store and came back with half a dozen "No Trespassing" signs and a dozen thick rolls of wire fencing.

At this sight, MJ cringed. She guessed they would have to attach that nasty mesh to the whole fence around the rear field—probably two or three days of backbreaking work.

Fortunately, even Anna the DIY queen realized the two of them would need help, and called upon the Pattersons. After she explained her concerns about trespassers, Walt showed up the next day with his father.

Sam Patterson turned out to be tall and bearlike, which surprised MJ, because Walt was less than six feet and more trim and agile than bulky. However, father and son did share one trait—outdated haircuts. At least Walt's was short enough to pass for a cheap barber-shop job. Sam's graying-brown hair covered the tops of his ears, an odd combination with his straight, short bangs.

I'll bet Dottie cuts their hair, to save money. If she does the whole family, I feel sorry for Walt's sister!

Anna already knew Sam from the role he had played in rescuing Dash. He checked on the buckskin now and seemed impressed by the progress the horse had made.

"Remember how scarred up and nervous he was when he first came here?" Sam asked Anna. "Me and Walt would go to the shows and see that guy spurrin' Dash and yanking on his mouth. Not during the competition, where the judges could see him, but in the practice ring. I said to Walt, it's just not right to treat any of God's creatures that way." Sam turned to his son. "You were askin' about that guy just the other day, weren't you?"

"Anna wanted to know his name."

"That's right. Name was Artie Jeffers. Don't hear about him on the show circuit anymore. If he's still riding, he probably moved away, where nobody knows his reputation."

"Let's hope!" MJ said.

She liked Sam Patterson better than his wife—he asked fewer nosy questions and passed fewer judgments. Because of his height, he was elected to post the "No Trespassing" signs on trees in a few critical spots. His skill and efficiency with a staple gun also meant their labor would go more quickly. Sam and Anna started on one side of the field's gate, while MJ and Walt worked from the other. Eventually, they'd meet and overlap the mesh at the far end.

Wearing her work gloves, MJ unrolled a length of the stiff wire grid and held it as tightly as she could against the first post and its three rails. Walt secured the mesh in several places before they moved on to the next section.

In between loud pops from the staple gun, he remarked on her absence from the farm for more than a week. "Anna said you went home."

"I needed to get my hair cut." MJ didn't add that she wouldn't have trusted any stylist within a twenty-mile radius of the farm. "Plus, I needed more clothes, and to spend some time with my mom and brother."

Walt fired off another staple. "That's all cool. But Anna sounded like she wasn't sure you were coming back."

"We did have an argument." While MJ rolled out another couple yards of the fencing, she summarized the crisis with Valentine. "I was pretty hurt by the way Anna yelled at me, but later she did say she was sorry. Anyway, I figured what we're doing here is too important for me to quit over just a stupid misunderstanding."

Walt cocked his head at her. "That's very...mature of you. Whatever the reason, I'm glad you came back." He faced away to tack the mesh to another post. "I'm sure Anna would have a tough time running this place without you."

MJ wondered if he'd just added that last bit so it wouldn't sound like he'd missed her. "I'll bet you're glad I'm back— otherwise, she might have you over here doing all my work! But she told me you got some other kids to pitch in."

"Yeah, two guys and a girl from my church group. I think they'd be happy to come again, any time."

This could be good news, MJ thought. "Hmm...I wonder if Anna would let them watch the farm when she takes Murphy to his big show. Otherwise, I'll probably be stuck here, and I'd really love to see it."

"Even if nobody else is free, I probably can watch the farm for you, if it's just for a few hours. How's Murphy been doing?"

"Pretty well, but he's still got some issues." She explained about the horse's nerves in the warmup ring. "Hey, are any of your church friends good riders? Maybe with horses of their own?"

Walt leaned against a post for a breather, resting the tool against his slim hip. "Charlene Boyd ought to be. She talks about having an Appaloosa that she rides on the trails. Why?"

"I just thought of a way we might be able to help Anna."

That Saturday afternoon, MJ and Walt rode side-by-side around the big practice field, with its newly repaired and reinforced fence, he on Dash and she on Valentine. A few paces ahead, Charlene sat aboard her tall, speckled Appy. Walt's brother Luke, about ten, led them all on one of the Pattersons' Quarter Horses. Anna had asked them to use only about a third of the field, and to form a big oval the size of a typical warm-up ring. While they stayed to the outside, she rode Murphy past them and gave more instructions.

"Charlene, Luke, Walt...you can jog, lope, or whatever it is you crazy Western riders call what you do," she teased. "MJ, stick to a walk. Slower riders stay to the inside, faster ones pass along the rail. I'll do my best to avoid the rest of you. If it all works out okay, I'll also go over those three jumps in the middle. Everybody ready?"

With a nod, Walt clucked to Dash and the buckskin broke into a jog, carrying his head low. MJ had no trouble holding Val back, and knew better than to overstress the sick mare. Still, she envied the others who got to ride faster.

Charlene, about her age, was doing what they called a lope—a very easy canter. She had a slim figure, rosy cheeks and a long, honey-colored braid that bobbed with the rocking of her horse. Walt hadn't mentioned that his friend from church was really cute.

I wonder if he likes her. MJ caught herself, annoyed. *If he does, why should I care? I'm not interested in Walt that way. The only guy I really care about is...*

With a pang, she remembered. Bobby Raser was no longer an option. He'd already demonstrated that he didn't think of *her* in "that way."

Her thought bubble burst when Anna swept past her on the outside. It had been awhile since MJ had seen her aunt practice on the big gray, and they looked great today. Maybe because the rest of the riders were taking it easy, the Thoroughbred seemed to fly by them. Anna did circle him once to rate his speed, but he didn't seem rattled by the unfamiliar horses and riders.

After a while, her aunt cantered Murphy into the middle and jumped the three hurdles. She made a big figure-eight and came at the combination from the other direction. The gray cleared everything again, ears happily pricked forward. On his way back to the rail, he did give a little kick, but it looked like just high spirits.

MJ noticed the other riders had either come down to a walk or halted, to better watch the performance. When Anna finally slowed and gave Murphy a long rein, they clapped. She did a mock bow in the saddle and rubbed the Thoroughbred's dappled shoulder.

Walt rode up alongside MJ again. "I don't know much about jumping, but he looks like he should do great in that show."

She nodded. "Guess that's the good news and the bad news."

"Why bad news?"

From afar, MJ noticed her aunt's beaming face. "If he ends up in the ribbons, he'll probably get adopted. Just seems a shame that Anna's done so much hard work with him, only to lose him."

That evening, while MJ watched a movie up at the house, Anna sat working at the computer in the office. Now and then she heard a snort from the paddock and got up to peer out the barn door. She saw nothing amiss, though, and no strangers hanging around.

Maybe the signs and the reinforced fencing are having some effect.

By eight forty-five, she had finished editing an article for *Good Life* about high-end wine cellars, and emailed it to Zack. After that, she tallied up her business expenses for the past week. Usually Anna dreaded that task, but it became easier to face now that she had sponsors for two horses. When she had first set up the website, she hadn't even thought of seeking sponsors as well as adopters, but their regular donations were a big help.

Like Lillian said, if this keeps up I might even be able to take in another horse or two. Maybe those PMU colts?

A lot would depend on whether she could find a new home for Murphy. That idea still made her nervous, because of the disastrous experience with Starbuck. She didn't want to place the Thoroughbred with someone who might neglect him, or run him into the ground with too many competitions.

I'd feel better if I knew something about this prospective adopter. Wonder why Josh was so mysterious about her? Could she be the same person he phones whenever he's going to be held up late at work?

Anna closed her budgeting program, powered down her computer, and listened to the crickets outside loudly calling for mates. She remembered, at least from the early years of her marriage, what it was like to have someone eager for her to finish work for the day and hurry home. *Though with Richard, it was usually the other way around—me waiting for him. So awful, to think that he put in those long hours swindling people!*

Whoever this mystery adopter might be, Anna hoped she'd

be as impressed with Murphy as Walt and his friends had been today. There was only one phase of the show that she and Murphy hadn't practiced yet at all. Josh said he would help them with it on Tuesday. Getting it right could make all the difference, but it might also be the most challenging part for Anna.

It could bring back memories of the worst day of her life.

CHAPTER THIRTY-NINE:

BONDING

Josh had set up five hurdles in the field, about the right number for the jump-off of a lower-level show. He stood just inside the gate with a stopwatch. As Anna cantered past, he punched a button and shouted, "Go!"

She touched her heels Murphy's sides and he shot toward the first jump, a simple upright fence. Going so fast, he reached it too soon and took off early. He still got over with no problem, but after they landed Anna reined him in a little.

Their first round would not be timed, but if they went clean and even one other competitor did the same, there would be a jump-off against the clock. Then they'd have to balance speed versus control, because both knockdowns and time faults would count against them.

They skimmed easily over the low oxer, then doubled back over a makeshift wall built of straw bales. By now, Murphy could turn tightly enough to shave a few seconds. His narrow, Thoroughbred build made him easier to maneuver than Duke, Anna thought.

It's like going from a Mercedes to a Maserati. Duke was smooth, steady and easy to handle. Murph is super-sensitive, hugs the curves...and has a sticky gas pedal.

They also cleared the triple-bar nicely, but came up too fast again at the spread fence. This time, Murphy misjudged the distance and Anna heard a clunk behind them.

They blew past Josh, who called out "Time!" and clicked his stopwatch again. In the show ring, Anna would ride past an electronic eye that registered her start and finish.

She trotted the gray for a minute, to cool him down, then walked him back toward the gate. Sunglasses hid Josh's eyes but not his slight frown.

"Your time was fine, but that last rail would've cost you four points."

"I know." Anna rubbed the crest of the horse's neck, anyway. Her error, not his.

"He's got so much speed that you'd do better to check him a little, so he doesn't run off with you. Remember to count your strides."

Anna took the criticism seriously. It was the kind of mistake she'd made with Duke at their last show, with disastrous results.

But that's not going to happen this time. The jumps will be low, so even if we knock something we won't really crash. And yet...we don't have to fall far to get hurt. The day Murphy tripped on that bottle, he almost went down on his knees and I nearly flew over his head!

Peering up at her, Josh tapped her boot. "Anna? Where'd you go?"

"Sorry. I was just thinking about...counting my strides."

They went through the exercise two more times, all the jumps a little higher for the last go-round. Anna used her weight to slow Murphy between hurdles, and though they lost a couple seconds they had no more knockdowns.

Back in the barnyard, Anna put the gray in the outdoor wash stall. While she sponged him off, she and Josh firmed up their plans for Saturday. Anna and Clint would trailer Murphy to the show grounds by six-thirty, where Josh would meet them. That would give them plenty of time to work with the Thoroughbred again before his first class at eight.

Anna dared to ask, "Will his prospective new owner be coming with you?"

Josh raised an eyebrow. "With me? No, I think she'll be with some friends. They've got a daughter riding in the Junior Hunters."

"Any reason I can't know her name?"

He hesitated. "I suppose not. It's Jessica. Jessica Coleman."

Anna just nodded. Unlike Lillian Gale's, the name meant nothing to her. She used a sweat-scraper to squeegee the moisture from Murphy's coat. "How well do you know her?"

"We grew up together—our families even vacationed together. She was like a sister to me."

Is she still? Anna was tempted to ask. Before she got up the nerve, though, Josh reassured her, "Don't worry. You know I'd never let your horse go to someone who'd mistreat him. Jess is an excellent rider, and I've taught her a lot of my techniques."

He didn't seem to notice the potential double-entendre, and Anna wasn't about to point it out. "Sorry. I guess after Starbuck's adoption turned out so badly, I'm a little paranoid. I just want what's best for Murphy."

Leaning against the pipe rails of the wash stall, Josh smiled. "I know, and that's refreshing. Most of my clients have agendas for their horses: This one should be doing fourth-level dressage, that one's got to take their kid to the National Horse Show. They spent a lot of money on the animal, and by God, they want results. If I ask what they think the *horse* wants—what kind of work he seems to like and be good at—they look at me like I've sprouted antlers. But you've always considered what's best for Murphy, Anna. You really get it."

She warmed at this compliment, which meant more than if he'd praised her riding to the skies. "Thanks. My only goal is that my horses have happier lives in the future than they did in the past." To mask her self-consciousness, she dried Murphy briskly with a towel and snapped the lead line to his halter.

She expected Josh to be on his way then, but he came along as she led the gray back to his pasture. Figuring he must have more instructions, Anna asked, "What should we practice between now the show? Work more on the jump-off, or—"

"Glad you asked. I think the reason Murphy's getting strong with you is that you're still a little tense riding him."

Anna realized that could be true. Compared to Duke, the Thoroughbred always remained a little unpredictable, so she felt she had to stay alert. She opened the pasture gate and brought him inside. "What should I do about that?"

"I'll show you." Josh came through the gate, too, and closed it behind them. "Go on, let him loose."

Curious, Anna slipped off the horse's halter and let him trot off to touch noses with Patches. Josh cupped her shoulder with one big, warm hand. "Come with me."

He brought her to a clean, level spot near the middle of the pasture and gestured for her to sit. He dropped down beside her, comfortably cross-legged in his sneakers and cargo shorts.

Anna felt a little unnerved by this cozy situation—as well as by Josh's long, very toned bare legs. She searched the lenses of his dark glasses for an explanation.

"Here's what I want you to do," he said. "Every day, for about half an hour, just hang with Murphy. Get to know him as a buddy, the way Patches does."

Horse-whisperer stuff. But Anna couldn't scoff. She actually had done that in the early days. Sat out in the pasture with Valentine and Starbuck, just to watch their body language, separately and together. Was that part of the reason why she'd always felt so bonded with her first two rescues?

"And you think that will help him to relax more when we jump?"

"It'll help *you* relax, and that'll help him." With the sun lowering toward the treetops, Josh slipped off his sunglasses and tucked them in a pocket of his shorts. Anna almost had forgotten that his eyes were that rare shade of pewter, with fine lines at the corners. "Horses are very tuned-in to a person's state of mind. Murphy knows you still don't quite trust him."

Even though it only referred to a horse, the observation drew a grim chuckle from Anna. "I admit, I may have some trust issues. And not just with horses."

Josh considered this with a squint. "I did notice a whole lot of 'No Trespassing' signs today, on my way in."

"Hey, you saw all the junk someone left up in our field. And you're the one who pointed out that the opossum had been shot."

"I know. Anyway, I shouldn't tease you about having 'trust issues.' Be amazing if you didn't, after everything you've gone through."

The casual statement hit Anna like a blow. Despite the fact that she'd moved all the way out here and gone back to her maiden name, the scandal had followed her. *Like Julie said, the horse world's a small community.*

"You know about Richard."

"Wasn't sure if I should bring it up." Scanning the treeline again, Josh added, "Divorce by itself is hard enough, I know. But in your case..."

"Finding out that the person I'd been married to for eight years was a thief and a con man? Yeah, that was tough." She shook her head at the memories. "But Richard wasn't the only person who betrayed me. I told you about my trainer selling Duke to the couple that sent him to auction."

"Some trainers only care about their own ambitions. That's one reason I went into the business. Would you believe I started out to be a lawyer?"

Having gotten to know a few during her husband's trial and their divorce, Anna laughed. "No, I wouldn't."

"Thought I'd be a public defender, helping people who were unjustly accused." His smile acknowledged how idealistic this sounded. "But in the summers off from law school, I worked at a big, public stable. I exercised horses for owners who couldn't come more than once or twice a week. And I saw a lot of stuff that I didn't like."

"People abusing the horses?"

"Once in awhile, but mostly trainers who were clueless about how to solve problems, and sometimes made things worse. They used old-fashioned methods without questioning what was right for that particular animal. Then they wondered why he behaved so much better when I got on him. I just approached each horse as an individual and kept an open mind. I insisted they show me respect, but I did the same for them."

"So instead of becoming a public defender, you became a horse advocate," Anna observed.

"Seemed like they needed somebody to take their case." Josh rotated to face her. "But you understand. It sounds like you had the same kind of turning point, when you decided to buy this farm."

She nodded, realizing she had never even told him about that fateful day at the auction when she'd rescued Valentine. Maybe she still would, someday.

His eyes held hers intently now. "You've got what it takes for this, Anna. I don't just mean the show jumping. You should be fine at that, even if it's not something you want to do very often. I mean the rescue and rehab work. You've got the gift to see what each horse needs. Just stick with it and trust your instincts."

With their faces inches apart, Anna was ready to trust her instincts in another way. Josh seemed about to kiss her, and she held her breath to avoid jinxing the moment. She stifled the familiar voice warning that she didn't need the complications of a new man in her life. Josh seemed to be everything Richard hadn't been, sensitive and honest—

A shrill arpeggio shredded the silence. He winced, rocked backward to pull his cell phone from his shorts, and checked the number. To Anna's disappointment he excused himself, got up and walked a few feet away. She could just barely hear his half of the conversation.

"Yeah, sorry," he told the caller. "I'm on my way. Be there about seven, okay? Love ya!"

Still seated on the grass, Anna felt something nudge her shoulder and looked up into Murphy's big, dark eye with its silvery lashes. She stroked the horse's long face, hard bone covered in plush.

Josh wandered back with a grin. "See, you're bonding already."

"Looks that way." But the intimate connection between her and Josh had been broken, and she got to her feet, too.

"Anyway, I have to run," he said. "Funny how I always seem to lose track of time when I come here."

Now what the heck does that mean? Anna wondered.

She accompanied him out the gate, and the gray horse looked almost disappointed when they left the pasture.

Striding briskly back to his SUV, Josh slid behind the wheel. "See you Saturday. Meanwhile, try to spend a little more 'down time' with Murphy. I think it'll do you both good."

276

Confused and frustrated, Anna watched him drive away. Would she ever get to spend any more "down time" with Josh? It seemed every time they started to connect, he dashed off.

Of course, maybe he had a good reason to keep things strictly professional between them. And maybe she'd be smart to do the same, if he could flirt with her minutes after telling someone else on the phone, "Love ya!"

I got my heart broken by one charming liar. I sure don't need to get mixed up with another.

MJ had just finishing measuring out the grain and medications for the horses' evening meal when she heard Josh drive away. She glanced out to see Anna gazing after him, and cleared her throat before speaking. "I wondered where you got to. I saw Murphy's tack on the stand outside, so I knew you were finished riding."

"Sorry, didn't mean to worry you. We took him up to the field, and Josh gave me a few tips on how to spend more time with him so we can really bond."

This statement brought the girl up short. "You mean...with Murphy, right?"

Anna chuckled, with an edge. "Yes, with Murphy. I suspect Mr. Buchanan has already bonded with someone else. By the way, he finally revealed the name of the person who might adopt Murphy. It's Jessica Coleman."

"Is she somebody well-known?"

"I've never heard of her, but I've been off the show circuit for a while." Anna carried her "good" saddle and bridle toward the tack room.

Her niece hovered nearby, burdened with a message she wished she could put off delivering. *Go on,* she scolded herself. *Remember how much trouble you got in last time, when you didn't tell Anna about your mom's phone call?*

"Speaking of people interested in the horses...y'know that guy who's been sponsoring Dash?"

"Jeb Andrews, yeah."

"You've got a phone message from him. He's going to be near

here on business Saturday, and wants to come have a look around."

Anna emerged from the tack room with a pained expression. "This Saturday? Boy, he couldn't have picked a worse time, could he?"

Her niece agreed. They already had worked it out for Walt to watch the farm, possibly with some of his friends, while Anna and MJ went to the horse show. The girl hoped this wouldn't screw everything up.

"Andrews lives kind of far away," Anna noted. "I guess if he's going to be in this area for some other reason, he wants to kill two birds with one stone."

Hopefully, MJ suggested, "Maybe Walt could show him around..."

"No...Walt doesn't know the farm's background like you and I do. Besides, if the man is going out of his way to visit, and neither of us can make time to meet with him, he might be insulted." Anna shook her head. "He's paying for Dash's feed and medications every month. We can't afford to tick him off."

"Well, you can't skip your horse show. That's important, too." MJ slumped against a post, having foreseen this result. "Guess I gotta stay here to give him the tour."

Anna studied her niece with a sympathetic frown. Meanwhile, they heard a shrill whinny from Valentine in the paddock.

"C'mon, let's feed," she said. "Then I'll call Andrews back, see if I can work something out."

Later, while her aunt did this, MJ loitered outside the office but resisted the urge to eavesdrop. Anna's tone of voice alternated between accommodating and bargaining. Meanwhile, the girl used her smartphone to search online for "Jessica Colman, N.J." Even after several minutes, she found no references that involved horses or riding. *Maybe another spelling?*

Anna came to the office doorway. "Okay, here's the deal. I told him I'll be unavoidably tied up this Saturday—I didn't say I'd actually be off the property—but if that was the best time for him to visit, you'd be able to give him the tour. I did ask him to come in the morning, though, because that's when you'd be less busy. He said he'll be here around ten."

Better than noon, the girl thought, since Anna's classes should be in the early afternoon.

"I'll talk to Walt and ask him to be here by that time, too," her aunt added. "There's no way I want you alone here with a man I've never even met."

That thought hadn't crossed MJ's mind; she was glad it had crossed Anna's. "Guess nobody's worried about leaving me alone with Walt anymore."

"Seems like the lesser of two evils," her aunt said, a teasing gleam in her eye. "Besides, Walt knows now that if he put the moves on you, his mother would kill him."

He doesn't seem so under her thumb anymore, MJ thought. "But I'll still be stuck here all day. Even if Walt would let me borrow his truck, I can't drive a stick. Unless...maybe he can teach me before Saturday."

"Oh no. You're not driving that old truck on the highway with so little practice." With a dismissive wave, Anna headed down the aisle toward the feed room.

Again MJ followed her. "What if Walt can get some friends to come by later and take over for us? Then he can drive me to the show. Maybe Charlene and Luke?"

Anna opened the lid of the grain bin. "I dunno. They're pretty young, Luke especially."

"They only have to watch over Dash, Patches and Valentine, and those guys never cause any trouble. Anyway, you got your cell phone fixed, right? So, they'll be able to reach you at the show."

Anna finally softened. "When I talk to Walt, I'll ask him." She scooped grain into a blue plastic bucket. "After all, it should only be for three, four hours."

"Sure." MJ grinned. "How much can go wrong?"

CHAPTER FORTY:

SHOW TIME

At the show grounds, Murphy unloaded like a veteran; tied to the back of the trailer, he glanced around with interest but stood quietly. Clint was able to take off his blanket and leg wraps with no problem.

Anna valued his help. A heavy rain the night before had left the ground muddy, with puddles in spots. In buff breeches, a high-collared white shirt, a lightweight navy jacket and polished boots, with her hair in a bun at the nape of her neck, she needed to keep herself clean until she entered the ring.

She just hoped everything went smoothly back at the farm. Walt had promised to be there by ten, and his father would take over by noon, so Walt could bring MJ to the show.

Anna had been lunging Murphy for a few minutes—gently, with no whip to alarm him—when Josh showed up. His teal-blue polo shirt played up his healthy tan and gave his short curls a coppery glint. He carried a thermal coffee mug and greeted her and Clint with a cheery, "Good morning, team!"

She laughed. "I'm glad someone's feeling positive."

Josh scanned her from head to toe with a smile. "You look ready to kick some serious butt. Got your number?"

"Not yet. I wanted to limber him up first."

"I can do that. You and Clint take a coffee break. Get a couple programs, too."

Figuring Murphy couldn't be in better hands, Anna took off toward the show barn with Clint. He glanced back once, as if to make sure the trainer wasn't having any trouble. "He charge you for comin' here today?"

"The usual coaching fee for a show. Not very much."

"Where's his lady friend, who's supposed to be buyin' Murphy?"

"I'm sure she's here somewhere. And she's not buying him, she's adopting him. She'll have to fill out the form, and we'll be entitled to check on him. I'm not running the risk of another Starbuck disaster."

"Better not, or I might stop bringing you my racetrack rejects. She know his history?"

He means about the flipping, Anna thought. "I hope Josh told her. At any rate, she must be a good rider. I checked her out online. She was jumper champion this spring in an A-rated show in Pennsylvania."

Clint shrugged. "Then whatever tricks Murphy pulls with her, she oughta at least be able to hang on."

Anna still wouldn't recognize Jessica Coleman if she fell over her. There had been a photo of the Pennsylvania show's six top award winners, but taken from a distance in the late afternoon, with all the riders' faces half in shadow.

Anna didn't need any more coffee. While Clint got some for himself, she stopped at the show secretary's table, picking up her number and two programs. Scanning one, she saw that her first class didn't start until ten. That would give her plenty of time in the warmup ring.

She'd compete in Green Jumpers, for horses new to showing. The first time around, the riders would need to complete a course of eight jumps, and anyone exceeding the time allowed would be out. Those who'd gone clear would ride again in a timed jump-off over a shortened course. Whoever had either another clear round or the fewest faults, along with the fastest time, would win the class.

By the time Anna and Clint reached Josh again, he'd finished lunging. Murphy grazed at the end of the line while his trainer talked on the phone. Anna overheard Josh say, "Yeah, at this point I think it's only fair. I don't know if it will make her any less nervous, but she has a right to know. Okay?" He signed off with,

"See you later."

Anna approached curiously, and he greeted her with a crooked smile. "I have news. Don't know if you're going to like it or not."

"Jessica's not interested in Murphy, after all?"

"Oh, nothing that bad. Would I let you waste all this time and effort?" He paused for effect. "But she's riding against you today."

"What? Why—?"

"She decided to try out another horse at the same time...'to make things interesting,' she said. She wanted to do it anonymously. But since I already told you her name, I figured I'd better give you some warning before you hear it over the loudspeaker."

Unnerved, Anna tried to figure out the implications. "In other words, if she does better on this other horse than I do on Murphy, she might buy that one, instead?"

"Well, she didn't say that in so many words, but..."

Anna pressed a hand to her forehead, the stress returning. Just when it seemed like things were going so well! "Josh, I know she's a top rider. What chance do I really have of beating her?"

He caught Anna's arm. "Take it easy. This other horse also is showing for the first time. So really, you're pretty much even. Two experienced riders on green mounts."

She spotted Clint standing a couple feet away and glanced at him for support. But though he obviously had overheard, he just grinned and toasted her with his paper coffee cup.

"Sounds like a horse race to me," he said. "May the best woman win!"

By eight-thirty that morning, MJ had finished feeding Val, Dash and Patches, grabbed a quick breakfast herself and put the animals back out together in their pen. All that remained before their visitor arrived was to clean up any droppings left in the stalls.

Delilah stayed out of the way during this chore, though she listened politely while MJ confided in her.

"My friends all think I'm crazy, y'know," she told the dog. "My mom probably does, too. They can't believe I'd rather do stuff like this than go off to some college. Man, I've already spent—what, twelve years?—sitting in a classroom all day. Why would I want to do it for four more?"

Delilah lay down near the office door and rested her head on her paws, as if she appreciated the seriousness of this dilemma.

MJ expertly forked damp shavings into the big wheelbarrow. "I guess I do have to make a living somehow. But I've been looking online, and they have degrees in something called animal husbandry. I know, it sounds weird, but it's about how to take care of livestock, run a farm and things like that. Maybe I could take those classes on the computer or someplace nearby. And if I want to learn more about website design, I can do that almost anywhere. So, I'd be able to stay here with you and the horses. And Anna too, I guess."

Delilah didn't get that last joke. When MJ started pushing her full wheelbarrow toward the barn door, though, the dog leaped up and trotted after her, as if she couldn't imagine a more fun outing.

"Whadya think, girl?" MJ asked, on the move. "If I agree to study something like that, will Mom get off my back? It's not an MBA, but at least it would be a college degree. Maybe she'd even give me her red hatchback, so I wouldn't have to beg rides from Anna or Walt."

MJ had dumped her load and was guiding the stubborn wheelbarrow back over the barnyard's muddy ruts when a truck jounced up the drive pulling a horse trailer. This confused her. Did Josh get his wires crossed, and think he was supposed to pick Anna up for the show? But he usually drove a late-model SUV.

It's got to be Andrews. He's almost an hour early! Not that the farm wasn't fit to show him, but after what Anna had said, MJ did feel nervous about being alone with a man neither of them knew much about. As the truck parked, she could make out two people in the cab.

The driver stepped out. Average in height, he had short, graying brown hair, a broad face and a full beard. Also a bit of a belly, MJ thought. Or it might just look that way because of his loose black rain jacket, which had one of those front pouches.

He smiled widely and held out his hand. "Hi! You must be MJ." His voice was big and hearty, like on his phone message.

She relaxed a little, because he seemed so friendly and knew her name. She also noticed the person in the car smoothing back long hair, and felt reassured that he was traveling with a woman. Delilah's presence at her side also gave MJ more confidence.

She shook his hand. "Mr. Andrews? Glad you could come. I... wasn't expecting you just yet."

"Yeah, sorry about that. My other appointment got rescheduled, so I had to fit this stop in earlier than I planned."

MJ eyed the trailer. "Taking a horse somewhere?"

He tucked his hands into the jacket's side pockets, though the pouch in front still sagged. "Not yet, but that is part of my business today."

Up close, she noticed his teeth were kind of yellow and his breath smelled a little like...tobacco? *But not the way a smoker's does.* "My aunt was sorry she couldn't show you around herself, but she's—"

"Off at a horse show," he finished, genially. "Yeah, I know."

That surpised MJ. *I thought Anna didn't tell this guy she'd be away from the farm, just that she'd be busy. Maybe she changed her mind, and emailed him later?*

"No problem," the visitor went on. "I'm sure you can give me the tour just as well. I mostly stopped by, anyhow, to meet my pal Dash over there." He nodded in the direction of the horses' pen.

Still a bit uneasy, MJ glanced toward his truck. "Does your... friend want to look around, too?"

"Naw, she's not feelin' so good today. Said she'd rather stay in there and nap."

MJ escorted him toward the barn. "Watch your step. After the rain last night, things are kind of muddy." Glancing down, she noticed for the first time that Andrews had on pointy-toed Western boots.

A chill like rainwater trickled down her back.

A lot of people probably wear those. Doesn't mean anything.

She spent a few minutes showing him the barn and the fields beyond. Figuring he might want to know how the horses were cared for, she explained they were turned out most of the time and only brought in for feeding and grooming. She told him Reboot Ranch was still a pretty young operation, but already had a board of directors and had applied for nonprofit status.

Andrews wore a slight smile throughout her spiel, but often looked over his shoulder at the horse pen. Taking the hint, the girl brought him out to meet the three occupants.

"There he is!" Andrews crowed over the buckskin. "Looks even better than on the website."

"He's been doing pretty well." MJ entered the pen and scratched the horse's withers. "He's had a rough time of it. Dash used to be a reining horse and won all kinds of ribbons. But his owner pushed him so hard he got arthritis in his back legs. Then the guy left him in a weedy field to starve, so the Humane Society placed him with us. We've been giving him rest and medicine, and now we're finally starting to ride him again."

"Huh. You'd never know there ever was anything wrong with him." When the man reached toward Dash's face, though, the horse backed a step and threw his head out of reach.

"Whoa!" MJ scolded. Andrews was paying the horse's keep, so he should at least be able to look him over.

"Maybe put a halter on him?" the man suggested. He happened to pick the right one from the fencepost, and handed it to her.

She slipped it onto the Quarter Horse and held him by the long, thick lead rope as Andrews ran a hand over his tan body and down his dark legs. MJ noticed the normally calm animal trembled the whole time.

What's with him today? I thought it was Murphy who had a phobia about men. Dash always acts fine with Walt.

But MJ couldn't blame the buckskin. She felt spooked, too. How did this guy know Anna had gone to a show, and why had he insisted on visiting today? It was almost like he'd planned to come when her aunt wasn't around. Like he'd been spying on them—

"Y'know," the visitor said slowly, "he reminds me so much of a horse I used to have. Name's similar, but a lot of Quarter Horses come from that bloodline. Hard to tell much from the photo on the website..." He squatted near one foreleg and pointed. "Lookit that! One splotch of white, just above the left front hoof."

Andrews straightened again to face MJ, and she realized what bothered her about his big smile. It didn't touch his cold eyes.

"I'll be darned," he said. "This *is* my horse."

CHAPTER FORTY-ONE:

HORSE THIEVES

J osh walked alongside as Anna rode Murphy toward the warmup ring. There, at least eight other riders exercised their mounts in both directions and at various speeds. Like a spy checking with her handler, Anna asked, "Is Jessica out there now?"

Josh nodded. "Number thirty-six, on the bay."

She almost didn't need to be told. Number Thirty-Six rode a big, sleek Thoroughbred with conformation to rival Murphy's, but a more easygoing demeanor. The bay cantered smoothly across the center of the ring and arced over the three practice hurdles with little effort. Jessica piloted him easily around all the other traffic, including one boy's kicking pony, with no drama.

Anna's spirits plummeted. *Oh, Murphy. We are screwed.*

To make things even dicier, no sooner had Josh let them into the ring than Number Thirty-Six rode over to say hello. In full show regalia, she had the bone structure and figure of a model. Though Josh said they'd grown up together, Jessica looked in her mid-thirties at most. Judging from her eyebrows and the hair netted below the back of her helmet, she was a striking, dark brunette.

Josh introduced them with a wry look that acknowledged the awkward situation. Jessica's smile was more poised.

"Great to finally meet you, Anna. I've heard many good things." She laughed a little. "Hope I didn't throw a wrench in the works by entering Hawkeye in the same class today. A friend's looking to sell him, and thought for his first show he should have an experienced rider. It seemed like a way to kill two birds with one stone."

As long as it doesn't kill Murphy's chances of being adopted. But the woman had not said, outright, that she planned to choose between the two horses.

Meanwhile, Jessica's bay stood statue-still beneath her, softly chewing his bit, while Murphy pawed restlessly.

"A little friendly competition never hurt." Anna tried to match the other woman's light tone. Then a new, uncomfortable idea struck her. "Has Josh been working with you and Hawkeye, too?"

"Not very much," Jessica said. "He works mostly with problem horses, and luckily Hawkeye is a sweetheart."

Great—my problem child against her model pupil. Suddenly Anna recognized the woman's voice. "You shot the training videos that Josh sent to me, right?"

"Guilty. I'm afraid they weren't the best—I'm no expert with a video camera. But anyone else he'd have to pay, right?" Jessica winked at the trainer. "Anyhow, I don't want to chat away your warmup time. We'll get out of here so you have one less horse-and-rider to work around. Be careful out there!"

She waved, and Josh held the gate open for Number Thirty-Six to leave the ring and Anna to enter. She would have thanked him, but Murphy carried her away at a trot. He tried to race a teenager's Quarter Horse until Anna made her first circle of the day to get him back under control.

So, Jessica's perfect. Her horse is perfect. And probably neither of us has a chance against them.

Maybe I should phone my niece and tell her not to even bother coming this afternoon.

Paralyzed with confusion, MJ tried to figure out what Andrews meant. *Dash used to be his horse...when? Before the guy who abused him, or—?*

Meanwhile, the visitor made a "come-on" gesture in the direction of his truck. His female friend, not looking either ill or sleepy, got down from the cab and started toward the paddock. MJ instantly recognized the woman who'd asked about Dash before, but balked at filling out adoption papers. What had Anna said her name was, Mandy?

What are these two trying to pull?

Andrews launched into a defense that sounded well-prepared. "From what you said before, honey, I think you were told a lot of vicious lies about me. I never mistreated this animal. It's true he was a top show horse. We won a few blues and even a state championship together. After awhile he stopped doing as well, so I gave him some time off to rest. My competitors turned all that around. They sicced the Humane Society on me, sayin' that I was 'neglecting' him. Fact is, Dash and I were winnin' so much, they wanted to keep him off the circuit."

MJ half-wondered if this could be true. By the time she'd come to the farm, the buckskin had looked pretty healthy and moved normally. Anna and Walt warned her not to ride him too hard, but were they just being extra-careful?

The girl came up with the only solution she could think of. "If that's so, you should talk to Anna. Maybe you can arrange to—I dunno—adopt him back."

Mandy, who halted just outside the pen, rolled her eyes, and Andrews laughed with a hard edge. "I ain't got time for that. Like I told your aunt, I'm just here for the weekend. 'Sides, I been paying this horse's keep for a couple months now. From what she told Mandy, that comes to about half his adoption fee. Dunno if you checked your website today, but I deposited the balance this morning. So, I'll save us all a lot of time and trouble, and take him with me today."

Andrews moved to snatch the lead rope from MJ but, heart thudding, she yanked it out of his reach. At the same time, Dash snorted and backed another step. Val and Patches sensed the new tension and sidled away. Delilah, on the other hand, stuck protectively close to MJ.

"Why do you even want this horse back?" she asked Andrews, stalling for time. "If you try to show him, he'll just go lame on you again."

"Oh, I dunno. The way he's dancin' around right now, looks like your aunt did a fine job of fixin' him. He's probably got a few more good years left."

Maybe, if you shoot him up with painkillers, she thought. *And when he finally does break down, you'll make a few more bucks by sending him off to auction...and slaughter.*

Now another vehicle rattled down the drive, somewhere behind Andrews' trailer. MJ felt a jolt of relief—Walt was early, too!

Jeb and Mandy also froze. They'd obviously thought they could bulldoze over the girl, but hadn't figured on anyone else getting into the act.

Walt cautiously circled around the horse trailer and truck, stopping short when he saw the couple in the barnyard. He asked MJ, "What's *that* guy doing here?"

"Trying to steal Dash!" she shouted back. "Call 9-1-1."

He did not reach for a cell phone, and she remembered in dismay that he seldom carried one. If she tried to use hers, though, Andrews would grab the horse.

Anyway, Walt seemed fixated on the man in the black nylon jacket. "That's Artie Jeffers, the one who almost killed Dash."

Andrews/Jeffers tried to argue his way out of this, too. "The horse rightfully belongs to me. He was taken away under false pretenses. Some jealous riders on the show circuit spread lies—"

Walt passed Mandy as if she wasn't there and stalked toward the paddock. "Lies, eh? I went to a couple shows with my Dad, and we *saw* you abusing him. Dad even reported you, once, to the show steward."

Jeffers reddened and opened his mouth again, but Walt talked over him.

"A while after that, Dad drove by your place one day and saw the same horse limping around a field full of nothing but nasty weeds. In the middle of summer, with no water. He called the Humane Society, and *that's* why they took Dash away from you."

Jeffers muttered, "I don't have to listen to this crap!" He ordered Mandy to open the paddock gate, but she hesitated.

Walt told them both, "You're not goin' anywhere. I'm parked behind you."

"Then you better the hell move!" Jeffers reached into the

sagging front pocket of his jacket and pulled out a revolver.

While Walt and MJ froze, the stocky man reached once more for Dash's lead rope. MJ's hands remained clamped onto it, but he shoved her aside. Near their feet, Delilah began barking furiously. Valentine and Patches started pacing around the paddock again.

Jeffers aimed the gun at Delilah and snarled at MJ, "Shut that mutt up."

"Sssh!" She squatted to hug the dog's neck, tears blurring her vision. *How can this be happening?* She glanced toward Walt, who stood tensely near the paddock gate. He seemed to be watching the gun.

Out of fear? Or maybe waiting for Jeffers to drop his guard?

Dash's former owner tried to lead him forward, but the buckskin planted his feet and laid back his ears. With another curse, Jeffers swung the end of the thick lead rope and smacked him hard on the shoulder. This only made the horse jump sideways, yanking his abuser off-balance.

MJ saw Walt lean forward like a sprinter on his marks. *Be careful!* she told him in her mind. Jeffers might be distracted right now, but he still held a loaded gun.

All at once, though, he howled in pain and shock. MJ saw that Valentine, from behind the man, had bitten him on the shoulder. She hung onto him, too, practically lifting him off his feet. Flailing at her, Jeffers lost the gun, and it skittered into the middle of the paddock.

The mare let him go so suddenly that he dropped to his knees. His jacket was torn, but he didn't look badly hurt, MJ thought—just furious. He cast around for his gun at the same time as MJ made a try for it.

Walt hollered, "Delilah! Get him!"

The dog charged forward to grab Jeffers by the right arm, the same side Val had bitten, which sparked another yowl of rage and pain. Mandy darted into the paddock, maybe to help Jeffers. But Patches, trying to escape the turmoil, bolted blindly across the woman's path and slammed into her at hip level, so she also went sprawling.

MJ snatched up the revolver, startled by its weight and by the idea of holding a lethal weapon. When Walt reached her side, she gladly handed it over. "Here. You probably know how to use this."

Able to catch her breath, she noticed Valentine and Dash standing off to one side of the paddock. They touched noses briefly, then looked on as Walt held the intruders at gunpoint. Patches trotted over to join them, and all three horses seemed proud of themselves.

Kneeling on the ground, with Delilah still attached to his arm, Jeffers managed to smirk at Walt. "Whadya gonna do, kid, kill me? Over a damned horse?"

Walt leveled the gun in a two-handed grip. "Probably not. But I'm a good shot, so I still could hurt you bad."

MJ stared at him for a second, impressed. Then she pulled out her phone—her own weapon of choice—and finally dialed 9-1-1.

Man. Are the cops even going to believe any of this?

CHAPTER FORTY-TWO:

COMPETITION

Anna had almost forgotten the joy of trying to shimmy back into stretch nylon riding breeches on a humid August day within the confines of a smelly Porta-John. This weather would have anyone sweating, even if she had not spent the last couple hours schooling a high-energy horse and then jumping him against some tough competition.

Clothes finally back in place, she rubbed her hands with sanitizer, pulled her riding gloves back on, and tucked a few strands of hair under her helmet without benefit of mirror. She stepped out of the toilet into the fresh air and faced her biggest challenge of the day.

She, Jessica and a male rider on a chestnut all had jumped clear in the first round.

Walking briskly back to where she'd left Clint with Murphy, Anna checked her cell phone. *No calls from MJ—that's funny.* During the lunch break, she had left her niece a message to say she was still in the running. *Maybe Sam Patterson got held up at his farm, and MJ and Walt are still waiting for him.*

All worries vanished when she got within sight of her horse and saw Walt holding him. Her niece offered Murphy a bucket of water while Clint adjusted the gray's short leather jumping boots.

When she spotted Anna, MJ ran up to hug her. "Josh told us you made it to the jump-off! That's so great!"

"Thanks, honey. I even surprised myself."

Clint glanced over. "Yeah, I think we had more faith in her

than she did."

"Who's minding the farm?" Anna asked Walt.

He gave her an odd, cat-that-swallowed-the-canary smile. "It's in the best of hands."

"Your Dad?"

"He's there."

"And Lieutenant Mertz," MJ added, with a mysterious smirk of her own.

"And a couple guys from the county sheriff's department," Walt finished, offhandedly.

Despite the smiles, they didn't sound like they were joking. "What on earth did you two do?"

"I like that!" MJ huffed. "What did *we* do?"

Clint chimed in, "From what they told me, sounds like they kept some guy from stealing one o' your horses."

"Some guy? You don't mean...Andrews?"

"Fake name," Walt said. "He's really Art Jeffers, the guy who used to own Dash."

Before Anna could make sense of all this, Josh returned from the direction of the show ring. "Hey, mount back up. The jump-off's started. Jessica just went in, and they'll be calling you next."

Still eyeing MJ and Walt in curiosity, Anna let the trainer give her a leg up. All of them walked alongside as she rode Murphy back to the ring. She wanted to ask more about what had happened at the farm, but Josh kept pulling her focus back to the competition at hand.

"Number Twenty-Four, the guy on the chestnut, had a knockdown. Plus, his time wasn't so hot. So it's probably just you and Jess."

Anna nodded. At first, thinking she didn't have much chance against the flawless Number Thirty-Six, she hadn't felt so much pressure. But now that they were virtually even, Anna heard the blood pounding in her ears. She tried to relax so she wouldn't transmit those nerves to Murphy.

Waiting outside the ring, she watched Jess and Hawkeye cruise around with their usual easy grace. The original number of hurdles had dwindled to just five for the jump-off, but had been raised few inches higher. They also were numbered in an order that required some sharp turns.

To no one's surprise, Thirty-Six jumped clean once again, and clocked a time that would be hard to match, much less beat. The loudspeaker duly announced this, and a contingent of Jess's admirers on the other side of the ring led the applause.

An official opened the gate to let her ride out. As Jessica passed Anna, she wished her good luck.

Like she knows I'll need it.

"Last in our jump-off, Number Thirty-Two—Anna Loehmeyer on Murphy Himself."

They trotted a few strides into the ring, then Anna put her horse into a canter and passed the start pole at a good clip. The first two jumps going away from the gate were simple verticals and, though they'd been set higher than before, Murphy cleared them easily. Anna noticed, though, that he wasn't pulling as hard as usual. She wondered if he might be tiring.

Maybe I didn't condition him enough for this, or maybe the heat is getting to him. Is he breathing harder than he was earlier?

Now's not the time to slow down! But I don't want to hurt him...

They had to make a quick half-turn, and she cut it as close to the jumps as she could. The ground in that spot was still damp from the morning rain, and she felt the gray dig in a little. They headed for the rising oxer, flanked by bright flowers, which before they'd jumped only in the other direction. Murphy started to shrink back from the fake plants, but when Anna clucked to him he sailed over the hurdle.

Needed a push on that one. She wasn't even carrying a crop, because the gray was so whip-shy. *But maybe I should have?*

Another tight turn, and they headed toward the double combination. Once again, Murphy slowed a bit as if to rebalance himself, and Anna worried. *He needs more juice here, or he won't make it!* She gave him a sharp squeeze with her legs.

Startled, the horse took off too soon for the first jump, and instead of just one stride after it needed to take two. This messed up his approach to the second jump. Though he made a game try and landed safely, Anna heard a clunk behind them. A groan from the audience confirmed that they'd brought down a rail.

Damn! she thought. Even Murphy gave a little kick of frustration.

But he powered toward the last "gate" with a vengeance, cleared it, and flew past the electronic eye so fast that Anna could not even read their time. She did hear clapping and cheers—MJ's voice especially shrill—but figured her friends were just trying to make her feel better. She cantered the horse in a half-circle to slow him and patted his damp neck.

"Sorry, boy," she whispered to him. "My bad."

The loudspeaker pronounced, "Number Thirty-Two had one knockdown, for four faults, and a time of—"

Riding out of the ring, Anna heard the results a split second before MJ ran up to her. "You beat Jessica's time!"

"I know. Would've been great, if we'd only jumped clear."

Walt and Clint also looked happy with her performance, but Josh asked, "What happened at the combination?"

"I thought he was tiring, so I gave him a push, but I threw off his rhythm."

The trainer frowned. "He was fine. If you'd left him alone, you still would have made that time."

"Really?" Anna felt chastened. "You told me to trust him... Guess I should've listened."

"I thought you both did great," Clint insisted. "Just think how this horse started out."

Anna felt disappointed tears rising, and wanted to escape them all for a minute. "I should walk him."

"Don't go far," Josh warned. "They'll want you for—"

The announcer drowned him out. "The results of Class Six: First place, Jessica Coleman on Hawkeye; second, Anna Loehmeyer on Murphy Himself; third, Martin Ross on The Cardinal."

She rode back into the ring and took her place between the other two competitors. Murphy flinched just a little when the red ribbon was hooked onto his bridle. Riding out of the ring with it did lift Anna's spirits.

Clint's right. Considering how wild Murphy was when I first got him, we accomplished a lot to come this far. I just hope my dumb mistake didn't blow his chance to be adopted.

She planned to congratulate her rival, but Jessica already had dismounted and was surrounded by enthusiastic supporters. They included a tall, athletic blond man of about forty, a middle-aged woman, and a girl who looked around ten. Anna wondered if they were Hawkeye's owners.

She's probably already forgotten about whatever interest she had in Murphy. I guess the good news is, I'll get to keep him a little longer.

Anna swung off the gray and led him to the trailer. Meanwhile, her own small entourage kept reminding her that she had done well.

Even Josh offered some consolation. "I bet I know what happened. Murphy started to mellow out and pace himself, and that surprised you. You're so used to him rocketing around that when he eased up, you thought he was losing steam."

He reads people as well as he does horses, Anna thought. "Exactly right." She took a long gulp from a cold bottle of water. "Anyhow, MJ and Walt have to take some of the blame, because I couldn't stop worrying about what they told me. So, what the heck happened at the farm?"

While Walt fed Murphy carrots, he and MJ filled Anna in on the whole story. It horrified her to learn that, despite her best intentions, she had left her niece alone to cope with such a dangerous situation. "Walt, thank God you showed up early and knew what to do."

He raised his hands in protest. "I can't take the credit. It's not like I disarmed Jeffers. Valentine did!"

Anna tried to picture the sweet mare sinking her teeth into a man's shoulder. "That's so bizarre. She's never even tried to bite anyone else."

Josh shrugged. "She's probably your alpha mare."

"Huh?"

"In a herd, if there's no stallion around, one mare takes over that role. When there's a threat, she leads the herd to safety and fights off any predators."

MJ appeared fascinated. "I guess that's how she saw Jeffers, when he started beating up on Dash."

"And after he dropped his gun, it was MJ who grabbed it," Walt added.

"Real brave of her," Clint said.

Josh wore a broad grin. "Sounds like excellent teamwork all around. I wish I'd been there to see it."

MJ lifted the saddle and its pad from Murphy's back and set them on the folding rack. "I'm just glad we didn't have to bother you guys here at the show. When I called 9-1-1, Lieutenant Mertz showed up right away." She elbowed Anna. "Guess he doesn't think you're paranoid anymore."

"At least none of you got hurt. Did you and Walt have any lunch?"

He shook his head. "We were in too much of a hurry to come here."

Anna got her purse from the trailer and handed him a ten. "Get yourselves something from the food truck. Josh said the wraps aren't bad."

The two of them set off, while Clint took over sponging the horse. Anna removed her hot jacket and saw her number still attached to the back. "I'd better return this."

"Let me," said Josh. "You stay in the shade."

After he'd gone, she dared to stroke the satiny loops of the red rosette and savor her accomplishment. She'd gotten a few blues on Duke, and had a good chance at another the day of their accident. But then, too, her judgment had been off, her mind not quite in the game.

Maybe I've never had the single-minded drive that it takes to be a great rider. At least this time my mistake didn't do either me or Murphy any real harm. Unless you count screwing up his first, and maybe best, chance at being adopted...

When Anna glanced back up again, she wondered for a second if she was hallucinating. But no, Jessica Coleman was striding across the field in her direction. She had taken off her helmet and let her dark hair out of its net. It flowed glamorously to her shoulders, as Anna figured it would.

Probably wants to break the bad news to me in person. Let me off the hook, so I can go home and post Murphy's profile on our website. At least coming in second today should boost his prospects.

Clint sneaked a peek over the horse's bare back as Jessica reached the trailer. Anna stood up to shake the brunette's hand and congratulate her.

"You guys did pretty well today, yourselves," Jessica responded.

"Thanks. He could've done better, though. That last knockdown was my fault."

The other woman laughed. "Girl, it was *so* your fault. Good thing you're not the one up for adoption."

Her tone raised Anna's hopes. "You mean, you're still interested? But you won on Hawkeye, and he was perfect."

"Hawkeye is a really nice horse, but I did have to push him in the jump-off. He's pretty, he's well-mannered, and he's fine over a low, easy course. He'll make some kid a great hunter prospect." Jessica sidled up to Murphy and stroked his neck. "But this guy has the fire in the belly! His eyes light up when he even looks at a jump. *He* can go a lot further."

"Just not with me," Anna joked.

"Naturally, I'll have to try him out myself," the brunette added. "Some time next week, when he's had a good rest, can I come by your farm?"

"Absolutely."

"I'll give you a call." With another fond glance at the gray, Jessica sauntered back to her own trailer. She passed MJ and Walt, returning from the food truck.

"Guess what," Anna challenged them.

"She still wants him?" MJ squealed.

Matter-of-factly, Walt noted, "You did beat her time."

When Josh rejoined them a second later, he acted unsurprised. "Jess knows horses. And I've bent her ear about Murphy a few times over the last couple months."

Anna tried not to picture the intimate circumstances of those conversations. "She was there when you were training him, wasn't she? She shot the videos."

"You're right. Funny, I'd half-forgotten about that."

Other trailers began to leave as the last classes wound up. Anna led Murphy into hers, while Josh commented that she didn't need his help to do that anymore.

Suddenly she felt reluctant to let this roller-coaster day end. "We were planning to go to the Broken Inn tonight for dinner." She nodded toward Walt, MJ and Clint. "Of course, I need to change, and after what happened at the farm, I have no idea what I'll find back there. But you're welcome to—"

"Oh, gee..." Josh raised his eyebrows, as if caught off-guard. And disappointed? "I'd love to, but I think the Colemans are going out somewhere, too—"

"I understand. Maybe another time."

"Sure, give me a rain check." Josh startled Anna with a quick good-bye hug. "Glad everything worked out so well today. Enjoy your celebration!"

As he headed off, MJ shot her aunt a knowing look, before climbing into Walt's truck. Anna got behind the wheel of her own pickup with Clint as her passenger, and they all started back to the farm.

"Too bad Josh couldn't celebrate with us," Clint said, after a while.

"*She's* still the winner," Anna observed.

"True. An' she's family."

"Huh? Jessica?"

"She's his cousin. You didn't know that?"

"No. How come you do?"

"Josh an' me got to jawin', while you was in the ring."

"He just told me they grew up together." *And that she was like a sister to him. Leave it to a man, to omit the most important detail.*

Clint looked at her sideways. "You like him, but you thought they were an item? Nah. Didya see that big, blond dude? That was her husband, and their little girl."

"No kidding?" Jessica may have bested her in that day's

competition, but any leftover resentment Anna might have felt quickly faded.

"S'what Josh told me. So maybe you got two breaks today. From the big ol' squeeze he just gave you, you might still be in the jump-off for him, too."

CHAPTER FORTY-THREE:

ADOPTION

The local papers loved the story of two teenagers thwarting an armed "horse thief" at a small rescue farm, with help from several of the animals. Soon after, MJ fielded calls from school friends she hadn't heard from in weeks, including Stacey and Kayla. They both asked her about Walt, whom they found much cooler after hearing that he'd threatened to shoot a bad guy. She even got a text from Bobby, who joked that it sounded like her summer job was turning out a lot more exciting than she'd planned.

MJ responded politely, but felt little desire to fall back in with that crowd. She realized now how quickly they could betray her.

She found Walt more intriguing now, herself, after the way he'd kept his head during the crisis and stood up to Jeffers. Meanwhile, their shared adventure versus the "horse thief" even seemed to earn MJ more credibility with the Pattersons. Dottie now answered more pleasantly when the girl called, and gave the phone to her son without stalling.

Erika went through a range of reactions when she heard about the standoff with Jeffers. She started to accuse Anna of negligence, but MJ explained, "Neither of us had any way of knowing Andrews wasn't legit, or would go to so much trouble to trick us."

Worried that her mother might insist she stop working for Anna, MJ floated the idea about getting an online degree in barn management. Erika conceded that, while it wasn't the fast-track career she'd imagined for her daughter, at least it would be some further education.

A few days later, Erika called to say she and Burt were in the area and wanted to drop by. Two flashy vehicles pulled into the barnyard—the ivory-colored SUV, driven by Burt, and the red hatchback, with Erika behind the wheel.

"I know your birthday isn't for another month," she told MJ, "but I guess if you're old enough to protect the farm from a crook while Anna's gone, you're responsible enough to have your own set of wheels."

Jessica dropped by a week after the horse show, with Josh, to try out Murphy. She first rode him in the round pen, then took him up to the practice field and went over a few jumps. When she brought the gray back to the barn, she still seemed enthusiastic.

"He's a bit of a challenge, but I like that," she told Anna. "I think once we get used to each other, he'll be great."

Jessica answered all the questions on the lengthy adoption form and quibbled over just one thing at the end. "Is this the fee?"

Anna clenched her jaw. She had set what she felt was a fair price, and was counting on the money to help pay down her charges with the farm's various suppliers. "I think he's worth that. He's young and healthy, and he's already proven himself..."

"Exactly. Plus, he was trained by the famous Josh McMahon." Jessica winked at her cousin, who hovered in the office doorway. "He's worth three times this much! I know it's an adoption, not a sale, but..."

The tension drained from Anna's body. "Well, I'm a rookie at this rescue business, so maybe I under-priced him. Why don't you give me what you think he's worth?"

Jessica wrote a check that would allow Anna to pay off even more big bills than she'd expected. After they shook hands, Jess went outside to get her trailer ready.

Anna cross-tied the gray and began to curry his silver dapples from neck to haunches. He was fitter now than when he'd first arrived at the farm, his muscles filled out from the steady training.

She whispered, "I didn't think letting go of you would be so hard. When you first got here, I was afraid to even get on you—I thought you'd kill me! But we got to be a real team, didn't we?"

Now Jessica will benefit, Anna thought. *She could take him all the way to the National Horse Show in Madison Square Garden, or the International Horse Show in Washington, D.C. She sounds as if she might be that ambitious. But will that be the best thing for Murphy?*

Polishing him with the soft brush, Anna gazed into the horses's big, dark eye, its pupil as wide as a horizon. She told him he was going to live with Jessica now, and he should behave well for her, too. "But don't worry. If she ever treats you badly, I'll make her bring you right back here."

Near the barn door, someone cleared his throat. Anna saw Josh there and tried to blink away a tear.

"Going to miss the big guy, eh?"

She nodded. "Even though we all worked so hard to make this happen. Like they say, be careful what you wish for."

Josh sidled up next to her, so the horse's body concealed them from anyone outside. "Don't worry about Jess. I think she'll use good sense, but I'll keep an eye on her. She might be family, but if I ever think she's pushing Murphy too hard, I'll rat her out in a heartbeat."

Anna smiled. "Y'know, when you first introduced us I didn't realize you two were related. I recognized her voice from the video, and I thought you—"

He laughed in surprise. "Guess I never mentioned it, huh? I assumed you knew. Your magazine even wrote about our connection once, in the society column."

"That figures—one of the few columns I didn't edit myself." Anna remembered another nagging question. "What about those calls you got every Wednesday night, when we were finishing up? Sounded like you had someone at home, expecting you."

Josh dropped his gaze. "I probably should have been more open about that, too. My dad. He's in an Alzheimer's residence in Morris County. I visit for dinner once a week, but sometimes he gets the time wrong and calls to ask why I'm late."

"Ah," said Anna. "I'm sorry. That must be rough."

Voices outside suggested that Jessica was wondering where her new horse was, and MJ was stalling her from going into the barn.

Anna squared her shoulders. "Anyway, I just wanted to thank you for your help with Murphy. You gave both of us back our courage."

He wagged his head, refusing the credit. "You already had plenty."

The half-joking voices outside got closer. Feeling pressured, Anna started to brush the horse again. She stopped when Josh turned her in his arms and planted a light kiss on her lips. When she froze in surprise, he seemed ready to back off. But she slid her arms around his neck and kissed him back, more warmly.

Josh's twinkling eyes said he'd gotten the message. "Look, I'll be in Ohio the next week or so, at another of those horse expos. But when I get back, I'll take you up on that rain check for dinner. Okay?"

"It's a date," Anna breathed.

On his way out of the barn, he slapped Murphy lightly on the neck. "Sorry, pal. This time, you're not invited."

By the end of the week, the farm lost another of its longtime residents.

Lillian Gale phoned Anna to find out more about the attempted theft of Dash. She praised the bravery and resourcefulness of the two "young people," and also congratulated Anna on placing Murphy with Jessica Coleman.

"Now that you don't need a companion for him anymore, why don't I take Patches off your hands?" she offered. "Via the full adoption process, of course."

I'm on a lucky streak, Anna thought. "That would be wonderful. I'm sure she'd get the best of care at your farm."

The day Lillian came to pick up the pony, Anna and MJ fussed over Patches and said their slightly weepy good-byes. While they lured the pony onto the heiress' trailer with some sweet feed, Lillian commented on all of the "No Trespassing" signs.

"We put those up because of Jeffers' antics," Anna explained.

"What you do need is something out by the road to tell people you're here," Lillian suggested. "I've got a guy out my way who does excellent signs. Would you let me help you out with that?"

"I'd appreciate it very much. MJ already came up with a kind of logo for us, so maybe you and she can work out the design."

As they closed Lillian's trailer, she asked, "Have you applied for nonprofit status?"

"Still waiting to hear back. I was told it would take a few months."

Lillian slipped into the back seat of the attached SUV, behind her driver. "Feel free to drop my name, as a donor. That might help things along."

⟨✺⟩

With only two horses left in their care, Anna and MJ planned to take a short breather. But Francie of the New York state rescue group soon phoned the farm again.

"Anna, are you still able to take these two colts? They've been gelded and vetted, and we need to move them along, if we can."

Anna told herself the group was doing important work, and she had room now for more animals. "What kind of training do they have?"

"You can lead them, groom them, and they'll behave in a stall, though they're better outside. We taught them all that. They don't learn *anything* at the PMU farms."

Swallowing her reservations, Anna told Francie to send the colts on down.

MJ and Walt arranged to be on hand for their arrival, a week later, and watched from a distance as they were unloaded.

"They're only a year old?" MJ asked Francine.

"Not even. Seven months."

"Big feet," Walt noticed. "They're still growing."

"Well, they're three-quarters Belgian Draft." Francie patted the nearest one, a burly golden beast, to quiet him. "We've been calling them Butch and Sundance."

Anna sized up the restless newcomers with a cautious eye. "Want to turn them out together in the last paddock? There's room for them to run a little, but not so much that they'll go crazy."

This done, Anna and Francie went into the office to finish up paperwork. MJ and Walt stayed outside watched the colts trot, canter and buck around Murphy's old pen. They stopped now and then to send piercing neighs to Valentine and Dash, who watched with calm curiosity. When MJ said she'd never seen a horse like Butch before, with white hairs sprinkled all through his chestnut coat, Walt explained that he was a red roan.

"Sundance is a palomino, right?"

Walt creased his freckled nose. "A little darker...more of a sorrel."

Francie's trailer pulled away and Anna joined the teens. "I hope I don't regret this. It's like taking on two Murphys! Anyhow, you guys ready for some lunch?"

Back at the house, she brought tuna sandwiches out on the porch. It was almost Labor Day, the summer heat had broken a little, and a mild breeze kept things pleasant. Anna sat in one of the rockers and MJ on the loveseat next to Walt. Delilah sprawled near their feet, probably hoping some tuna would drop.

"I asked Francie what these colts can be trained for," Anna said. "She figured Western, trail riding, pulling a wagon, maybe dressage... but so far they've had no training at all. And I don't know how to teach a horse any of those things."

MJ couldn't resist pointing out the obvious. "You'll need help from a top-notch trainer. Gee...do we know anybody like that?"

Her aunt blushed a little. "Lucky that we do. Seriously, these foals are just 'bypoducts' of the PMU industry. Draft mares are more...productive than other breeds while they're pregnant. Then they have these big babies, but no one needs them anymore for farm work."

"That's crazy," said Walt, with a scowl. MJ reflected that it felt good to hang out with somebody who cared about these issues as much as she did.

"When you add in the number of other horses bred for racing or showing that don't work out, and end up neglected or put down, it just boggles the mind." Anna ran a hand back over her hair, looking overwhelmed. "It's impossible to rescue all of them. The little bit we can do here is just a drop in the bucket."

MJ remembered saying that to Walt, a couple months ago, and elbowed him with a stage whisper. "I think Anna needs to hear the starfish story."

"Starfish story?" Her aunt faced him.

"You never heard it, either?" Walt asked, in amazement.

"C'mon," MJ ribbed her. "*Everybody* knows the starfish story."

Anna looked blank but curious.

"Walt, you can tell it the best," the girl prompted.

He finished the last bite of his sandwich and washed it down with a swallow of lemonade, then rose to the challenge. "Okay. An old man is walking on the beach, after a big storm..."

Delilah rested her chin on her paws for a nap, MJ noticed. Probably, having come from the Pattersons' house, she'd heard the story before.

In the paddocks beyond the porch, four of the farm's rescued "starfish" also half-dozed in safety and contentment, their manes ruffled by the late-summer breeze.

ACKNOWLEDGMENTS

First and foremost, thanks to Beverly Dee of Bright Futures Farm in Cochranton, Pennsylvania, whose real-life tales of her rescue experiences have inspired many of the incidents in this book. Decades ago, Beverly also provided a safe home for my chronically ill mare, Brenda, who lives again in the character of "Valentine." Also, thanks to Dorothy Nadon of Hidden View Farm in Monroe, New Jersey, and Laura Hensley Trouard of Perfect Fit Equine Rescue in Morgan Hill, California, who provided me with further information about starting a horse rescue.

Finally, I owe much gratitude to the members my north Jersey critique group: Elisa Chalem, Susan Moshiashwili, Harry Pollack, Ed Rand, Jeremy Salter, Janice Stucki, and Joanne Weck. Because none of them were horse experts or even equine fanatics, I think they helped me develop a story that will appeal to a range of readers.

Thank you for taking the time
to read *Reboot Ranch*.

COULD YOU TAKE A MOMENT TO GIVE THE BOOK
A SHORT REVIEW ON AMAZON.COM? YOUR REVIEWS
MEAN THE WORLD TO OUR AUTHORS, AND HELP
STORIES SUCH AS THIS ONE REACH A WIDER
AUDIENCE. THANK YOU SO MUCH!

Find links to
Reboot Ranch
AND ALL OUR GREAT BOOKS
ON AMAZON OR AT WWW.WHOCHAINSYOU.COM.